MW00788671

RELIGIOUS TOURISM IN NORTHERN THAILAND

RELIGIOUS TOURISM IN NORTHERN THAILAND

Encounters with Buddhist Monks

BROOKE SCHEDNECK

UNIVERSITY OF WASHINGTON PRESS

Seattle

Religious Tourism in Northern Thailand was made possible in part by a grant from the Charles and Jane Keyes Endowment for Books on Southeast Asia, established through the generosity of Charles and Jane Keyes.

Rhodes College provided additional support for this publication.

Copyright © 2021 by the University of Washington Press

Composed in Minion Pro, typeface designed by Robert Slimbach

25   24   23   22   21   5   4   3   2   1

Printed and bound in the United States of America

All rights reserved. No part of this publication may be reproduced or transmitted in any form or by any means, electronic or mechanical, including photocopy, recording, or any information storage or retrieval system, without permission in writing from the publisher.

UNIVERSITY OF WASHINGTON PRESS
uwapress.uw.edu

LIBRARY OF CONGRESS CATALOGING-IN-PUBLICATION DATA
Names: Schedneck, Brooke, author.
Title: Religious tourism in northern Thailand : encounters with Buddhist monks / Brooke Schedneck.
Description: Seattle : University of Washington Press, [2021] | Includes bibliographical references and index.
Identifiers: LCCN 2020052172 (print) | LCCN 2020052173 (ebook) | ISBN 9780295748917 (hardcover) | ISBN 9780295748924 (paperback) | ISBN 9780295748931 (ebook)
Subjects: LCSH: Tourism—Religious aspects—Buddhism. | Tourism—Thailand—Chiang Mai. | Buddhism—Social aspects—Thailand—Chiang Mai. | Buddhism and culture—Thailand—Chiang Mai. | Globalization—Religious aspects—Buddhism. | Buddhism—Relations.
Classification: LCC G156.5.R44 S33 2021 (print) | LCC G156.5.R44 (ebook) | DDC 338.4/791593—dc23
LC record available at https://lccn.loc.gov/2020052172
LC ebook record available at https://lccn.loc.gov/2020052173

The paper used in this publication is acid free and meets the minimum requirements of American National Standard for Information Sciences—Permanence of Paper for Printed Library Materials, ANSI Z39.48–1984.∞

For Jet and William

CONTENTS

PREFACE

My interest in Buddhist encounters in Chiang Mai began as a result of living in the city from 2013 to 2017, when I taught in a study abroad program, hosted by Chiang Mai University, called the Institute of Southeast Asian Affairs. During this period, the influence of tourism and urbanization on Buddhist temples, temple schools, and student monks was obvious. In particular, I noticed that student monks in Chiang Mai were eager to meet and discuss Buddhism in English with foreign tourists. As a result, I had many opportunities to facilitate discussions between my study abroad students and student monks about their lives, Buddhism, and Thailand. These initial encounters became the basis for this book.

The Buddhists whom foreigners meet during formal and informal encounters at temples are typically student monks. These monks are usually of high school or college age and are part of the monastic education system. The city of Chiang Mai has two Buddhist universities and multiple monastic middle and high schools, and many of these monks are studying English. I became close with several monks who audited my classes and participated in our class excursions, providing insight into Buddhism for my students and myself. These encounters and varying perspectives between student monks and foreign students began to intrigue me more and more, and I decided to research this topic by including the broader category of international tourists to Chiang Mai City.

As a foreigner who speaks Thai and researches Buddhism, I moved between groups of foreign travelers and Buddhist monks. For their assistance with my research, I endeavored to give back to these interlocutors as much as I could. As an academic trained in religious studies, particularly Buddhism, I volunteered my services, informally answering questions for tourists about Buddhism that were more easily answered in native English. I also gave formal lectures to larger groups of tourists, foreign students, and student monks. Student monks were happy to listen to my answers and lectures. My presentations helped inform the ways some of the student monks learned to translate Buddhism and Thai culture to the international community.

Additionally, I volunteered to teach "Buddhist English" and had informal topical discussions with student monks at the Buddhist universities. During each of our meetings, we discussed topics such as Christian missionaries, temple economics, media coverage of Buddhism, and problems in Thai Buddhism. In many of the sessions, the monks were enthusiastic about these issues and happy to have a chance to express themselves. I did not see these monks as providers of data; rather, our mutuality was accentuated in our separate but related educational projects.

Student monks often wondered why I sought out their opinions, as they were not used to being positioned as authoritative or knowledgeable on these topics. Instead, Thai lay Buddhists, academics, and media outlets often sought the views of abbots and senior Buddhist leadership. Although I also interviewed some senior monks and abbots involved in Buddhist education, student monks were crucial for my research not only because they are the ones involved in most encounters with tourists and who experience the changing nature of the temple space, but also because they are an understudied group, as the monks themselves understood. Because of Thai and Buddhist hierarchies, which favor seniority, student monks have few opportunities to express their opinions about the monastic life. However, the thoughts and ideas of these more ordinary monks present a more comprehensive sense of the issues affecting contemporary Buddhism, as opposed to the opinions of high-ranking, nationally and internationally known monks, whose high-profile monastic experience is atypical.

My interest in Buddhist encounters also grew out of earlier work on international meditation centers (Schedneck 2015), during which I discovered programs where foreigners could experience Buddhism outside of its most popular practice of meditation. Since the early 2000s, opportunities for encounters in Buddhist monastic educational settings—including volunteering in temples, temple stay programs, temporary ordination, and monk chats in which tourists ask monks their questions about Buddhism—have been on the rise, especially in Chiang Mai Province. I have termed these possibilities for engagement "Buddhist cultural exchange programs." For monks who live in popular tourist temples, encounters occur on a daily basis, either formally within programs designed for exchange or informally as monks meet curious visitors. For other Buddhist monks included in this study who live outside of the main tourist areas, volunteer tourists may come to their temples or monks may travel to temples where tourists are likely to visit. For travelers, these encounters can include short-term visits to Buddhist temples as well as long-term engagement with the religion. Both tourism and education are processes of urban mobility that serve to create these encounters. Tourism brings travelers from around the world to view Buddhist temples and seek religious encounters. Education has traditionally framed mobility within Buddhist monasticism and continues to at a rapid pace. These networks are entangled within the urban space of Chiang Mai, both connecting people across countries and reconfiguring local contexts as young men move away from home, while urbanization has altered the economic and social structure of the city.

The focus of this book is not interreligious dialogue or interfaith alliances, but rather societal and global forces that define and shape the encounter between Buddhist monks and the international community. The idea of encounter may connote confrontation or struggle. Especially because of its renunciatory practices, Buddhism can appear challenging to foreigners. As well, understanding foreigners' varied lifestyles and cultures is a struggle for Buddhist monks. However, this initial challenge often leads to growth and self-transformation for both parties. Such encounters are not one-dimensional but illustrate multiple ways to understand global developments within Buddhism. For Buddhist monastics, these encounters demonstrate self-conscious and selective constructions of religion, revealing the scope of Buddhism as it reaches multiple audiences. Buddhism, as a traveling religion, has always transcended geographical and cultural boundaries with universal messages; but recently the reverse is occurring as curious travelers make their way to Buddhism. Pertinent questions are: What are the economic implications of Buddhist tourist encounters in Chiang Mai? How do contemporary Buddhists view the religious others they encounter? How do Buddhist monks spread Buddhism to foreigners? How do travelers come to understand Buddhist traditions? What are the possibilities for change and self-transformation in these encounters? This book explores these questions within this particular setting but maintains a wide analytical frame of global Buddhism within the context of religious encounters.

ACKNOWLEDGMENTS

The main voices of this book, besides my own, are the student monks of Chiang Mai, Thailand. They attend university, learning English, Buddhism, and other subjects while pursuing the monastic lifestyle of supporting rituals, laboring for the temple, and participating in meditation retreats. I was always impressed with their energy and vitality as they continued to enthusiastically discuss Buddhism with tourists and international students, creating programs and opportunities for further exchange. I thank them for their willingness to share their knowledge and perspectives with me.

Much of the research for this book was conducted during 2013–17, when I taught international students at the Institute of Southeast Asian Affairs at Chiang Mai University. I thank these students for their curiosity and interest in their encounters with student monks. The other important institution to recognize is Mahachulalongkorn University (MCU), where I often met and spoke with monks who were studying on the English-language track toward a bachelor's degree. Dr. Wisuttichai Chaiyasit, chair of the English major, supported my guest lectures and presentations, and my good friend Steven Epstein, an instructor at MCU, coordinated workshops and opportunities for me to speak and interact with the student monks. One former student monk, Phra Maha Milan Shrestha, became my research assistant, and I appreciate his diligence.

Since 2017, Rhodes College in Memphis, Tennessee, has supported my research. In the summers of 2018 and 2019, I returned to Chiang Mai to conduct research and lead students on a study tour of Buddhism in Thai society. I thank the Rhodes students in these classes for helping me to see the encounters between international tourists and student monks anew through their eyes. I also thank Rhodes College for funding my research in 2018 with a Faculty Development Endowment Grant.

This book benefited from the invited lectures I gave at MCU, Bridgewater State University, the University of Copenhagen, and the City University of Hong Kong, as well as presentations through the Association of Asian Studies, the International Convention of Asia Scholars, the International Conference on Thai Studies, the American Academy of Religion, and the Theravada Cultures and Civilizations Conference.

I profited from the feedback of colleagues. Jillian Schedneck and Elizabeth Williams-Oerberg recommended important ideas for the introduction. Andrew Johnson, Alexandra Denes, and David Geary offered helpful suggestions for chapter 1. Nancy Eberhardt and Michael Jerryson read chapter 2 with much attention and useful comments. Chapter 3 is a revised version of an article published in *Modern Asian Studies* as "Religious Others, Tourism, and Missionization: Buddhist 'Monk Chats' in Northern Thailand" (Schedneck 2018). Chapter 4 benefited from the careful reading of Jack Meng-Tat Chia and Ann Gleig. Chapter 5 is also a revised version of an article published in *Journeys: The International Journal of Travel and Travel Writing* titled "Beyond the Glittering Golden Buddha Statues: Difference and Self-Transformation through Buddhist Volunteer Tourism in Thailand" (Schedneck 2017a). I thank the editors of *Modern Asian Studies* and *Journeys* for their permission to use this material. Both of these chapters contain additional and updated research.

The executive editor of the University of Washington Press, Lorri Hagman, has been supportive of this project since my first meeting with her. The two anonymous reviewers provided crucial feedback. William Starner, my husband and proofreader extraordinaire, deserves much appreciation and thanks. Jet, my child, was always willing to accompany me on research trips to temples, bringing joy to me as well as the monastics we met.

NOTE ON TRANSLITERATION

This book follows the Royal Thai General System of transcription for all Thai words from interviews and textual sources, except Thai names and Buddhist temples and terms, where I have followed the common romanization (e.g., Wat Phra Singh, thammacarik, Phrajao Tanjai, Chalermchai Kositpipat).

RELIGIOUS TOURISM IN NORTHERN THAILAND

INTRODUCTION

Encountering Buddhism

AT WAT CHEDI LUANG, ONE OF CHIANG MAI CITY'S MOST FAMOUS Buddhist temples, a tourist usually finds a line of international travelers waiting to pay a small entrance fee. After receiving a ticket, the tourist walks down a narrow corridor displaying information in English and Chinese concerning the rules of the temple space. Billboards communicate appropriate ways to behave, dress, and comport oneself. After the tourist reviews these guidelines, a security guard takes the entrance ticket and evaluates whether the tourist needs to borrow loose clothing to cover an immodest outfit. Inside the temple and approaching the main Buddha worship hall, or *wihan*, the visitor is greeted by more signs indicating one should take off one's shoes; again, dress appropriately; and sit down inside the hall. Toward the temple's center and main attraction, the stupa, or *chedi*, another set of signs informs the visitor not to climb onto the structure and in which direction one should walk around it.

A cursory look at recent media reports in Thailand concerning Buddhism and tourism shows why multiple signs and staff are necessary. Thai media outlets often publish stories of tourists disrespecting Buddhist sites through inappropriate behaviors. In the age of social media and instant news, negative impressions of tourists have quickly spread among the largely Buddhist population in Thailand. In response, temple management teams across the country have taken steps to deter behavior they consider harmful to Thai Buddhist sites. But while some tourists' actions garner media attention, cultural misunderstanding and ethnocentric disrespect

3

are far from the only results of such encounters. In many popular tourist temples, Buddhist monks argue that tourist presence can benefit both the religion and the tourists. Travelers are actively being shaped by experiences of Buddhism, while Buddhist monks use the popularity of Buddhism among tourists to spread their teachings.

International travel, volunteer tourism, and urbanization within Asian cities have created new contexts for encounters that illuminate much about contemporary Buddhism. These encounters reveal a diversity of reactions to and interpretations of the spaces, traditions, practices, and beliefs of Buddhism. Thailand has a long history of foreign encounters with Buddhism. Chiang Mai, considered the country's second city in regard to its cultural influence, has recently become a significant space wherein global audiences readily encounter Buddhism. Using insights from religious studies, Buddhist studies, the anthropology of tourism and religion, and Thai studies, this book explores the conjuncture of religion and globalization in Chiang Mai, arguing that these encounters reflect (1) contemporary realities of temple economics; (2) Buddhist relations with cultural and religious others; (3) Buddhist techniques and understandings of missionization, or spreading the teachings of Buddhism to non-Buddhist audiences; and (4) possibilities for self-transformation for Buddhist monks and tourists. In all of these outcomes, global connections are constantly creating new encounters.

A useful approach for theorizing such encounters is anthropologist Anna Lowenhaupt Tsing's (2005) notion of interconnections as friction. She understands friction as the "grip of worldly encounter," and investigates the ways universal aspirations can only be fulfilled and enacted through "the sticky materiality of practical encounter" (1). Friction implies neither compromise nor resistance, but instead highlights the fact that global motion is not always smooth (5). Tsing uses the metaphor of friction to capture the complexity of global connections. In Chiang Mai, friction arises from two levels of global encounters between Buddhist monks and non-Buddhist visitors: the temple space and the modern urban tourist space. Both levels of global encounters in Chiang Mai produce their own kinds of friction, including misunderstandings and debates as well as opportunities for exchange and spreading Buddhism. Like Tsing, I am interested in the unequal and unstable but also "creative qualities of interconnection across difference" (4). This metaphor of friction explains how, despite the economic power differential between tourists and student monks, temples maintain agency as they draw from tourist resources. Tsing notes that globalization does not simply depict "global force and local response" but creates "moments of conjuncture" that produce "connections" (272). The main conjunctures that have produced global connections in Chiang Mai are education, tourism, and urbanization. Rather than accommodating the global force of tourists' expectations or desires, Buddhist monks have drawn from their understanding of Buddhist teachings and practices to maintain the temple space while taking advantage of this curious global audience to spread the teachings of Buddhism.

Another useful analytical concept is entanglement, which theologian Kenneth Fleming (2014, 17) uses to write about the encounter between Christians and Buddhists in Thailand: "Entanglement emphasises the multidirectional interplay of ideas and actions that influence people during encounter." In this way, the labels of "Buddhism," "other religions," "Thai," and "foreign" are fluctuating reference points, constructed through encounter with others. Modern historical and global forces are entangled with Buddhist monks and groups of travelers, which all work together to form the productive friction of Buddhist encounters.

Encountering Buddhism in Chiang Mai

Chiang Mai, Thailand's northern capital, is known for its dense concentration of temples and more than seven centuries of history. Much of the mythical history of Chiang Mai is captured in temple chronicles (*tamnan wat*) that contain stories marking the space as a Buddha land (*buddhadesa*). Chronicles about relics of the Buddha, Buddha images, and footprints place the Buddha within Chiang Mai and the greater northern Thai region (Sarassawadee 2005, 4). These chronicles, written by monks, link the presence of the Buddha to the space of Chiang Mai, and the place's geographic features are believed to have allowed for the ongoing agency and presence of the Buddha (Chiu 2017, 20). King Mengrai (1239–1317), when he founded the city in 1296, followed Buddhist cosmological principles in its construction. The center of Chiang Mai City is Wat Chedi Luang, which symbolizes Mount Meru—the center of the Buddhist universe. In strategic locations surrounding this center are eight more temples, representing the eight directions analogous to Buddhist cosmology (Sarassawadee 2005, 60–61).[1] The indigenous spirit cult cosmology is also part of the old city geography, with the Inthakin City Pillar now located within Wat Chedi Luang. This pillar contains the spirit of the city and is worshipped annually for the continued protection of Chiang Mai. This premodern marking of sacred space not only empowered the monarchy but also offered a sense of security to the urban society.[2]

The twentieth and twenty-first centuries have seen Chiang Mai rapidly urbanize, with construction of modern facilities like shopping malls, hotels, and international restaurants. However, the old city's historic markers remain evident, with forty temples located within the boundaries of its moat and walls. The entire city boasts about three hundred temples, about 80 percent of which are supported by northern Thai people (*khon mueang*), practicing the Lanna style of Buddhism.[3] Lanna, meaning "a million rice fields," is the name of the northern region of Thailand. Lanna Buddhism is a form of Buddhism distinct to this region and identifiable through temple architecture and ritual practices. Although the majority group of Lanna Buddhism in Chiang Mai is the subject of study here, Chiang Mai is a diverse location. The city is also home to indigenous groups such as the Shan (Tai Yai) and Karen (Kariang), who sometimes establish their own temples on the outskirts of the city or mix with Lanna Buddhism inside the city.[4] Indigenous religions are represented through spirit mediums and worship of spirit shrines and the city pillar, and there are communities and places of worship for Christians, Muslims, Hindus, and Sikhs.[5] However, because the dominant form of religion in Chiang Mai is Buddhism, and because Buddhism is inextricably related to state and royal power within Thailand, this is the religion most tourists encounter and seek to engage with when visiting the city.[6]

Tourism is an important component of the Thai economy and accounts for about 10 percent of the country's gross domestic product, as the country hosted nearly thirty million visitors in 2015 alone.[7] In 2017, about ten million tourists visited Chiang Mai, and three million of these were international visitors.[8] Chiang Mai City has almost three thousand Buddhist monks living in its temples.[9] As Thailand's second city, Chiang Mai is often depicted in Thai movies, TV, music, and art as a place distinct from the urban sprawl of Bangkok, a place where international and domestic tourists can be immersed in the ancient Buddhist history that remains.[10] Tourism has become an important financial contribution to many of Chiang Mai's Buddhist temples.[11] In fact, on the Tourism Authority of Thailand website, under the article "Religion," Chiang Mai is highlighted for tourists as a place that allows "visitors to chat with monks in order to gain general knowledge about Buddhism or to study Buddhism more seriously."[12] Most tourists arrive in Chiang Mai City by plane, bus, or train from Bangkok, but an increasing number of direct flights are operating from many locations in

Asia.[13] Tourists staying at one of the many centrally located hotels and guesthouses can easily visit temples within the city by local transportation. Besides the multitude of temples in the old city of Chiang Mai, of which the most well known are Wat Chedi Luang and Wat Phra Singh, historic and popular temples in the outskirts of the city are also easily accessible, the most famous being Wat Doi Suthep, sitting atop Suthep Mountain, overlooking the city from the west.

For the purposes of this book, and because this is the way my student monk informants discussed different types of tourists, I distinguish between Western (*farang*) tourists and Chinese (*khon chin*) tourists. Because of their arrival in large numbers beginning in 2013, Chinese tourists are a large part of the story of Buddhist encounters in Chiang Mai. The introduction to Chiang Mai for Chinese tourists was the 2012 blockbuster comedy hit *Lost in Thailand* (Mostafanezhad and Promburom 2016). Most of the movie's plot takes place in Chiang Mai, with Buddhist temples featured in key scenes. With the success of this movie, along with the rising middle class of Chinese citizens and the ability to receive a visa on arrival to Thailand, Chinese tourist numbers to Chiang Mai increased dramatically.[14] Although the tourist revenue from Chinese tour groups, and increasingly individual travelers, is important for Thailand's tourism industry, it has not come without conflict. After hundreds of articles reporting on "Chinese behaving badly," published internationally and in China, along with hostility from Thais on social media, Chiang Mai experienced a temporary boycott by mainland Chinese travelers in the summer months of 2016.[15] Living in Chiang Mai during this time, almost every day I heard a story involving the behavior of Chinese tourists from other expatriates, Thai people, and Buddhist monks. However, the Tourism Authority of Thailand has worked to win back Chinese tourists with shops displaying stickers that welcome Chinese and services geared to Chinese travelers.[16] This influx of Chinese tourists in their temples, along with the steady numbers of domestic Thai tourists and Western tourists to Chiang Mai, has presented both challenges and opportunities for monks.[17] This book does not include interviews with Thai and Chinese tourists, focusing instead on city and student monks involved in Buddhist education and their perceptions of these varying groups, along with the perspectives of volunteer tourists who have taught in Buddhist temple schools for an extended period and who are mostly from Western countries.[18]

While tourists may be convinced that Chiang Mai is an important Buddhist destination through magazines, social media platforms, and photographs of temples on Instagram, Buddhist monks come to Chiang Mai as a center of a particular kind of Buddhist education. The Thai monastic education system incorporates both secular and Buddhist subjects at the high school and college levels. Young men from various provinces in northern Thailand enter middle and high schools designed for novice monks in Chiang Mai. Further north, near the border between Thailand and Myanmar, members of ethnic minority groups in Thailand such as the Shan, Karen, Palaung, and others ordain as novice monks in order to take advantage of the educational opportunities. Within Chiang Mai City are two Buddhist universities representing the two sects of Thai Buddhism.[19] International monks from many places within the Theravada Buddhist world of Southeast and South Asia value the English-medium education available in Chiang Mai and the ability to study Buddhism along with secular subjects in English, something less accessible in their countries. Therefore, Chiang Mai is a center of Buddhist education but also English education for these Buddhist monks.

The monastic educational institutions under study here consist mainly of male monks. Occasionally, a precept nun or female monk will join a class or degree program at a Buddhist monastic university; however, this remains rare because the monastic system, and subsequently its education system, is set up for males.[20] Consequently, this book is concerned with the male monastic institution and the encounters that urbanization and education have created.

Most of the student monks represented here moved to Chiang Mai City for the exclusive purpose of education. As one monk explained when I asked a group of college monks why they had chosen to attend school in Chiang Mai, "We are all very poor. This is our only chance to learn English."[21] They all had heard about this opportunity to study and practice English in Chiang Mai from a senior monk friend or teacher. Many of these monks reside with others from their home countries in the same temple. But in the classrooms, they get to know monks from other countries. In this way, they encounter not only Thai Buddhism in Chiang Mai but also Buddhism from other regions and nations. These international monks may arrive in Chiang Mai by flights purchased with their savings, by benefactors from inside or outside their families, or with scholarships from their local temples. When they arrive they are assigned a temple, which in some cases might be up to an hour away from the university via the local transportation system.[22] Usually, after a year or two, student monks are able to move to a temple closer to the city so they can travel more easily and cheaply to their university. Because of all of these educational opportunities, there are many Thai, ethnic minority, and international monks who are eager to converse with international visitors. All of these are ways of thinking about Buddhism and the particular space of Chiang Mai—a place of beautiful temples, a movie set, a center of Buddhist education.

Along with the space of Chiang Mai as a platform for encountering Buddhism in different ways, this book analyzes the results of these global encounters. When I asked two monks who teach and study in Chiang Mai's Buddhist universities, Phra Ajahn Kaew and Phra Gamon, about tourism in the temple where they live, Wat Phra Singh, they saw mostly benefits. Wat Phra Singh is one of the landmarks of the old city of Chiang Mai and attracts hundreds of tourists each day. These monks listed many positive aspects for the tourists: the tourists can (1) become curious about Buddhism, (2) learn about Thai culture and the life of the monk, (3) participate in meritorious activities like chanting and worshipping the Buddha, and (4) get used to (*khoei chin*) temples and Buddhism, and, because of all of these aspects, tourism (5) spreads Buddhism and promotes Thailand. As one monk put it, "Visiting the temple is better than going to Central [the name of a ubiquitous department store in many of Thailand's malls]." Buddhist monks realize what some observers of Thai society have noted is occurring especially in Bangkok—the mall is replacing the temple as the center of activity (Sophorntavy 2011, 72). These monks find most tourists are a curious and interested population and are hopeful that although initially attracted by the unique art and aesthetic difference of the temple, they will be able to learn some of the basics of temple life and seek to find out more (*phoem khuen*), little by little (*khoi khoi*). These monks were optimistic that tourists will continue to learn about Buddhism through books or research on the Internet. The only downside these monks could think of to the large influx of tourists to their temples was that sometimes the tourists act inappropriately in the space. But they did not see this as a large problem because it is easy through body language to tell the tourists to speak more softly or to sit down in front of a Buddha image. These are the dominant views of student monks concerning tourism, demonstrating that they are mostly encouraged that the foreign interest in temples can lead to further engagement with the religion.

However, some monks and Thai Buddhist laypeople have negative feedback about tourism in temples. When tourists do not recognize the correct ways to act in the temple space, the site can lose some of its sacredness. The negative reactions to tourists that I have heard from student monks and read in Thai media concerning Buddhist tourism include (1) the tourists do not know Thai culture and they do not adapt (*prap tua*) to it as much as they should; (2) if the tourists do not behave correctly, this makes Thai people upset, feeling as if they have lost ownership over the temple; (3) the temple should not be responsible for educating the tourists about appropriate behavior; and (4) Chinese tourists in particular are very loud and behave inappropriately. Because of these varying views, when tourism meets Buddhism in Chiang Mai, it is not a superficially positive or negative engagement. Instead, these global connections produce friction and debates about the city's entanglement with tourist and urban encounters. Issues related to tourism ultimately reveal deeper debates concerning the nature of the temple space, the appropriate activities that can take place in it, and the best ways to manage the site for diverse populations of Westerners, Chinese, and Thai lay Buddhists.

Religious Encounters

"Encounters" occur both between distinct groups of people and within particular places. They can be long- or short-term, chance or planned, between individuals or representatives of groups, and take place with people across cultural and national boundaries (King 2015, 498). Encounters are central to the tourist experience, as a result of increasing mobility. Factors of movement, relations, exchange, and contact are key to understanding how religions make meaning for people and transform over time (Tweed 2006).

   Much writing about religious encounters concerns analyzing a meeting of different worldviews or cognitive maps.[23] Tourism is not just something that happens to less-developed countries, but involves cultural and economic encounters on a "complex, historically constituted world stage" (Liechty 2017, xii). An important example in this regard is cultural anthropologist Marshall Sahlins's (1985) analysis of the European trade ship sailors, led by Captain James Cook, and their encounter with the people of the Hawaiian Islands. These European sailors did not understand the social norms and taboos of the Hawaiians surrounding food and gender, resulting in unfortunate consequences. When the sailors invited Hawaiian women to eat with them, the Europeans found themselves desecrated and polluted in the eyes of the Hawaiian men. Men and women eating together was a taboo for Hawaiians because Hawaiian men ate the sacrificed food for the gods, which was off-limits to women. Before the European men ate with Hawaiian women, they could enter the temple as a place to repair their sails, recover their sick, and bury their dead; however, after the Europeans dined with women, the Europeans became polluted and desecrated according to the Hawaiian cultural logic (Sahlins 1985, 9). Cultural encounters occur within the fluctuating conjunctures of each situation. Encounters are partly based on group norms, contributing to assumptions and stereotypes concerning cultural and religious others. However, these assumptions are nuanced with each new encounter. Because of this, encounters occur in concert with established cultural and religious practices while constantly remaining in dialogue with specific spaces, individuals, and groups.

Moments of encounter can resist fixed group identities. Encounters between distinct religious groups in the same space, such as Muslims and Christians in Africa (Soares 2006) and Christian and Jewish populations in the United States (Chireau and Deutsch 2000), break down assumptions about religious boundaries. Although necessarily dividing and separating groups of people, encounters are complex and multifaceted. Individuals do not always act as representatives of their group, but instead act according to their own particular context of encounter. The concept is thus a productive way to appreciate the dynamics within and between religious groups, but also a way to recognize the dynamic between religion and the city.

A common misunderstanding about cities is that they are modern and therefore secular.[24] In contrast, the city can be understood as a space where religion becomes transparent and a more obvious part of one's self-identity as new populations come in contact for the first time (van der Veer 2015, 9). In urban Asian cities today, travelers explore new societies and commodities, but importantly also seek out cultural and religious sites. Buddhism began as an urban religion, and cities throughout its history have been centers of Buddhist kingdoms and cosmologies (Heine-Geldern [1942] 2013; Veidlinger 2016). Cities with majority Buddhist populations have also been hubs for Buddhist education and, more recently, tourism. These conjunctures make city centers within mainland Southeast Asia ripe for exchange opportunities. Some cities have an informal monk chat, such as the one on top of Mandalay Hill in Mandalay, Myanmar, where novice monks gather, hoping to engage in conversation with the many tourists who visit at dusk each day. Other cities, such as Phnom Penh in Cambodia, have programs arranged for volunteers to teach English in Buddhist temples. And yet other cities, such as Bangkok, have not yet capitalized on the conjunctures of tourism and Buddhist monastic schools, as there are few formal opportunities for exchange. The city itself, through programs and individuals, must be open to encounters. The history and culture of Chiang Mai have created

a unique environment for encounters between Buddhist monastic education and tourists, with both urban infrastructure and creative programs to
facilitate encounter.

Another example of Buddhist encounters occurred in Sri Lanka, where
urbanization and colonialism created a new social class, in turn affecting
Buddhism. The encounter between Buddhism and colonialism produced a
form of Buddhism distinct from its manifestations in villages. Because of
the urban bourgeoisie's contrasting religious values, Sinhalese Buddhism
was opened up to internal diversity. Indologist Richard Gombrich and
anthropologist Gananath Obeyesekere (1988) argue that urban Buddhism
had taken on characteristics of Protestantism, such as Buddhist Sunday
schools and Young Men's and Women's Buddhist Associations. They labeled
this phenomenon Protestant Buddhism because of its incorporation of
Protestant values and protest against traditional Buddhism (215).

Instead of change, another perspective of Buddhist encounter highlights
continuity. Sri Lankan Buddhists in the colonial period used resources
within their Buddhist tradition and monastic life and thus were not as
greatly influenced by Protestant Christianity as earlier interpretations suggest. Through investigating the historical evidence from this period, especially the life and work of Buddhist monk Hikkaḍuvē Sumaṅgala, one of
the most central figures in British-period Lankan Buddhism, historian of
religion Anne Blackburn (2010) argues that imported discourses did not
always displace those that existed previously. Sumaṅgala and his monastic
colleagues instead selectively added European forms of knowledge and
expression to their writings as occasional ways to strengthen arguments. If
needed, they would use "modernist" discourses to galvanize support from
Southeast Asia, in order to seek approval from the king of Siam, who was
in the midst of modernizing his kingdom. During the encounters between
Sri Lankan Buddhists and colonialism, Buddhist educational interests,
ritual, and monastic power remained important, and were not transformed
based on the model of Protestant Christian practices (Blackburn 2010, xiii).

Within urban settings of encounter, both change and continuity need to
be taken into account. Instead of seeing Sri Lankan Buddhism as "emphati-
cally marked" by colonial rule, Blackburn pays attention to "responses" to
colonialism, understanding colonialism as part of Sri Lankan Buddhists'
lives, but not encompassing all of it (2010, 202). Student monks in Chiang
Mai also use internal Buddhist resources when presenting their religion to
outsiders or debating for or against recent temple changes brought about by
urbanization, such as the introduction of temple fees for foreigners. They

are influenced by the presence of non-Buddhists and the fact of tourism and globalization, but their arguments about the nature of the temple space and the best ways to spread the teachings are grounded in Buddhist beliefs and practices.

Along with scholarship of encounters between religions and religious encounters with urbanization, there is a body of scholarship specifically focused on encounters with Buddhism through anthropological, historical, and theological angles. The few anthropological works on encounters between Westerners and Asian Buddhists in Asia focus on commodification of sacred sites and practices. Ethnographies of travelers encountering Tibetan Buddhism in Nepal and meditation retreats in Thailand highlight commodification of religious practices, religious identity, and the complexities of religious donations (Moran 2004; Schedneck 2015). Some edited volumes have dealt with the question of travel to Buddhist sites in Asia, including analysis of temples as cultural heritage and the ways domestic tourism can contribute to the revival of religious sites (Hitchcock, King, and Parnwell 2010; Oakes and Sutton 2010). These encounters with Buddhism reveal the parts of the tradition that become representative—practices such as meditation and physical landmarks such as temples—as the main face of Buddhism for domestic and international tourists to Buddhist locations. Beyond this, much anthropological scholarship within Buddhist studies focuses on Buddhist encounters located outside of Asia.[25] A good portion of this work highlights the struggles that arise and the adaptations that must be made in these contexts. Instead of focusing on Buddhists establishing temples and diasporic communities abroad, *Religious Tourism in Northern Thailand: Encounters with Buddhist Monks* reflects on the ways foreign audiences and Buddhist monks interact with one another within the context of Buddhist homelands.

Scholars of religious studies have also paid attention to the ways Buddhists have encountered religious and cultural others through historical and theological approaches. Studies of interactions between Buddhism and Islam from the eighth to the late nineteenth century and of Christian-Buddhist relations in the nineteenth century remind us of the flexibility of the tradition during premodernity, colonialism, and modernity (Elverskog 2011; Harris 2006). Scholars have taken theological approaches to understand Buddhist attitudes toward non-Buddhists, mapping Buddhist attitudes onto terms like "tolerance," "inclusivism," "exclusivism," and "pluralism" (Jayatilleke 1975; Kiblinger 2005; Schmidt-Leukel 2007). Instead of investigating Buddhist relations with religious others theologically, I draw out the emic perspectives of student monks, describing and analyzing their views within the context of contemporary life in Chiang Mai. Although anthropologists have set their books in Chiang Mai, writing about meditation in a Chiang Mai temple (Cook 2010) and urban development and spirit mediums (Johnson 2014), *Religious Tourism in Northern Thailand* is the first ethnography to analyze contemporary Buddhism in Chiang Mai. The chapters that follow demonstrate the results of these encounters: economic agency, varying attitudes to religious others, missionization, and self-transformation. All of these outcomes are informed by global perceptions of Buddhism, the tourist economy, and the city of Chiang Mai.

Fieldwork and Methodology

This book is based on fieldwork conducted in the city and province of Chiang Mai from 2013 to 2018. My field sites included many temples within the city of Chiang Mai, including Wat Chedi Luang, Wat Suan Dok, and Wat Srisuphan, where there are regular programs for tourists to engage with Buddhism. I also interviewed monks at temples such as Wat Phra Singh, Wat Palad, and Wat Buppharam, which do not hold formal programs for tourists but are still busy tourist sites. I was able to conduct this research periodically during each semester while working at Chiang Mai University. This long-term research in the city was useful in building connections and maintaining contacts with research participants. However, I also conducted research trips further from the city in spaces that regularly hosted foreign students, volunteers, or travelers. This research was conducted during the months of July and August, when I did not have teaching responsibilities. In June and July of 2018, I returned to Chiang Mai in order to update my research with site visits and interviews within the city. This combination of intense and periodic research provided depth to this study and a breadth of experience to draw from.

To a lesser extent, foreign travelers are a part of this study. As tourists are a transient group, it proved more challenging to locate and interview them on a regular basis. However, I was able to interview long-term travelers who engaged with Buddhism in Chiang Mai as volunteer tourists on trips ranging from two weeks to a month or more. When I began this research in 2013, four organizations advertised the ability to support and place volunteer tourists in temple schools or universities to teach monks. However, over the course of my fieldwork, two of these organizations emerged as the most enduring and focused on offerings for teaching in monastic schools.

I worked with Friends for Asia and the Wat Doi Saket Project, which transitioned into the FutureSense Foundation, because both of these organizations have solid relationships with Buddhist temple schools and place volunteers consistently throughout the year. In addition to interviews with tourists and travelers in English, I have also used public accounts of engagements with Buddhism in Chiang Mai on the Internet in various blogs, discussion boards, and personal websites. I also utilize the expertise of student monks to characterize the questions asked them by the majority of tourists they have spoken with. Because the student monks have interacted and spoken with foreign tourists on a daily basis over many years, their impressions were most valuable to my research. My interviews with foreigners are highlighted in chapter 5, but the majority of this book focuses on the monastic side of the encounter, as the group that has deeply reflected on Buddhism and travelers' understandings of their religion. Because of that, I pay close attention to the ways student monks make sense of Buddhism in Chiang Mai, and how they see their role as Buddhist monks.

Besides qualitative interviews, I used participant-observation while attending Buddhist cultural exchange programs. I sat in on question-and-answer sessions between visitors and monks, observed volunteer tourists teaching English to novice monks, and watched as study tours learned about the monastic lives of those who reside in rural temples outside of Chiang Mai City. I used semi-structured interviews with both foreign travelers and monks. For Thai monks not yet proficient in English, such as novice monks in high school or monks just beginning college, and senior monks who felt more comfortable speaking in Thai, the interviews were conducted in Thai. However, some of the more senior college monks like to practice English, so those with better fluency spoke English with me. If they had trouble communicating a difficult idea, then we switched to Thai. For all foreign monks attending Buddhist universities from Bangladesh, Cambodia, Laos, Myanmar, Nepal, and Vietnam, English was the main medium of communication.[26] In this book, I offer direct quotations from these interviews and conversations in English or provide my translations from Thai. In addition to spoken discourses, I also collected written information, mostly pamphlets or small books, introducing Buddhism to foreigners.

I refer to the monks I spoke to as "student monks," or more broadly to monks in Chiang Mai as "city monks," and the group they encounter as "international travelers." As should be clear by now, student monks cover a wide range of backgrounds and nationalities—although the most common age group here is between the typical college ages of eighteen and twenty-two. As well, international travelers come from a variety of places. Although for the most part these are Westerners and Chinese, I include within this category the entire non-Thai international community. They come for many different purposes as well: tourism, volunteering, commitment to Buddhism, or interest in Thailand and Thai culture. However, even though these are broad categories, they refer to important distinctions student monks make between those who are inside Thai Buddhism and those who are outside. Throughout the book, I refer to the groups in these general ways and, when necessary, delve into more specific identities. Because student monks and volunteer tourists are not public figures, I use pseudonyms when quoting their opinions and perspectives. I have retained the names of temples because an accurate discussion of the Buddhist landscape and geography of Chiang Mai is vital for this study. I also use real names for the few references to temple leaders, with their agreement. These interviews are all listed in the references section at the back of this book.

Spaces of encounter are a significant lens through which to understand how Buddhists operate in transnational settings. Encounters in Chiang Mai point to the insufficiency of the commonly employed sacred-profane, authentic-commodified dichotomies used to evaluate Buddhist encounters with the international community. Although the book is grounded in a particular city, its analysis of temple economics, attitudes toward religious others, missionization, and self-transformation contributes to the field of Buddhist studies more broadly. Buddhist encounters in contemporary Chiang Mai are part of the entanglement and friction of tourism, Buddhism, and the urban landscape in Chiang Mai.

CHAPTER 1

A MODERN HISTORY OF
BUDDHIST ENCOUNTERS IN CHIANG MAI

BUDDHIST RELICS AND IMAGES CONNECT THE LANDSCAPE OF Chiang Mai to Buddhist history. The Thai chronicle *The Sheaf of Garlands of the Epochs of the Conqueror* (Jinakalamalipakaranam), details the Buddha's visit to the Ping River, an important tributary in the region of northern Thailand. After preaching and receiving offerings, the Buddha predicts the discovery of one of his relics at a particular spot near the river. His prediction was fulfilled in the eleventh century when a stupa and temple were built around the relic (Swearer 1987, 107–8). *The Chronicle of the Sihing Buddha Image* (Tamnan Phra Buddha Sihiṅga) elucidates the complex history of the Phra Buddha Sihing image, located today at Wat Phra Singh. This chronicle narrates the movement of this Buddha image, associated with a lion because of its robust chest and its origin in Sri Lanka, through many kingdoms of central Thailand before finally landing in Chiang Mai (Chiu 2017, 25–31). These chronicles detail the legendary relationship of Chiang Mai and Buddhism.

Three more important sources for the legends of Buddhist Chiang Mai include *The Chronicle of the Relic of Doi Suthep* (Tamnan Phrathat Doi Suthep) and *The Legend of Doi Kham* (Tamnan Wat Phrathat Doi Kham), both works highlighting the sacredness of two mountains surrounding the valley of Chiang Mai, and *The Legend of Queen Cama* (Camadevivamsa), which focuses on the queen Chamadewi and the construction of her kingdom, Haripunchai.[1] *The Chronicle of the Relic of Doi Suthep* describes how the Buddha traveled to northern Thailand and received food from a family of giants, or *yakkhas*, named Grandfather (Bu) Sae and Grandmother (Ya) Sae, and their child, Wasuthep. The story in the Doi Suthep chronicle concerns the possession and enshrinement of a Buddha relic (Swearer, Premchit, and Dokbuakaew 2004, 72). In contrast, the Doi Kham chronicle focuses on the giants as the main part of the story. On Doi Kham, one of the central mountains of the northern Thai region, the Buddha eventually persuades Bu Sae and Ya Sae to stop killing and eating humans. In the chronicle, the Buddha's meeting with the family of giants is described in this way: "When they saw the Lord Buddha approaching together with his disciples they were intent on capturing and eating them as was their custom. The Lord Buddha, knowing their nature, extended loving-kindness to them and by the power of his great merit prevented their defilement from arising" (Swearer, Premchit, and Dokbuakaew 2004, 84). The Buddha preached to them "to tame their evil nature" (84). After he conveyed the negative consequences of their actions, the giants decided to become Buddhists. They reached a compromise that instead of killing humans they would eat a buffalo once per year. In this way, Buddhism acts as a civilizing force, taming the cannibal giants. The giants' son, Wasuthep, after this encounter with the Buddha, founds the nearby city of Lamphun, placing his mystically born daughter, Chamadewi, as the queen (Johnson 2014, 43).

In *The Legend of Queen Cama*, two sages choose this daughter, who becomes Queen Cama, or Chamadewi, to rule over a walled city, Haripunchai, bringing civilization to the indigenous people of the forest (Swearer and Premchit 1998, 6). She is chosen because of her high moral virtue and her possession of the ten traits of a wheel-turning monarch, or *cakkavattin* (Swearer 1987, 107). Queen Chamadewi is also part of an interlocking story with the family of giants. Together these two stories attempt to reveal and unravel tensions between chaos and order, wild and tamed. Chamadewi represents Buddhist civilization, which must triumph over the wild forces of the forest-dwelling animists and their king, Wilangkha. Wilangkha, from the forests of Doi Kham, courts the city-dwelling Chamadewi with gifts but also with spears, showing his crude form of power. Chamadewi defeats Wilangkha with her cleverness, sending him a gift of a turban, which is secretly made out of her menstrual undergarments. This polluting substance, when placed on Wilangkha's head, causes him to lose his powers, ultimately leading to his downfall. Both the Buddha and Chamadewi cleverly compromise with these untamed forces to bring them into Buddhism's orbit (Johnson 2014, 43).

These stories from the northern Thai chronicles highlight the power and significance of Buddhism in making northern Thailand into a Buddhist land, or *buddhadesa*, transitioning the people from wild forest-dwellers to cultured, urban Buddhists. These myths are still important for Chiang Mai locals through the story and tradition of Grandmother and Grandfather Sae as well as Chamadewi's spirits, all of which inhabit contemporary spirit mediums (Johnson 2014, 45–47).[2] Although these are significant legends in the founding of Chiang Mai as a center of Buddhism, these stories are not the way the city is marketed as a Buddhist destination today. Instead of myths involving giants, spirit mediums, and the lingering presence of the Buddha, the Buddhist aspects of Chiang Mai themselves have been tamed in a different way for the modern tourist audience. The aesthetic beauty and density of temples, friendly monks, and the numerous ways to engage with Buddhism take center stage in advertising today's Chiang Mai.

Marketing Chiang Mai

Chiang Mai is a place of multiple layers. It is the capital of northern Thailand, one of Thailand's largest cities, and promoted by the Tourism Authority of Thailand to be the "city of culture" for national and international tourists (Johnson 2014, 39). Although Bangkok may be considered "a space of irredeemable unnaturalness" and "modernity gone awry," Chiang Mai is still imagined as a nostalgic element of the mythical past and origins of Thai culture (Taylor 2008, 13). With activities such as ethnic "hill tribe" treks, elephant riding, and shopping for local handicrafts, encountering Buddhist monks fits within a broader package of cultural day trips. Many travel agencies trade on learning the "way of life" of Thai people, whether they are northern Thai silk weavers, silversmiths, or monks—the commodification of difference is good business.[3]

Modern-day Chiang Mai is identified as a Buddhist tourism destination because of its dense concentration of temples and the relative ease with which one can talk to monks (Choe and O'Regan 2015, 199).[4] The United Nations World Tourism Organization (UNWTO) lists Chiang Mai as an important part of Thailand's religious tourism because of "the opportunity provided to approach monks, talk to them and learn about Buddhist practices" (Citrinot 2011, 30). Religious tourism is a rapidly increasing tourism segment, which comprises both domestic and international tourists (Kom 2011, 276). Profit is not the only factor driving Buddhist tourism. The Thai government and tourism agencies seek to promote Buddhism as a symbol of the nation-state. The positive global associations with Buddhism make for a better national brand than sex or even beach tourism (Schedneck 2014, 442).

Many of the imaginaries of the city itself are linked with Buddhism. Travel magazines list Chiang Mai as a top destination, showing photos of monks in lush temple spaces. The Chiang Mai municipality also seeks to enhance these ideas of its city through its promotion as a UNESCO World Heritage site. In 2015, UNESCO added Chiang Mai to its list of tentative World Heritage sites. Over seventy of the nominated properties included in the city's official submission are Buddhist temples.[5] Through these venues touting Chiang Mai as a top tourist destination and cultural heritage center, visiting the sites of Lanna Buddhism has become one of the principal tourist activities. Along with highlighting temple scenes and architecture, the Tourism Authority of Thailand has developed products around Buddhism and marketed the "scientific" benefits of Buddhist meditation. Diverse Buddhist activities including festivals and meditation retreats are readily available through websites and guidebooks (Choe and O'Regan 2015, 198). Not simply possessing culturally significant temples but marketing them in a way that promotes an accessible spirituality for different tourist interests is part of the success of Chiang Mai as a Buddhist destination. The Chiang Mai portion of the Tourism Authority of Thailand's website highlights the city's combination of traditional and modern: "Chiang Mai is one of the few places in Thailand where it is possible to experience both historical and modern Thai culture coexisting side by side: the city features centuries-old pagodas and temples next to modern convenience stores and boutique hotels."[6] In this way, the Tourism Authority of Thailand depicts Chiang Mai as the best of both worlds, with the convenience of the modern and the authenticity of the ancient.

Guidebook websites promote the possibilities to engage with Buddhism in Chiang Mai. The Lonely Planet website for Chiang Mai adds a tagline to the city—"temples galore."[7] Out of the top eight recommended sites, the first three are Buddhist temples. The "Chiang Mai Travel Guide" on the Rough Guides website writes of Wat Phra Singh, Wat Chedi Luang, and Wat Chiang Man: "These elegant *wats* may be Chiang Mai's primary tourist sights, but they're no pre-packaged museum pieces—they're living community centres, where you're quite likely to be approached by monks keen to chat and practise their English."[8] The Frommer's web guide to Chiang Mai highlights Monk Chat as a top activity, describing the conversation between tourists and monks as "a mostly informal discussion about one's own country or sports (young novices are nuts about English Premier League football), but the more senior monks can give you some insights into Buddhist practice and monastic life."[9] These travel guides equate temples with the most popular and important sites to see in Chiang Mai. But temples are also spaces to engage with Buddhism, especially its monks, through both casual conversations and deeper teachings.

Buddhist monks also seek to promote Thailand as the land of Buddhism. Phra Thiraphat Burawatnukoon (2009, 5), in the small booklet titled *Thai Buddhism: Monk Chat*, writes, "Life in Thailand today, as throughout the past, would be unthinkable without the Buddhist faith, and without the monkhood which is the cornerstone of that faith." Similarly, the well-respected Thai scholar-monk P. A. Payutto (1984, 11), in his *Thai Buddhism in the Buddhist World*, characterizes Buddhism as the state religion because "under the Constitution, the King, as a symbol of the nation, although protector of all religions, must be a Buddhist." Payutto continues, "The charm that has earned Thailand the reputation as the 'Land of Smiles' undoubtedly comes from the influence of Buddhism over her people" (42). The similarities of Buddhist monks promoting Buddhism to foreigners and tourism companies are apparent here, as they both equate Thailand with Buddhism. As well, professor of Thai Buddhism Saeng Chandra-ngarm (1999, 1), writing from a Buddhist perspective based on talks given to foreign tourists, states that "Buddhism is regarded as the national religion of Thailand." He goes on to assert four reasons why: (1) there is a large majority of Buddhists in Thailand; (2) the king must be Buddhist as stipulated by the constitution; (3) Buddhism has been rooted in Thailand for over a thousand years; and (4) Buddhism has connections to Thai culture, expressed in many forms of art. Officially, however, the Thai constitution makes no provision for a national or state religion. This conflation of "Thainess" (*khwam pen thai*) with Buddhism, which occurs through selected culture and traditions, shapes the foreign encounter with Buddhism.

This packaging and presentation of Buddhism to tourists maintains the civilized "face" of the country to the world. The focus on the connection between Buddhism and Thailand suppresses darker sides of Thai society—sex tourism, political conflicts, corruption, and underdeveloped infrastructure. Just as Buddhism tamed the demons and unruly spirits of northern Thailand, it continues to tame more obvious demons for the international community. Well-known Buddhist monks, travel magazines, the Tourism Authority of Thailand, and guidebooks all market Chiang Mai as a Buddhist city, where one would, as a matter of course, encounter Buddhism. Along with tourism, Buddhism in Chiang Mai has also encountered the urban environment.

Buddhism and Urbanization in Chiang Mai

In Chiang Mai, a city identified with and tamed by beliefs and actions inspired by legends of the Buddha, the urban environment and Buddhism are inextricably intertwined. While Buddhist sacred spaces in the city are important visible and symbolic landmarks, aspirations linked to Buddhism within Chiang Mai's population can also be seen throughout the city. As with urban religious aspirations expressed elsewhere in Asia (van der Veer 2015), there are multiple conjunctures between Buddhism and urban aspiration in Chiang Mai. Wealth, a favorable rebirth, and prestige through temple sponsorship are part of the fabric of the society. It is easy to find donation boxes for temple building projects and invitations to join in making merit (*ruam tham bun*) in businesses across the city. These smaller-scale aspirations lead to the city being seen as a site of multiple possibilities, social mobility, and transformation through the cosmological framework of Buddhism. The Buddhist city also provides large-scale possibilities of aspirational transformation to young men through ordination and education. This rural-to-urban migration of young men allows them to remake themselves in the city, while being exposed to different forms of Buddhism, secular worldviews and institutions, and middle-class lifestyles.

From 2009 to 2019, the degree of urbanization in Thailand increased more than 8 percent.[10] Although Thailand is still much more rural than other developed nations, with an urban population of over 50 percent, this recent growth demonstrates a marked shift from what was several decades ago a predominantly rural country.[11] In Thai society, urban space increasingly extends toward and embraces the countryside. In Thailand, urban and rural are often constituted in relation to each other. City space consists of ideas, practices, and habits that are contrasted with the rural landscape's (*chonnabot*) lack of opportunities. The Thai city, for the most part, undermines the countryside's backwardness while at the same time praising its maintenance of traditional lifestyles (Taylor 2015, 221). The city is loved and hated in Thailand. It is the site of cosmopolitanism and development, but it is also the site of loss—increasing traffic, overcrowding, air pollution, and Westernization. For most Thais and foreigners, the Thai city that immediately comes to mind is Bangkok, which holds approximately 8 million residents; however, the much smaller Chiang Mai, with a population in the city's metropolitan area at about 250,000, is also included in this critique.[12] I have heard Chiang Mai locals, on several occasions, comment that the city has grown too much. These locals are beginning to prefer smaller cities of the north such as Chiang Rai, which are compared to what Chiang Mai was like twenty years ago—a city of a small and manageable size. Anthropologist James L. Taylor observes that "Thais are delving into an imagined past while feeling a sense of time and space compression caused by urbanization and late modernity" (2015, 229).

Urban religion highlights the fact that religious innovation and creativity have often taken place in cities, partly due to the diverse cultural influences (Berger 2018, 27). During his founding of Chiang Mai in 1296, King Mengrai drew on cultural influences from numerous ethnic groups such as the Lawa, Mon, and Khmer in building the city. Highlighting this fluidity makes it clear that Chiang Mai is not simply a "Thai" city. In fact, Chiang Mai maintained closer connections with the north, east, and west than it did with central Siam until significant trade with Bangkok began in the late nineteenth century (Easum 2018, 195–96).[13] The dynamism of northern Thailand can also be seen when diverse Buddhist regional ways of practice come together and are negotiated. In Chiang Mai, one can witness the lottery (tan kuai salak) ritual of northern Thais, where laypeople make offerings to individual monks based on a random matching-number system. The Shan (Tai Yai) novice ordination ceremony for boys, Paui Sang Long, is also part of the cultural diversity of Thai Buddhism. Temples in the Lanna style, such as Wat Chiang Man, and Burmese-style structures in temples like Wat Chedi Luang and Wat Buppharam can be found within the city. Chiang Mai as a space of urban Buddhism highlights the diversity and aspirations of its inhabitants as well as its magnetism as a host for multiple kinds of Buddhism.

Although neither a world city nor a megacity, with no business or financial center to speak of, Chiang Mai is significant within northern Thailand as the urban space connecting diverse rural areas.[14] Chiang Mai has grown rapidly over the past decade, as attested to by a tremendous increase in road and air traffic, mostly due to tourism and education (Rimmer and Dick 2009, 94). Other factors in Chiang Mai's urbanization include growth in manufacturing and development of leisure and entertainment options (A. Cohen 2009, 164). With three large shopping malls within the city and two on the outskirts, Chiang Mai's consumer culture is flourishing. Many Thai teenagers from the north move or commute to the city, not primarily for its Buddhist influence but for educational opportunities and access to fashion, movies, and international commodities. Although all cities contain manifold secular influences, in Chiang Mai urbanization also creates a need for cosmological explanations and connections with sacred spaces for reassurance (Johnson 2014). Through this paradox of the city, in Chiang Mai we can still find moral claims of Buddhism as an urban, taming, civilizational influence. But we also find critiques of this same place, teeming with secularism and consumerism and lacking a moral core. This urban environment has also attracted foreign missionaries, businesspeople, and, more recently, tourists. In their encounters with Buddhism in the cities of Thailand, they have presented a wide range of reactions.

Historical Encounters with Buddhism

Today, Christianity is, for the most part, the main "other" religion with which student monks in Chiang Mai are in dialogue. The history of foreign Christian encounters with Buddhism in Thailand can be located mainly in the writings of missionaries and early travelers to Siam.[15] The earliest Catholic missionaries failed to win any converts because they lacked indigenous terms to explain their religion, making it seem alien to Thai people (Keyes 1993b, 270). It was challenging for Thai people to disentangle Christianity from Western culture and colonialism, and they often grouped missionaries and colonialists into the same category (Chansamone 2003, 16). By the twentieth century, missionizing strategies had become more sophisticated, adapting the Christian message to the local cultures; however, "the aura of foreignness" has not been shed (Keyes 1993b, 273). Catholic author Benedetto Philachan Kornkrai (1991, 61) believes that "it is quite difficult to separate Buddhism from Thai culture. Many Thai people think that both are one and the same. It is quite difficult for Thai Catholics to adapt Christianity to their culture." A professor of Christian theology, Saad Chaiwan (1999, 65) continues with this same point, stating, "In fact, the majority of the Thai people feel that to be truly Thai means to be Buddhist. Consequently, when someone becomes a Christian, or embraces another religion, he usually experiences considerable family pressure and village opposition, but he is rarely physically persecuted."

Philosopher Warayuth Sriwarakuel (2009, 95) finds that for Thais, in general, "Islam is the religion of the Khaeg ['guest,' but in this case it is a slang term referring to Muslims], and Christianity is the religion of the Farang [a slang term referring to Europeans, usually indicating white foreigners]. Many Thai people still believe that those who are Christians are not authentic Thais. Some may say that the Thai Christians are Thais by nationality but Farangs by spirit." Here we can see clearly the connection between Christianity and foreignness, Buddhism and Thainess, which sets the terms for the encounter on both sides.

A general sense of the historical encounters between foreign Christians and Siamese Buddhists can be gleaned through the following overview of several historical moments: exchanges between Siamese Buddhist monks and Christian friars in the sixteenth century, Dutch East India Company employees' view of Buddhism, a Greek Jesuit's royal relations during the seventeenth century, nineteenth-century Christian missionaries in Chiang Mai, a twentieth-century French missionary, and, finally, a 1970s incident involving Mormons and a Buddha statue. These moments reveal both the possible range of reactions foreigners have when encountering Buddhism and the varying responses Thai Buddhists have exhibited toward these foreigners.

Portuguese friars arrived in Ayutthaya, Siam, in 1511 and "were invited into temples and exchanged ideas with Buddhist monks, engaging in substantive debates on such subjects as the transmigration of souls" (Pascal 2016, 13). Because of their similar dress, the friars were treated in a comparable way to the Buddhist monks by Buddhist laity, who received them warmly and with admiration. The friars as well were impressed by the discipline of the Siamese monks they encountered (13). Although their beliefs were very different from their own, the friars understood how doctrines such as rebirth could serve as "sources or inspiration for religious devotion and good morality" (15). This case of early Buddhist-Christian encounters in Thailand demonstrates that a positive evaluation of the two religions was possible for both sides.

Lay Christian practitioners had more neutral encounters with Buddhism. Two representatives of the Dutch East India Company, Gijsbert Heeck and Engelbert Kaempfer, encountered Buddhism in the seventeenth century. Their subsequent reaction and writing about the encounter revealed that, without context or information, foreigners are more likely to make negative assumptions about Buddhism. The travel accounts of Heeck contained much misinterpretation because he did not consult any expert

about Buddhism while touring temples in Siam. Heeck's confusions indicate the difficulties involved in such a short-term visit for someone who
cannot communicate with the local people. He draws conclusions from his
own observations, which must have been colored by the views of other
European residents. This led to Heeck calling Siamese Buddhists heathens
and stupid, simple people (Terwiel 2016, 72). In contrast, Kaempfer exercises
respect when he observes Siamese in rituals of worship. He describes the
rituals and Buddha statues without judgment, trying to learn the Siamese
understanding of the sacred, and attempting to comprehend the doctrines
of the religion from Catholic priests who were knowledgeable about Buddhism (Terwiel 2016, 81). Although both Dutchmen were Protestants, one
had a more open, interested, and curious attitude toward Buddhism. Given
that response, the student monks of Chiang Mai today would find Kaempfer, as well as the Franciscan friars, to be suitable conversation partners.

Other travelers to Siam were interested more in power than in Buddhism. The Greek adventurer and Jesuit convert Constantine Phaulkon
(1647–1688) came to Ayutthaya with the British East India Company in
1678. He soon became a close adviser to King Narai (1632–1688). Through
this relationship Phaulkon became convinced that the king would convert
to become a Jesuit (Wyatt 1969, 100). Because of the high profile of this
attempted conversion, anti-Christian sentiment grew in Ayutthaya. This
tension eventually led to a revolution after the king's death in 1688 and the
murder of Phaulkon (104). Siamese Buddhists reacted strongly against
foreign, Christian power. However, missionaries who were not interested in
being connected to political power did not cause as much concern within
Chiang Mai.

In 1869, Daniel McGilvary (1828–1911), the first Christian missionary to
arrive in Chiang Mai, made his first convert to Presbyterianism, a former
Buddhist monk and abbot named Nan Inta. In McGilvary's description of
this conversion he relates the ways that Nan Inta came to see Christianity
as superior. McGilvary writes, "But Buddhism had never satisfied his deep
spiritual nature. What of the thousands of failures and transgressions from
the results of which there was no escape? The doctrine of free and full pardon through the merits of another, was both new and attractive to him, but
it controverted the fundamental principle of his religion" ([1912] 2012, 96).
Although Princess Bua Kam of Chiang Mai never converted, McGilvary
recounts her appreciation of his preaching. He states, "I believe that the
Gospel plan of salvation struck a chord in her heart which her own religion
never did. From Buddha she got no assurance of pardon" (81). McGilvary

also believed that this idea of pardon captivated the abbot of Wat Umong. McGilvary describes what he assumed to be the thoughts of this monk: "Very early in our acquaintance he came to see that the universe could not be self-existent, as Buddhism teaches. On his deeply religious nature the sense of sin weighed heavily. He was well versed in the Buddhist scriptures, and knew that there was no place for pardon in all that system" (82).

In all three cases, McGilvary finds that Buddhism appears to be lacking a doctrine of forgiveness and a theory of creation. Because of that, McGilvary believes that all three of these Siamese Buddhists to whom he preached realized the truth of Christianity, although only one converted. The others, he believes, were Christians in their hearts but felt unable to formally convert due to their social positions in Siamese society. What these people actually felt internally about Christianity and Buddhism, we will never know. However, McGilvary writes of one way these two religions had been reconciled by Princess Bua Kam: "A favorite theory of hers—and of many others—was that, after all, we worship the same God under different names. She calls hers Buddha, and we call ours Jehovah-Jesus" ([1912] 2012, 81). This perennialist conclusion is not the best outcome for McGilvary, but he does not expand further on his reaction to this idea. Although McGilvary apprehended parts of the Buddhist religion and tried to learn about Buddhism, he maintains a clear sense of Christian superiority.[16] This encounter with Buddhism represents a view that respects the Buddhist people but does not place Buddhism on equal footing with Christianity.

Christian missionaries were also known to portray a negative response to the hybrid coexistence of elements of Buddhism, animism, and Brahmanism. One of the earliest and most significant missionaries in Bangkok, Dan Beach Bradley (1804–1873), stated to an official of the Thai government that if the Siamese wanted to be taken seriously within the international community, they needed to "abandon the worship of idols and sustain the worship of the living and eternal God" (quoted in Chansamone 2003, 22). Some missionaries blatantly yelled at the Siamese that their religion was wrong and would lead them to hell (Chansamone 2003, 23). This kind of encounter only bred contempt from Thai Buddhists. After incidents like these, Christian missionaries found it necessary to implement more friendly conversion methods. They turned to focus instead on their well-known projects of developing medical, educational, and printing facilities.

Edmond Pezet (1923–2008), a French missionary sent to northeastern Thailand, did not display the negative attitudes of his predecessors toward Buddhism. For ten years he felt he had failed to convey the Christian message to Thai Buddhists. He then sought to understand the lifestyles and teachings of Buddhism as a way to better frame Christianity (Huysegoms and Liesse 2012, 13). From his many years living, practicing, and studying in a monastery in Bangkok and a forest temple in the northeast, he came to deeply respect the Buddhist religion (50). He sought to present the Christian message as connected with the authentic values of Buddhists, "to ensure that those values are salvaged, adopted, taken deeper and indeed enriched, on the path which they have decided to take, namely that of faith in Christ" (89). In vain, he attempted to convince the Catholic missionary hierarchy to change its portrayal of Christianity in order to take into account the Buddhist doctrines and values he had observed—describing Catholic missionary strategies as opposing, competing, and conquering (82). Thai Buddhist laity and monks were impressed with Pezet's practice, asking him to give lectures about Buddhism and to help translate publications. This mutual respect between Buddhists and Christians in the modern period indicates that when one lives in a temple and attempts to understand a Buddhist way of life, Buddhists may respond with a welcoming attitude.

In contrast, in the "Sukothai incident" of the 1970s, a negative attitude toward Christianity emerged after Buddhist sacred sites were not respected. When pictures of two Mormon missionaries sitting atop the head of a Buddha statue in Wat Sri Chum, Sukothai, surfaced, they became a flashpoint in Thai media for debates about the perils of Westernization and how to preserve Thai culture. The media coverage reveals disbelief that Mormon missionaries, as religious people, could treat the Buddha statue in this way, because Thai officials and students receive training on how to behave respectfully when sent to foreign countries. In response, the two Mormon missionaries were arrested on charges of insulting Buddhism (Strate 2016, 186).

The Sukothai incident highlights how the Thai nation and the religion of Buddhism are perceived as fragile and Thai people feel responsible for them (Strate 2016, 195). In the media, blame was placed on guides, caretakers, and passers-by of this site. Surely, there were Thai people who witnessed the disrespectful actions of the Mormon missionaries toward the Buddha statue and did not stop them. This attitude is also seen today in Thai media as tourists continue to behave inappropriately—it is up to Thai people, who know better, to intervene. Historical encounters with Buddhism demonstrate a range of possibilities on both foreign and Thai Buddhist sides, from disparagement to mutual respect, from suspicion to understanding. Because Buddhism is such an important part of Thailand's national culture and heritage, Thai society, by and large, seeks to protect the religion from any disrespect. Buddhism, as linked to the nation-state, is still related to the taming agent of its urbanity. Thai Buddhists seek to enhance the urbane and enlightened image of Buddhism for tourists and are disappointed when tourists, in turn, do not respond appropriately to this importance.

Contemporary Encounters

Contemporary encounters with Buddhism follow patterns similar to those of the historical moments described above. The Thai Buddhist reaction is dependent upon whether or not visitors display proper respect in Buddhist spaces. Foreign tourists should exhibit and contribute to the perception of Buddhism's taming nature. There is some anxiety over tourists behaving in uncivilized manners in temples, with inappropriate outfits and actions; however, criticism is not directed at monks for the tourists' behavior in their temples. The commentary on tourists' misbehavior is instead directed at laypeople for not being brave enough to explain temple behavior. One reason for this criticism is that the temple is not just the space where monks live but also a community center for laypeople to worship in and make merit. Therefore, it is the role of laypeople to shield monks from viewing these behaviors. In 2018, the *Bangkok Post* reported an incident similar to the one involving the Mormons in Sukothai—a young woman was photographed sitting in the lap of a Buddha statue at Wat Yai Chai Mongkol in Ayutthaya. The images quickly surfaced on Facebook, where the *Bangkok Post* reported that it "drew ire" and "attracted a lot of criticism." The author of the article suggested that to eliminate such behavior the community should be posting signs, making tour guides aware of the problem, and filing a complaint with the police against this woman.[17] The nationality of the woman is unclear, but Thai tourists also misbehave at these historic and religious sites.

In February 2018, also in Ayutthaya, a group of five Thai tourists were charged with climbing the ruins, an offense that could damage the ancient stones, and displaying inappropriate behavior at a historic site.[18] Thai Buddhist practitioners at Wat Nong Ket Yai, a well-known historic temple in Pattaya, criticized Chinese and Vietnamese tourists and their Thai tour guides in June 2018 after the tourists placed "good luck" stickers throughout the temple grounds. These stickers, given out by the tour company, were meant to identify members of its tour group, but instead of throwing away the stickers after the tour, the tourists stuck them on trees, leaves, walls, and temple buildings. According to newspaper reports, the local people believed this act was inappropriate and made the temple look dirty.[19]

Thai Buddhists have also criticized foreign tourists for displaying inappropriate behavior in Chiang Mai and Phuket. In Chiang Mai, two people were photographed doing a "couples' yoga" workout on the grounds of Wat Suan Dok, with the famous white pagodas in the background. In Phuket, a young Russian woman was photographed entering Wat Chalong wearing a see-through cover-up, revealing her bikini underneath. The Thai public, via Thai media outlets, labeled these actions inappropriate, disrespectful, and scandalous. The solution, according to this coverage, is to employ security guards and to have Thai Buddhists be brave enough to admonish the tourists (Schedneck 2020). Thai Buddhists clearly have a low tolerance for tourists disrespecting Buddhism, but they lack the ability to confront these tourists directly. Thai Buddhists are continually policing tourists by sharing photos and videos of their behavior on social media platforms. However, these are not the only types of engagement that tourists have with Buddhism.

Another article in the *Bangkok Post* describes the annual monastic ordination in April when one thousand Malaysian tourists come to the southern province of Nakhon Si Thammarat. Not only does this activity "give local tourism a life," but the local Thais feel "as if the visitors [are] relatives."[20] As the Dutchman Kaempfer above hinted, if foreigners display an interest in Buddhism—a curiosity to learn more and take steps to become part of the religion—then the attitude toward these non-Buddhists shifts to one of pride and joy. When the final contestants on *The Bachelorette* took a romantic trip to Chiang Mai for the TV show's 2018 season, they visited temples and received advice from a Buddhist monk about creating long-lasting relationships. The dramatic tension of this reality-show trip was that this couple could not touch or kiss on the "sacred grounds" of the scenic Wat Palad. Despite this struggle, they were able to obey the religious and cultural norms. Following the lead of an English-speaking interpreter-monk, the American couple paid respect to a senior monk before being blessed and learning how to live a happy householder life. The bachelorette herself commented that the experience felt "very old and cultural," and her date found the advice of the monk to be incredibly wise.[21] Regardless of the mismatch between a romantic excursion and the space of a temple, the couple did follow the behavioral expectations of the temple and were impressed by its peacefulness. Because many Buddhist monks in Chiang Mai had seen evidence of foreign travelers' curiosity and interest in Buddhism, what I term

"Buddhist cultural exchange programs" have been established as venues open for foreigners to encounter Buddhism further.

Buddhist Cultural Exchange Programs

Learning about Buddhism is part of a broader outreach to educate travelers in Chiang Mai. Because of this desire, abbots of temples popular with tourists have initiated cultural exchange programs geared toward international travelers, particularly those seeking to speak with monks about meditation and the monastic life. These programs extend Buddhism's reach by allowing non-Thai Buddhists to be transformed and tamed by this religion. Since the early 2000s, Buddhist cultural exchange programs have formed in a variety of temples in northern Thailand. International partners, in affiliation with Buddhist monastic community leaders, offer these opportunities for students and volunteers, as do local temples themselves, mostly for tourists. Besides a temple visit, there are two types of Buddhist tourist encounters possible in Chiang Mai: Buddhist meditation practice and Buddhist exchange programs. For those interested in Buddhist practice, international meditation centers offer retreats for English speakers that focus on the Buddhist practice of meditation as taught by Buddhist monk meditation teachers. These centers often downplay the value of learning about aspects of Buddhism beyond meditation (Schedneck 2015). A retreat involves many hours of meditation, leaving little time to chant, attend rituals, or ask questions about the Buddhist tradition that are unrelated to meditation. In contrast, Buddhist exchange programs offer opportunities to experience life in a Buddhist temple. The size and scope of Buddhist exchange programs vary depending on the nature of the exchange. These programs tend to be locally produced and do not emerge from formal sangha structures.

There are four kinds of Buddhist exchange programs, each with different priorities and levels of engagement: the Monk Chat program allows tourists to learn about the monastic life and Buddhism by providing informal conversations with monks; volunteer English-teaching opportunities in temple schools offer unique experiences to travelers; gap year and study abroad experiential learning trips enable participants to learn a Buddhist way of life in a temple setting; and a temple stay and retreat program offers the ability to become part of a Buddhist community by living in a Buddhist temple, along with the possibility of ordaining as a novice monk for male participants. These programs all facilitate encounters between international visitors and monks within immersive experiences ranging from an hour to several months. The majority of the international visitors who attend these programs are English speakers from North America, Europe, Australia, and New Zealand, along with a minority group from East Asia.

The Monk Chat program is available in three temples in Chiang Mai (Wat Suan Dok, Wat Srisuphan, and Wat Chedi Luang) for English-speaking tourists and is conducted primarily by college student monks. This program began in 2000 for the purpose of giving monks a chance to practice their English and teach about Buddhism.[22] Daily Monk Chat sessions usually consist of five to ten monks having small group conversations with tourists seated at rectangular tables. The number of monks and tourists varies according to the monastic academic calendar and the tourism seasons. During North American school holidays, senior monk facilitators of Monk Chat give lectures and discussions to groups of students.[23] Tourists learn about this program through guidebooks, online recommendations, or the Monk Chat websites.[24]

Two organizations have advertised their ability to support volunteer tourists by placing them in temple schools in Chiang Mai to teach English to monks: Friends for Asia and the FutureSense Foundation.[25] The Teaching English to Monks program of both organizations is featured in this book. In the FutureSense Foundation program, participants have the opportunity to teach English to Buddhist novice monks in the Doi Saket District, forty minutes outside of Chiang Mai.[26] Friends for Asia is affiliated with and places volunteers in a number of temple schools in Chiang Mai City. From interviews with volunteers, I learned that their motivations for participating in the Teaching English to Monks program typically include gaining teaching experience, making a contribution, and pursuing an interest in Buddhism.[27]

Study groups to Thailand often include a multiday Buddhist immersion experience. An example of a Buddhist exchange program that frequently hosts educational groups is that of the Plik Wiwek Dhamma Center, located three and a half hours northwest of Chiang Mai City, in the town of Wieng Haeng. The founder and head monk of Plik Wiwek is Phra Ajahn Dr. Thani Jitawiriyo. Situated near the border of Thailand and the Shan State of Myanmar, this center was established to provide a home to the many orphaned and poor boys in the community. The main purpose of the center is to give these young men skills to be able to contribute to society inside and outside of the monastic life, to be able to take care of themselves and others. Plik Wiwek therefore offers many unique experiences for foreign university and gap year students to learn from and contribute to the space. These groups stay for varying lengths of time, from a few days to several weeks. They participate in activities such as teaching English to novice monks, learning meditation, chanting with the monks, visiting temples close to Thailand's border with Myanmar's Shan State, and farming with the novice monks.[28]

The most immersive of the Buddhist exchange programs is the temple stay program. Currently, Wat Sri Boen Ruang is the only temple in Thailand that I am aware of that offers a temple stay program for interested individuals. This temple, like Plik Wiwek, is also located far from any tourist area, in the town of Fang, three hours north of Chiang Mai City. Participants find out about this opportunity through the program's website or by word of mouth while traveling in Chiang Mai. Its aim is immersive learning about Buddhism through experience and interaction. The program has been offered year-round since 2013, with space for about four or five guests at any given time.[29] Wat Sri Boen Ruang has about fifty novice monks in residence, about one hundred novices who attend the school on the monastery grounds, and a handful of fully ordained monks. The abbot of this temple, Phra Ajahn Dr. Abhisit Pingchaiyawat, estimates that 70 percent of novices at Wat Sri Boen Ruang have families that cannot take care of them for a variety of reasons, the most significant being poverty.[30] Because the temple's community would benefit from exposure to international visitors, Phra Ajahn Dr. Abhisit created this program where foreign guests come to stay at his temple.[31] Instead of managing the program himself, Phra Ajahn Dr. Abhisit relies on program coordinators and other local volunteers to promote and orient the guests. Since 2016, a foreign monk named Ajahn Clyde Jarudhammo has been the head coordinator and meditation teacher for international guests, and the Temple Stay and Retreat program has directed its focus to primarily serve as a place to practice *vipassana* meditation.[32] However, unlike the strict schedules of most meditation centers in Thailand, the schedule of Wat Sri Boen Ruang is flexible and "beginner friendly," with two group practice sessions in the morning and evening along with time for instruction and study about Buddhism.[33]

The monks who participate in Buddhist cultural exchange programs are mostly student monks, novices, or fully ordained monks, and they attend Buddhist temple high schools and colleges. These monks display a wide range of English-language proficiency, from a thirteen-year-old novice monk beginning to speak English at a temple high school to an almost fluent twenty-two-year-old who is about to graduate from college. A second group, consisting of abbots and teachers in temples where these programs are hosted, interact less frequently with the travelers. These religious leaders also vary in their levels of English fluency. Because these abbots have busy schedules and are more involved with Thai Buddhist laity, the majority Buddhist populations that foreigners meet in Chiang Mai are student monks. They take on most of the labor in helping expose foreign tourists to the teachings, and they hope that foreigners will come to understand the taming nature of the Buddhist religion. This does not necessarily include conversion to Buddhism but suggests being transformed or touched by its teachings and people in some way. Buddhist cultural exchanges are located within the temple but exist outside of traditional temple purviews, creating a kind of hybrid space. Part of this hybridity is a result of Buddhist education, which consists of both secular and Buddhist curriculums.

Student Monks' Education

Since the sixteenth century, foreign travelers to Thailand have engaged with Buddhism, and Thai Buddhists have responded to this interest in various ways. The other aspect of Buddhist encounters—the lives and educational pursuits of student monks of Chiang Mai—is also an established part of the history of the city. Since the religion's inception in Thailand, many members of society have demonstrated their belief in Buddhism's ability to tame young men, especially through education. The curriculum student monks learn at Buddhist educational institutions in Chiang Mai has been shaped historically by national, political, and historical factors. Buddhist universities in Chiang Mai follow the national curriculum, which was first developed by Prince Patriarch Wachirayan (1860–1921) (Keyes 1975a, 64). It is hard to overestimate Prince Wachirayan's influence on Thai Buddhist education. In the 1890s, Prince Wachirayan, along with Prince Damrong (1862–1943), established the two monastic colleges, the Thammayutnikai's Mahamakut College and the Mahanikai's Mahachulalongkorn College. Wachirayan's intention was to promote study of the Buddhist scriptures, the Pali Canon, and other authoritative commentaries, which he believed would develop monks who could teach the dhamma, or Buddhist teachings, to Thai Buddhists, like the Christian missionaries who could teach the Bible (Dhammasami 2018, 134).[34] Wachirayan worked with both sectarian colleges to formulate not only the national monastic curriculum but also the systematic study of Pali and correlating annual examinations (Phibul 2015,

432).[35] By the 1920s, these Pali exams (Parian) came to be seen as a way to safeguard and preserve the Buddhist dispensation (*phra phutthasatsana*) (Dhammasami 2018, 124). However, after 1899, when the previous supreme patriarch, Somdet Sa, passed away, Wachirayan, an ordained member of the Thammayutnikai, promoted Mahamakut College as the national center of monastic education. From 1902 to 1921, there was a monopoly of power in the Thammayutnikai, at the expense of the Mahanikai's Mahachulalongkorn College (Phibul 2015, 434).

The sectarian rivalry flipped its fortune in the 1950s and 1960s when, Mahachulalongkorn University (MCU) introduced a curriculum that included secular subjects.[36] The significance of purifying the sangha with textual study was replaced by a new perception that the purpose of monastic education should not be just textual study, but should also include meditation practice and "modern" subjects like education and social science (Phibul 2015, 440). Today these secular subjects are important for the student monks of Chiang Mai, at both Mahachulalongkorn and Mahamakut universities. Very few of the student monks I have spoken with are interested in climbing the sangha hierarchy by studying for the Parian degrees.[37] Although a few monks we will meet in this book have reached the upper levels of Pali study, most of them hope either to contribute as monks to the development of their hometowns or countries or to disrobe and find a job, using their English skills, possibly in the city of Chiang Mai.[38]

The sectarian rivalry and debates over monastic education in Bangkok eventually reached the northern region. Both the hierarchy and the curriculum of premodern Lanna Buddhist education were informal and independent. Local authority and popularity determined leadership positions in the sangha and the subjects one learned in the temple. The choice of topics as dissimilar as Pali scriptures and carpentry depended entirely on the interests of the monk teacher or his novice students (Ratanaporn 2018, 85). Because of this autonomy in the nineteenth century, it was difficult for the centralizing powers from Bangkok to integrate the Lanna people. Part of the way the center tamed this periphery was through education. Because the sangha was the strongest social organization in the Lanna kingdom, education was used as a way to benefit the local population while bringing them into the central Siam fold (81). The Sangha Act of 1902 solidified these changes by standardizing the education as well as the hierarchy of Lanna Buddhism (87).[39] Although these changes brought resistance, they were gradually accepted because of the educational development and the assurance that the high-level status of Lanna monks would be maintained and promoted

(Ratanaporn 2018, 95). Chiang Mai, once integrated into what would become the Thai nation-state, continued to develop its educational institutions.

Today Chiang Mai is a diverse center of Buddhist education with monks from such distinct locations as Bangladesh, Cambodia, Laos, Myanmar, Nepal, and Vietnam. Within MCU at Wat Suan Dok, both English and Thai tracks are offered. The curriculum has many options for bachelor's, master's, and doctorate degrees. But the most popular degree program for international monks is the bachelor of arts in English. These monks learn secular subjects such as language and communication, introductory linguistics, and basic mathematics, but also Buddhist subjects including Pali composition and translation, Tipitaka studies, and Buddhist meditation, among others. Out of 140 credits for the bachelor's degree, 40 of them are devoted to Buddhism and applied Buddhism courses.[40] Although mostly monks attend this university, the campus has opened up its degree programs to lay students since 2004.[41]

The most popular degree for monks interested in learning English in the Mahamakut Buddhist University (MBU) at Wat Chedi Luang is the bachelor of education program in teaching English, which is conducted in Thai. Along with instruction on English grammar, phonetics, and pronunciation, courses in Buddhism include History of Buddhism, Meditation Practice, and Sanskrit for Buddhist Research.[42] Only about half of the students are ordained, and due to the language of instruction, almost all of them are from Thailand. Because of the cost of study, compared to private colleges, there are many young women and men from disadvantaged backgrounds studying at this university.[43] When I volunteered to teach a Buddhist English class at this university, I noticed that many of the non-monastic students were Christians from the indigenous groups of Thailand.[44] Because of this student population, participants in the Monk Chat program at this university differ from those at Wat Suan Dok, with all its international monks. When foreigners arrive to chat with monks at Wat Chedi Luang, they may, surprisingly, be greeted by Christian students hoping to practice their English. Phra Ruang, the president of Monk Chat from 2015 to 2017, set up many programs for monks to improve their English, including recruiting foreigners to offer lessons and evaluate levels of proficiency achieved by the monks. Phra Ruang had to disrobe after his graduation in 2017 in order to serve in the Thai military. This situation highlights the fluctuating and unstable nature of these cultural exchange programs. Their infrastructures depend on people to fill and stay in leadership roles. When new leadership enters and students graduate, older initiatives may fade and new ones might emerge.

There are two other types of Buddhist temple schools in Thailand that connect Chiang Mai's monastic education system to cultural exchange programs and Buddhist encounters. The first type is the Pariyattitham Saman, or general education school. Some of these schools, such as Wat Phra Singh's Thammaraj School, educate students from first grade through high school and are open to both monks and non-monks and both girls and boys. But other Pariyattitham Saman schools like Pali Satit at Wat Suan Dok, also in Chiang Mai, only allow ordained boys. The Pariyattitham Saman schools normally teach a curriculum of general subjects, including Thai language, mathematics, science, social sciences, physical education, technology, art, and English, through middle and high school. These students also study additional subjects about Buddhism, including religious practice, Dhamma Vinaya, and Pali language. The second type of temple school focuses only on Pali and Dhamma exams. In Chiang Mai City there are fourteen Pali and Dhamma schools and six Pariyattitham Saman schools.[45] Today some monks still believe that monastic education should consist mainly of learning Pali and studying the Buddhist scriptures. In fact, outside of Chiang Mai City, one Pariyattitham Saman school for novice monks was forced to move to a new temple because its original temple location wanted the school to focus exclusively on Pali studies. The principal of this new Pariyattitham Saman school believed strongly, in contrast, that young novice monks must learn real-life skills and secular subjects, as most of them disrobe after graduating high school.[46] Many of these Pariyattitham Saman schools host volunteer tourists who teach English. One of the advantages this city center of Buddhist education offers both monks and foreigners is the opportunity to participate in Buddhist cultural exchange programs.

These educational options are part of the reason why Buddhist encounters are so readily available in Chiang Mai. With this population of ordained young men learning Buddhism and secular subjects, and travelers interested in Buddhist sites while in the city, the development of cultural exchange programs took root. Volunteer tourism organizations as well as Chiang Mai city temples noticed the benefit of bringing these two groups together. While these monks and travelers have commonalities, their individual stories offer a picture of their motivations and specific interests in Buddhism and Buddhist education.[47]

Student Monks' and Travelers' Stories

There are many reasons why Thai and international monks choose to study in Chiang Mai.[48] Narratives of the student monk participants whom I interviewed over the course of my fieldwork reveal some of these reasons. Some young monks attend Buddhist universities because of the low cost or scholarship opportunities. Although the tuition is less expensive than it is at public or private universities, there is still some cost. For example, Phra Ruang, from northeastern Thailand, decided to take the scholarship he received to attend MBU in Wat Chedi Luang because, he said, "[I wanted] to keep being a monk and learn what I am interested in—language and children—and be with the people." Phra Ruang was focused on his role as a community member and his future career, which he could envision himself achieving through monastic education.

Phra Le came from Vietnam to study at MCU at Wat Suan Dok. When asked what motivated him to come to Chiang Mai, he replied:

> I came here by my own choice. Four years ago my monk senior was studying here and I asked him to help. Before that I intended to study in an ordinary university in Vietnam but when I looked at the curriculum with so much communism involvement, I did not want to enter anymore. Actually, you will easily hear of this fact if you live in Vietnam. They even try to bring communism subjects to Buddhist schools. Then when I heard my senior describe the study here [Chiang Mai], which focused on English, I liked it and applied. Also, the international environment was very appealing, for sure![49]

Similarly, Phra Sonalin, from Laos, heard about studying in Chiang Mai through his senior monk friends. As he explained, "I met several senior monks who have finished from Chiang Mai and they suggested to me about studying there. I also studied English at that time so they told me that I am going to do well if I go there." Word of mouth based on the positive experiences of their senior peers seems to be the primary way that these monks learn about and are convinced to study in Chiang Mai. Phra Thet is a fourth-year college student who moved to Thailand from Myanmar in order to enroll in the English program at the Wat Suan Dok campus. He heard from his Burmese monk friends living in Thailand that Chiang Mai has a degree program where one can learn not only about Buddhism but about other subjects in English as well. By contrast, monks in Myanmar typically do not have the opportunity to learn much English, study with foreign teachers, or study subjects outside of Buddhism. Phra Trilok, from India, has been living in Thailand for eight years. He left India when he was seventeen because he wanted to live in a Buddhist country, and he had lived in Bangkok and southern Thailand before coming to study for a bachelor's degree in Chiang Mai in 2015.

Other monks from outside of Thailand attend Thai temple high schools and subsequently become fluent in Thai and English. Phra Maha Mitra, from Nepal, moved to Thailand in 2009. He studied Thai for one year and then entered high school for three years in a Thai temple school before beginning the bachelor's degree program at Mahachulalongkorn. Naen (novice monk) Samrin is a Khmer Krom monk from southern Vietnam who attended a Thai high school as a novice monk and graduated from Mahachulalongkorn in 2017. During the next academic year, he taught at the Wat Suan Dok Pali Satit School, obtaining an English-teaching certificate. He came to Chiang Mai because his brother asked if he wanted to go to monastic school in Thailand. Naen Samrin considered that impossible since he did not know Thai. But he always thought he would ordain after high school or college to make merit for his parents. After Naen Samrin visited his brother in Thailand for one month, he liked it and decided to ordain. He enrolled in the monastic high school, studying in Thai along with the native speakers.

Interest in English is the primary, initial reason for many young men to choose to enter monastic colleges. Naen Maha Tri is a frequent participant in Wat Chedi Luang's Monk Chat program, even though he does not attend college yet. Before beginning college, he hopes to be fluent in English and pass the ninth level of Pali exams. Achieving this highest level of Pali study is a rare achievement for a novice monk and would allow him to be ordained as a monk with the king of Thailand present. Phra Decha had been a novice monk for seven years at a temple school in Lamphun, the neighboring province where he was raised. He recalled, "I love English because when I was in fifth grade, the teacher asked a question in English and no one could answer but me. I feel like she appreciated me, and then speaking English is like I have power." He began his study at Mahamakut as a monk in order to be a part of the humanities program and learn English. After the initial encounter with Chiang Mai and the monastic college, these student monks usually move beyond their interest in English. As they continue through college, studying both English and Buddhism, they begin to see how English can help them explain and spread Buddhism to foreigners. The friction of the student monks' encounters with the city and with the Buddhism of

Chiang Mai, along with foreign non-Buddhist tourists, challenges many of these monks to create new goals beyond learning English.

Novice monks usually have less agency in the choice to study at a monastic school. For this reason, I use discussions with monastic school teachers, rather than the novices themselves, to portray their motivations for attendance. Monastic and lay teachers at Wat Nong Bua's Pariyattitham school estimated that the novice monks attend this school for three reasons: their family is poor, they are orphans, or their parents think the temple and robe offer their boys protection and safety. There are a few novices who want to become fully ordained monks, but the majority disrobe after completing high school and do not continue on to monastic college education, as they would prefer to find a job right after graduation. A few of them do go on to enroll in Mahachulalongkorn's English program or a public university.

Travelers engage in a different kind of Buddhist education when in Chiang Mai. They seek to explore difference within the city, and much of this difference comes in the form of Buddhist temples and monks. Viewing the many temples within the old city of Chiang Mai or the mountain-top temple of Doi Suthep is among the most popular activities in Chiang Mai for all visitors. Some choose to visit for longer periods through companies that run volunteer tourism programs. Jen, a twenty-year-old American, describes why she chose Chiang Mai—the elephants and the monks. "I originally decided to go to Thailand to volunteer. I just wanted to partake in an elephant nature park. However, I stumbled upon a program, through GapGuru, that combined an elephant experience with a volunteer teaching program at a Buddhist temple. I was intrigued by this program because I believed it would put me out of my comfort zone. I had never taught, let alone to young monks, and I knew it would be a good cultural experience."[50]

Difference is a factor in Jen's choice of Chiang Mai because the place offers access to both elephants to care for and monks to teach, two opportunities she would not encounter in her home country. Another volunteer tourist was interested in the actual experience of encountering monks. Jim, a college-aged American, states, "I think I wanted to see the monks in Thailand with my own eyes, more so than actually learning about Buddhism here [Chiang Mai] academically. I also wanted to see the cultural background and atmosphere of the relationship between monks and laypeople."[51] The chance to experience Thai Buddhist life in person led Jim to Chiang Mai, where as a volunteer tourist he taught monks in Buddhist monastic schools. Felix, a volunteer from Germany, had more personal reasons for traveling to Thailand. A Buddhist since the age of twelve, he recalled,

"I wanted to see the culture I cannot see in Germany. I can visit places and see the respect everyone has for each other. In Germany I have no community, only a few people to talk about this with, but here Thai people value meditation and Buddhist practice and teachings." These examples help illustrate how the difference of the Buddhist culture attracts many foreigners to Chiang Mai.

A number of tourists who visit Monk Chat keep online journals and blogs about their travel experiences. These travelers, by and large, are interested in Thai Buddhism and culture, and they are surrounded by it in Chiang Mai. The writers often describe visiting monks and learning about their lives as a positive experience. One blogger, Ileana, links Monk Chat to spirituality, explaining that for those searching for spiritual answers or those just curious about Buddhism, Monk Chat is a worthwhile way to spend your time.[52] Seema, in her blog, writes that Monk Chat made her fall in love with Chiang Mai even more. She recounts her whole conversation with Phra Thet, a Burmese monk, in dialogue format. From this conversation, she concludes that monks are just like the rest of us—they take selfies, post on Facebook, and listen to pop music.[53] Seema, although seeking difference, is surprised and excited by the fact that Buddhist monks are closer to her modern lifestyle than she had expected.[54] Another tourist blogger, instead of just looking for a unique cultural experience, is testing out Buddhism as a personal religion. After his conversation with a monk, David was disappointed by the monk's demeanor as he chatted on his cell phone instead of paying attention to David's questions. Despite that, David still decided that he is more closely aligned with Buddhist beliefs than with other religions.[55]

Other tourists, anxious about the experience, post on forums such as TripAdvisor, asking if Monk Chat is worth the time and effort. Almost universally, respondents concur: "[It is] one of my highlights of Chiang Mai . . . the monks love chatting in English with Westerners . . . they are friendly" and "It was really interesting talking to them."[56] Some respondents also noted that the monks who shared their life story and personal experiences were the most interesting, as opposed to those who enumerated Buddhist doctrines and teachings.[57] Nelson, in his blog, recounted that instead of chatting, one monk gave a proselytizing lecture about the destructive nature of desire.[58] A number of posts, along with displaying pictures of "my monk" or the one the blogger spoke with, note for the general reader that although one can go to the formal Monk Chat temples at the regular times, many monks in Chiang Mai are students, and when they have free time they are often open to having a conversation in any temple. In addition, tourist guidebooks on Thailand and Chiang Mai recommend the Monk Chat program. Fodor's Travel reports that Monk Chat can help visitors answer any questions they have, as the monks "eagerly welcome foreign visitors."[59] Lonely Planet states that this experience will allow the tourist to "find out about the inner workings of monastery life."[60]

In the city of Chiang Mai, Monk Chat offers an especially notable experience, for both monks and travelers. Other exchange programs, including gap year, study abroad, and volunteer tourism, although engaging in different ways, have fewer but longer-term participants. All of these programs were generated because of the Buddhist education and tourism conjunctures in the city and surrounding area of Chiang Mai. Foreign Christian missionaries, European businesspeople, and contemporary travelers have left a mixed record of their encounters with Buddhism. However, those Christian friars, missionaries, and tourists appreciative of Buddhism and seeking to engage with its communities have been welcomed by Thai Buddhists. That is part of the reason why Buddhist cultural exchange programs work in Chiang Mai. Besides the availability of tourists and student monks, there is a willingness to allow non-Buddhists into temple spaces to experience the religion.

Chiang Mai is a place of Buddhist encounters. Since its earliest history, myths about the Buddha and the ability of this religion to tame any uncivilized force have linked the city to Buddhism and urbanity. Today Chiang Mai stays connected to its Buddhist identity through tourist branding. As promoted by both tourist guidebooks and Buddhist monks, Chiang Mai remains the city that was tamed by Buddhism, with its hundreds of temples and thousands of monks. Taming not only the city from demons and uncivilized forces, Buddhism today can function to tame the international community's image of Thailand, young Buddhist men, through ordination, and tourists' behavior, through their engagement with the religion. Because of this religious identity, Chiang Mai has been a place to encounter Buddhism. At first, Christian missionaries and business travelers did not engage much with the religion, either misunderstanding it or declaring Christianity superior. For those few who were able to relate to the temple and the monastic life, Thai Buddhists reacted positively. But when visitors behaved disrespectfully, Thai Buddhists felt belittled and upset. Modern encounters reveal a similar dynamic. When tourists disrupt a Buddhist environment, whether a temple or Buddhist ruins, Thai Buddhists argue that someone or something—a guard, a Thai observer, or at least a sign—should indicate norms of proper respect.

But these types of superficial encounters are not the only outcomes of Chiang Mai's Buddhist identity. Cultural exchange programs were created so that travelers could deepen their understanding of Buddhism and benefit young monks. Monk Chat programs in the city are what many tourists encounter, as they are a short-term option available almost every day of the week. Gap year, study abroad, volunteer tourism, and temple stay programs require more commitment and advanced planning. However, foreign participants of these programs often receive a more immersive experience and deeper understanding of a Buddhist way of life.

Buddhist educational opportunities in Chiang Mai are the main reason for the large population of student monks in the city. Because monks can learn secular subjects in English along with Buddhist topics, young men from all over South and Southeast Asia come to Chiang Mai as a center of education. Travelers are intrigued by the difference of a city infused with Buddhism and highlight their encounters with Buddhist monks. These encounters underscore the friction of global connections created through education, tourism, and urbanization. Both foreign and monk participants in all of these cultural exchange programs are challenged to communicate with and understand the norms of religious and cultural others. Buddhism as a taming force upon the city does not stop negative perceptions of Buddhists by non-Buddhists and of tourists by Thai Buddhists. At the same time, the struggle to understand perspectives of others can have significant consequences—economic, social, religious, and personal.

CHAPTER 2

THE AGENCY OF BUDDHIST MONKS
IN THE TOURISM LANDSCAPE

THE TOURISM INDUSTRY AND URBANIZATION CAN SEEM LIKE unstoppable forces that make local communities bend to their current preferences. But tourism and the urban environment are not simply altering Buddhism; instead, Buddhist monks creatively engage this new audience and opportunity, revealing their agency within transnational settings. Monks residing in city temples popular with tourists use their location and the positive image of Buddhism internationally, actively engaging with the fluid and mutable forms of tourism in their urban environments. As international visitors began treating the temple as a tourist space, monks responded by charging tourist fees and allowing souvenir shops on the premises. When temples are located within newly significant urban areas, temple coffee shops have become a place to sit and relax. At the same time, because of the many signs located at these city temples reminding foreigners how to behave and dress, and shops located just outside the main temple environment, many monks argue that, for the most part, the temple does not shed its Buddhist atmosphere. Even with new audiences and commerce, the temple, from a Buddhist perspective, can still display a sacred environment, demonstrated through Buddhists' behaviors and appearances and the reverence paid toward Buddhist objects and monks. Besides monetary resources, volunteer tourism can bring educational benefits to Chiang Mai's large population of novice monk students. Temples located outside the city

of Chiang Mai host tourists through special temple stay or gap year programs. Buddhist monks engaged in these interactions have rules in place
so that foreigners can participate only if they show sincere and genuine
interest. Instead of resisting or totally accommodating outside forces such
as tourism or globalization, Buddhist monks engage modernity on their
own terms.

Theravada Buddhist nation-states entering modernity did not simply
adapt to Western norms and values during the colonial period, or more
recently due to tourism or urbanization.[1] Recent scholarship has sought to
reframe the discussion of Asian Buddhist modernities and agency, in light
of "secular bodies of knowledge, scientific technologies, globalizing networks and novel social practices" (Schober and Collins 2017, 8).[2] Despite
these profound effects of modernity in Theravada Buddhist nation-states,
their encounters with modernity are "fundamentally different than the
Judeo-Christian framework of modernity," as they "demonstrate regional
differentiation, employ different networks, technologies and knowledge
formations" (Schober and Collins 2017, 9). Theravada Buddhists have not
been passive in response to Western influences, with many examples of
reform within Buddhism arising in Asia in the beginning of the twentieth
century, including institutional, monastic, and broader Buddhist ethical
conduct.[3] In present-day Thailand, the temple space has been reframed in
certain respects as a tourist space, but important concepts within the Buddhist worldview remain, such as the economy of merit and proper lay-
monastic relations. When monks engage in the resources that tourism and
the urban environment bring, they offer explanations of the monetary
practices as beneficial to the temple and its community of laity and monks.

In the intersections of Buddhism, urban space, and the tourist economies in Thailand, Buddhist monks demonstrate agency. Among the factors
that influence this agency, the type of monk and his activities are the most
crucial in understanding different Buddhist attitudes toward money. Three
distinct types of monks in northern Thailand—city monks, forest monks,
and Kruba monks—all have different relationships with money, depending
on their interactions with laity and primary monastic activities. These differing attitudes demonstrate the necessity and importance of city monks'
agency over economic resources. Although city monks are enmeshed in the
capitalist economy, this does not mean that all monks agree on the best ways
to participate. Diverse opinions among city monks as well as the broader
Thai monastic population concern not only how temples should raise
money but also how much money is needed for a temple. Some monks, in

their conception of Thai Buddhism and the temple space, see deprivation. These monks are more open to integrating the sacred and the profane and working within the capitalist economy. Those who see the temple as having enough resources delineate between the sacred and the profane more starkly and would like to see less of the capitalist economy in temple spaces. The dichotomy of sacred and profane becomes an important indicator with regard to tourism and the urban environment.

The state of the Thai economy and the application of Buddhist teachings to economic practices called "Buddhist economics" are not of concern here,[4] nor are monastic rules or texts as the basis for appropriate monastic action (Schopen 2000). Instead, the ambivalent relationship Buddhism has with capitalism is relevant (Obadia 2011). This ambivalence has been expressed in scholarship on Wat Dhammakaya, located outside of Bangkok, which contextualizes understandings of wealth and how economic activity relates broadly to Thai Buddhist society (Scott 2009). The city monks in Chiang Mai's popular tourist temples illustrate the range of responses to and perspectives on the temple's relationship to money.

Buddhist Monks and Monetary Practices

Buddhism has its own internal economy known as the economy of merit. This economy is linked by an exchange between laypersons, who give clothing, food, and other support (*dana*) to the monastic community, and monks, who serve as a field of merit for these practitioners. Through their renunciant lifestyles, monks are able to accumulate and give merit to laypeople. Buddhist laypersons engage in donor practices in order to gain merit that will have a positive effect on their current situation as well as the next life and negate the effects of past evil deeds (Schedneck 2014, 441). Thus merit making is the central component in lay Buddhists' lives, and monastics maintaining their ascetic lifestyle is crucial to being able to serve as a field of merit. The practices within this economy are well known to Thai Buddhists; however, to international travelers, this aspect of Buddhism is very foreign. As one of the coordinators of a temple stay and retreat program told me, when the foreign participants arrive at the temple, he must teach them about the economy of merit. If he does not, it would be difficult for the program to run on donation. The culture of donation must be explained and passed on to the foreign participants. Anthropologist Peter Moran (2004, 65) points out the different ways of understanding donation: "In the Buddhist idiom it is the *donor* who is ultimately tamed (and ideally, liberated) by the *giving*, whereas in Western aid programs, it is the *recipient* who is improved by the *gifts*" (emphasis in the original). The economy of merit functioning correctly is a key component in the continued monetary support of Buddhist temples. Because this economy does not exist for non-Buddhists, and the donations received through the merit system are not always enough support, the capitalist economy becomes crucial for the survival of Buddhist temples.

Monks using cell phones, handling money, and fundraising seem strange to international travelers. Anthropologist Jiemin Bao (2015, 77), discussing the economic lives of monks in a Thai temple in California, explains, "A Buddhist monk in real life, however, is different from the monk who lives in the Western imagination—the ascetic monk who wanders along 'like a rhinoceros' in the forest, sits at the root of a tree in deep meditation, and has cut all ties with the world." Of course, this ascetic monastic ideal was hardly ever a reality, as Buddhist monks have been involved in economic activities since the tradition's inception, depending on the time, place, and circumstances (Brox and Williams-Oerberg 2016, 504). This push and pull between renunciation and the material world, between the economy of merit and the capitalist economy, exists on a practical level within the daily lives of temples and monks.

Historian of religion Gustavo Benavides (2005) has also noted this tension in Buddhism between money and asceticism, writing that "[as renunciants] monks explicitly distanced themselves from the economy; but this happened only to a certain extent, inasmuch as they engaged in elaborate ruses in order to participate in the economy without, for example, having to handle coins" (82). Although monks, according to their rules, should not handle gold and silver, many monks, including city monks in Thailand, use money. The eighteenth rule of the Vinaya category *nissaggiya-paccittiya* (the class of offense involving an item a monk wrongly possesses or has wrongly used, which necessitates confession and forfeiture) states, "Whatsoever Bhikkhu shall receive gold or silver, or get someone to receive it for him, or allow it to be kept in deposit for him—that is a Pacittiya offence involving forfeiture" (Terwiel 1975; cited in Strong 2008, 249). Therefore, if a monk handles money or saves it, his punishment would be to surrender it. However, few monks in Thailand follow this rule, as it is much more convenient for them to handle money themselves.[5] As well, laypeople often give money directly to monks living in the city. Because of that, within Thai society it has become convention for monks to manage their own money when they need to pay for transport, buy something for their education or for themselves, or take care of other basic needs. Buddhist monks in the city of

Chiang Mai discuss money as a necessary compromise between the renunciant life and engaging with the contemporary world.

As a result, the relationship between monks and money in Chiang Mai City is more nuanced than the complete separation of religion and the economy, the sacred and the profane. From the Buddhist perspective, money and Buddhism can be aligned; however, the money must be used for the benefit of Buddhism.[6] In light of that, we must rethink the connection between sacred and profane domains from the emic Buddhist perspective. In classical religious studies theories, Mircea Eliade and Émile Durkheim both found that the nature of the sacred was defined by its opposite, the profane. They posited that sacred and profane spheres must maintain complete separation.[7] Although some Buddhist monks included in this study found the sacred and the profane to be distinct, others believed these two poles were not so distant. The intersections of Buddhism and the urban tourist environments in Chiang Mai reveal various Buddhist perspectives concerning the relationship between the sacred and the profane, and between the economy of merit and the capitalist economy. The differing views and flexibility on this subject demonstrate the agency of Buddhist monks. Because the capitalist economy is not always separated from the Buddhist temple, there is room for commodities, tourism, and urban trends to move into the sphere of the temple.

Although city monks are among the most populous group of monks in Thailand, their use of and connections to money have not been the focus of scholarship. To contextualize city monks' attitudes toward money, I compare two monastic groups in Thailand that have been well studied: the Thai forest monks of the northeast and the Kruba monks of the Lanna region. The Thai forest tradition was begun as a distinct part of the reform movement of the Thammayutnikai by the famous wandering monk Ajahn Man Bhuridatta (1870–1949) in the 1930s.[8] Within the first generation of this movement in the early twentieth century, forest monks often did not keep money as they wandered through the north and northeast of Thailand (Kamala 1997, 59). However, when traveling between temples, they used the donation money they were given for train tickets (187). Forest monks, while using money outside of their wandering, only mentioned money in terms of their practical needs. They did not announce publicly the names of donors and how much they donated, as urban monasteries did (222). Forest monks were more concerned with teaching villagers how to exert themselves spiritually than funding construction projects or facilitating merit-making opportunities (238). The particular monastic orientation toward money is based upon the monastic relationship to laity, along with the kinds of activities and circumstances of the monk.[9]

From Ajahn Man the tradition moved into two main forest tradition lineages—Luangda Maha Bua Nanasampanno (1913–2011) and Luangpu Ajahn Chah Subhaddo (1918–1992). A short guide titled *Discipline and Conventions of the Theravada Buddhist Renunciate Communities*, on the Thai forest tradition for its western sangha, which is part of the Ajahn Chah lineage, instructs that any renunciant within this tradition is forbidden to have personal funds, including any coins, banknotes, or credit cards. Instead of personal accounts, forest monasteries are managed financially by the laypeople. The guide states that for laypeople, "financial donations should not be made directly to an individual *samana* [monastic renunciant], but placed in a donation box, given to one of the *anagarikas* (monastic postulants) or to one of the lay stewards of the monastery, making it clear whether such an offering is intended for a particular item or for the needs of a certain *samana*."[10] Monks within the forest lineage of Ajahn Chah are not even allowed to touch a bag that might contain money, let alone handle money directly.[11]

Although there was some flexibility in the first generation of the forest tradition's attitudes toward money, the tradition became stricter in the second generation. Anthropologist James L. Taylor (1993, 230n12) quotes a forest monk he interviewed in the northeast of Thailand as asserting that there is "'no place for money' in the life of a forest monk." As well, when the forest temple received a large amount of donations, it would distribute the money within the local community. The forest monks see "this as a pragmatic and expedient means of regulating excessive monetary support to the forest monastery, maintaining an equilibrium, and preventing spoiling inside the monastery" (253). The forest monks' orientation toward money centers on its possible dangers, seeing the life of the forest monk as having a sacred quality that might be risked by the profane nature of money. In this way, they have less flexibility than city monks, who must, given their location, participate in both the economy of merit and the capitalist economy.

At the other end of the spectrum of monastic attitudes toward money are the Kruba monks of northern Thailand and the Shan State of Myanmar. Monks who acquire the title "Kruba" are considered venerable teachers in the northern region and labeled as having charisma (*barami*) by the lay Buddhist community. They possess morality and knowledge, as well as skills, both magical and practical, which they have gained through study from teachers and Lanna texts (P. Cohen 2017, 7).[12] Included with this charisma is a concern for construction projects, mostly related to Buddhism.

Although Kruba monks have characteristics aligned with the forest tradition, such as strict asceticism and meditation, they do not maintain distance from their lay communities for long. Instead, they are actively and compassionately involved in supporting the lives of their disciples (P. Cohen 2000, 142). In this dynamic, Krubas are able to combine renunciation with this-worldly activism that is aimed toward material development and economic prosperity for lay followers.[13]

The newest generation of Krubas and their relationship with the economy has been labeled "charismatic capitalism" (Horstmann 2017). However, the money used by Kruba monks is not considered to be the same as the money being used in the regular economy. Because of the status of the Kruba, he can redistribute money to produce positive effects within Buddhist communities. This is the case for Kruba Sriwichai (1878–1939), one of the earliest monks to earn the title through the attraction and accumulation of labor and wealth for his building and renovation projects throughout the Lanna region. Kruba Bunchum (b. 1964), one of the most recent and well-known inheritors of the title, has many followers who donate large sums of money as a way to pay respect to him and make merit (Amporn J. 2016, 384, 388). All of their money is generated within the economy of merit because of the *barami* of the Kruba. City monks' orientations toward money are less dramatic than those of either the forest monks or the Kruba monks. City monks do not eschew money but, unlike the Krubas, are not able to amass large donations for their building projects.

Although the forest monks, Krubas, and city monks have different approaches to money, that "does not mean that Buddhist thought is infinitely plastic" (Keyes 1993a, 370). Instead, each group is making interpretations based on its population of supporters and individual goals. The relationship between Buddhism and economics is much more ambivalent than Max Weber had portrayed it, as it is "located both *within* and *against* the market" (Obadia 2011, 111).[14] Chiang Mai's city monks do not resist global capitalism, but they do not embrace it either. They have a practical orientation to money—knowing they need it to survive. Therefore, the agency they demonstrate over the capitalist economy through tourist and urban encounters is seen to be necessary for the future of their monastic life and temples. Globalization, in particular tourism, is perceived less as a threat than as an opportunity to acquire more resources. One must differentiate among different periods of monastic history and evaluate these on their own terms (Schopen 2000, 86); in the same way, one must also distinguish between different types of monasteries and monks, to understand the varying attitudes toward the economy. From the position of city monks, one can see the ways both the capitalist economy and the economy of merit mix, the ways that sacred and profane are positioned, and, ultimately, how agency is established. City monks utilize their agency over the capitalist and merit economies for the benefit of their communities, drawing on the assets of each temple, which depends on its location, attractions, and history.

The Business of Buddhist Temples

The sacred and the profane are not simply collapsed or totally separated in Thai Buddhist city temples but are understood by Buddhist monks in varying and complex ways. In October 2017, an order by the Sangha Supreme Council banned the sale of sacred items in any Thai temple's ordination hall (*ubosot*). The order states that the ordination hall should be free of commerce in order to facilitate meditation and prayer, while sacred items may be sold in areas outside of this sacred space within the temple. An article in the *Bangkok Post* about this order portrays varying reactions, with one monk in the northeast of Thailand stating that it will increase faith in Thai Buddhism, while another temple representative in central Thailand felt that it would have a negative impact on the temple's earnings.[15] Despite the Sangha Supreme Council's discomfort concerning this intersection of business and Buddhism, the problem is not with the selling of sacred items, but with the location of their sale. Additionally, in Wat Phra Singh, a famous temple in Chiang Mai City, there are shops in the front area of the temple, with a sign demarcating the locations where no merchandise (*sinkha*) can enter except as approved by the temple.[16] In both cases, there is a separation imagined within the temple space between sacred and profane, as well as varying degrees of sacredness, which reach their peak in the center of the temple.[17] The space of the ordination hall and the areas in general where Buddhist practices take place are considered sacred, where no commodities for sale should enter. However, they may be sold in areas not deemed as sacred within the temple gates.

In perhaps the most heavily touristed temple of Chiang Mai, Wat Doi Suthep, there is a thriving tourist economy. Along the stairs leading up to the temple are multiple shops selling food, drinks, jewelry, clothing, and other souvenirs. Within the outer part of the temple itself, at the top of the stairs, there are additional souvenir shops, Buddhist amulet stalls, and a coffee shop. With the exception of photographers hoping to take visitors' picture for a fee, the inner part of the temple, with the stupa containing a

Do and Don't in the temple

- Dress politely, do not wear shorts
- Show respect in the temple and shrine
- Take off your shoes before entering the platform around the Golden Chedi
- Keep your head lower than Buddha images and monks
- Don't touch the Buddha images
- Don't display affection for another person in public
- Always keep clean

2.1. A foreign national ticket purchased at Wat Doi Suthep for thirty Thai baht (US$1) lists the rules of behavior and dress inside the temple. Photograph by the author.

relic of the Buddha at its center, maintains distance from the economic spheres around it. However, to maintain its sacred nature, this inner part of the temple has become filled with directives about how to act in a Buddhist setting. "Do not disturb others," "Be quiet," "Dress modestly," "Sit down in the [temple] hall while taking a photo," and "Do not push the bells" are some of the signs directed toward tourists who might not understand the sacred nature of this temple for Buddhists. In addition, after foreign nationals pay the thirty Thai baht (US$1) entrance fee, they receive a ticket containing a list of proper temple etiquette (figure 2.1). In this way, a Buddhist temple's accessibility to foreigners opens up economic possibilities for community members, but must, at the same time, be managed to create the distinct nature of the space as different from a typical, profane tourist attraction. The capitalist economy is engaged through commodities for sale and the diverse and populous audience this temple attracts, while the sacred atmosphere allows for the economy of merit to be produced alongside.

This aspect of the temple space—as a community center where local people can make a living by selling food and worship items, and where merit making takes place—is, for the most part, accepted as normal. However, scandals regarding temple business practices do occur. Because of these scandals, Thai Buddhist society is engaged in continual conversations about the appropriateness of the intersections of Thai Buddhism and money.[18] Three examples characterize Thai Buddhist encounters with the capitalist economy: monks playing the lottery, the teachings of merit making within the controversial Wat Dhammakaya, and the 2018 alleged embezzlement of funds by five senior monks in Bangkok.

On Thai online discussion boards there is much traffic concerning whether monks may play the lottery and whether it is against their rules. Interest in the topic surged after a monk won approximately US$175,000 playing the lottery in 2016. Phra Prawit, a monk of ten years at a rural temple in the northeast of Thailand, had a habit of buying lottery tickets every month until he chose the lucky numbers. This monk "saw" the numbers of the winning ticket in the texture of a teak tree on the monastery grounds, a popular practice for selecting lottery numbers among laypeople.[19] The virtual discussion on the Dhamma Study and Support Foundation's website about whether buying a lottery ticket is against the monks' rules (*kan sue lottoeri phit sin mai*) centers on the intention of the monk—was he trying to help the lottery salesperson when purchasing the ticket and will he help Buddhism and the community with his winnings? Many argue that lottery playing is a form of gambling, exhibiting greed, which is an offense (*abat*) for the monk and not appropriate (*mai mosom*). But if the monk buys the lottery ticket because he pities the person selling it (*hen khon khai nasongsan*) and uses his winnings for Buddhist purposes, then it might be acceptable.[20] On another Thai discussion forum for more general topics, Pantip, members of the virtual community relate that there are many kinds of monks, some who are pure and follow the path and some who do not (*mi lay phra . . . phra tae phra tiam*).[21] Because there is no specific monastic rule against the lottery, this type of activity remains ambiguous and causes many to wonder about its legality and what monks can and cannot do in the world today.[22] The sacred and the profane are not clearly defined in these online discussion forums, with some arguing the lottery is profane and others finding ways it could connect with the sacred.

Wat Dhammakaya, the largest and most controversial temple in Thailand, is seen by mainstream Thai Buddhist audiences, especially as represented by the media, to be a fringe heterodox group within the Thai sangha. The group's particular ideas of merit making are closely connected to promises of wealth, so that a certain donation amount corresponds to a desirable realm in the next rebirth. *Bangkok Post* columnist Sanitsuda Ekachai reports that all temple abuses in Thailand pale in comparison to those of Wat Dhammakaya, where merit "is quantified in material terms," such that "the amount of merit gained and the levels of heaven you will go to depends on the amount of money you donate to the temple."[23] In addition, the abbot of the temple, Phra Dhammachayo, has been connected to financial scandals that have caused much concern. In 1999, he was accused of embezzlement, which led to both ecclesiastical and criminal investigations (Scott 2009, 129). However, both of these bureaucracies failed to reach any kind of satisfying resolution (139). In 2016–17, the scandal resurfaced when Thai police surrounded and infiltrated Wat Dhammakaya, forcing the abbot into hiding. The authorities ultimately abandoned their efforts when, after twenty-three days, they were unable to locate the abbot.[24] These controversies have been of particular concern in the media and demonstrate the importance of Buddhist economic practices in the Thai public sphere.

The Thai media are prone to view Wat Dhammakaya's activities as acts of manipulation that lack genuine religious piety. This is because of preexisting doubts about the temple's marketing campaigns for the construction of its Mahathammakai Chedi (Scott 2009, 90). The fund-raising techniques for this *chedi* were perceived to be aggressive, with new modern methods used such as "satellite networks, credit-card donations, and glitzy complementary gifts." These modern ways of fund-raising have aroused suspicion toward Wat Dhammakaya, as have its large promotional billboards, mass mailings, and "direct sales" techniques, all of which were used during the Asian economic crisis in 1997 (91). The temple's sales techniques appeared to be too businesslike—a term that for the student monks of Chiang Mai is synonymous with the profane, material world. This criticism is despite the fact that Wat Dhammakaya also employed traditional Theravada practices of merit making that related the cultivation of merit through good deeds to receiving positive results (103). Instead, traditional aspects were overlooked and Wat Dhammakaya became a prominent symbol of the commercialization of Buddhism in contemporary Thailand. In this case, insiders viewed Wat Dhammakaya's activities as lying within the sacred traditions of Buddhism, while onlookers, for the most part, found the merit-making techniques to be profane, positioned outside the realm of traditional Buddhism.

Wat Dhammakaya was not the only temple with a controversy sullying its reputation. In May 2018, the scandal of five monks arrested for alleged temple fund embezzlement in three Bangkok temples (Wat Sam Phraya, Wat Sa Ket, and Wat Samphanthawong) had again caused Thai Buddhists to shake their heads at the state of their religion. The *Bangkok Post* reported that two hundred police commandos raided the temples after complaints from the National Office of Buddhism that seven monks were involved in the embezzlement of funds meant for temple activities. Five were arrested on May 24, 2018; the sixth later surrendered to police, and the seventh fled to Germany.[25] Articles in the Thai media report that Thai Buddhists are still attending these temples, although in lower numbers, and that the response of a majority of Thai lay Buddhists has been to put faith in the religion, not in individual monks. The comment sections and articles in Thai media outlets also reveal a wish for the police to do more to stop these monks and restore the good name of Buddhism in Thailand.[26] In this case, of course, embezzling temple funds would be considered profane. Some Thai lay Buddhists hope the government can help Thai Buddhism rid itself of the profane, while others believe that the religion itself remains sacred but that certain individual monks have ventured into profane territory.

Beyond the major scandals and national media debates, everyday practices in temples are another site where money and its relationship to Buddhism comes under scrutiny, not only by Thai Buddhist laity, but by monks as well. How should money and the temple space come together, if at all? In the city temples of Chiang Mai, the debates around this question center on the specific cultural and historical contingencies of increased urbanization and tourist numbers, especially among Chinese citizens.

Tourism and the Buddhist Economy

City monks in Chiang Mai have readily drawn from the resources of their urban tourist environment in two ways: establishing an entrance fee for foreigners and allowing commerce and shops within temple spaces. There are a few theories concerning the origins of these temple business practices. Phra Ajahn Kaew, a resident of Wat Phra Singh, which charges twenty Thai baht (US$0.70) to enter the main Buddha image hall, or *wihan*, thought that head monks borrowed the idea to charge a fee for tourist entrance from famous Bangkok temples. Another possibility is that when monks travel abroad and see how different Buddhist temples elsewhere manage themselves, they get new ideas. These ideas are shared with other monastic leaders once they return. I was told by several student and senior monks living in Chiang Mai's old city temples that although the government subsidizes temple costs each month, temple abbots actually need much more money to meet their basic operating costs. One group of people who could help make up this deficit is the tourists who come to visit the temple. Instituting an admission fee is a way for this group to contribute. Tourism is a particular issue because it involves considering the nature of the temple space in new ways and distinguishing between people who visit the temple primarily for its aesthetic appeal and those who participate in the economy of merit. The latter distinction is located between the economy of merit and the capitalist economy. Because of their identity as non-Thai foreigners, tourists are considered to be non-Buddhists and subsequently excluded from the economy of merit, albeit involuntarily. Because of that, there is what I call a "rhetoric of deprivation" within the temple space. In this rhetoric, the perception is that the government and lay support is not enough to maintain the temple's needs. Since such is the case, the temple has to consider new ways to maintain itself. In contrast, some monks find that the temple is not deprived, but already has enough in terms of resources. Other monks seek a balance between these two views of the temple's monetary situation.

But in some cases, economic entanglements just seem to happen without a plan or consideration of the temple's financial situation. Phra Ajahn Kaew related a story that reveals how these economic entanglements occur. At the temple in Bangkok where he used to live, located in the business district of Sathorn, there was a parking lot, but no fee was charged to park there. Eventually, Thai locals came to ask for money from the car owners in exchange for "protection" of their car. If the car owners did not pay, then the protectors would scratch their cars. Because of this situation, the temple began collecting money for the service of the parking lot and hired people to look after it. Such economic entanglements seem to be borne out of necessity, in response to particular situations where money can be obtained. In fact, a few temples not popular with tourists, but located in areas of Chiang Mai where parking is difficult to find, gain a portion of their monthly budget from providing this service.[27]

Each temple has its own specific characteristics—its location or unique features—that must be considered along with the nature and purpose of the Buddhist temple in general to understand the city monks' relationship with money. Phra Ajahn Jong, a monastic professor of English at Mahachulalongkorn University (MCU) at Wat Suan Dok, balanced the sacredness of the temple space with its practical needs in his response to my questions about commerce in temples. He argued that if the temple does not have too many shops and uses the money to support the temple and community, then it is all right.

The temple belongs to the community. Some temples rent space for free as *tham bun* [giving merit] for the shop owners, or sometimes rent is very cheap each month to help out the Thai shop owners in the community. Some temples need much money to maintain [them] and we cannot always ask for money from the community, so we have *phapa* [a formal donation offering ceremony organized for a temple at any time of year] and *kathin* [the monastic robes offering holiday held annually after the three-month monastic rains retreat, which takes place during the months of July– October]. Times change. We have electricity now. As long as the money is not for the abbot but for the community, it is okay.

This is the balanced approach of some city monks—maintaining sacredness but allowing for adaptation, upholding the economy of merit while being open to the capitalist economy. Others fall more into the extreme camps of either deprivation or having enough, when asked about the financial status of their temples. Buddhist temples in Chiang Mai are not solely in alignment with the tourist industry, nor are they only following the urban city trends, but instead there are numerous responses and actions within their repertoires. In addition to monetary resources, Buddhist monks utilize tourism to improve the education of their monastic communities and maintain their temple spaces. Examples from recent intersections between the business of tourism, the urban environment, and Buddhism include fees for tourists, commerce, and volunteer tourism in temples.

TEMPLE ENTRANCE FEES FOR FOREIGNERS

Temples must sometimes find creative ways to engage with the capitalist economy. Monastic leadership must be able to fundraise in order for temples to survive. But what are the appropriate ways to manage a temple? What is the purpose of the temple? These questions get to the heart of the contested views of religious spaces and perceptions of the sacred and profane. Data collected from staff taking tickets at temple entrances, student monks in Chiang Mai, especially those living in temples that charge foreigners fees, and senior monks involved in monastic education and temple management illustrate how Buddhists debate about and utilize tourism for their benefit.

Wat Buppharam was not a temple popular with tourists, despite its location on a main road leading to the heart of the old city and its picturesque garden featuring characters such as Donald Duck, statues of giraffes and zebras, and real roosters. In fact, this temple was mainly known among monastics as a good school for learning Pali. However, that changed in 2012 following the release of the Chinese blockbuster *Lost in Thailand*, in which a scene in the movie takes place in Wat Buppharam. When large Chinese tour groups started to arrive as part of movie-fan tourism, a fee structure was put in place. I discussed the fee with Naen Maha Tri, a monk in residence there:

NAEN MAHA TRI: At my temple, Wat Buppharam, there is a fee.

AUTHOR: Yes, because of the movie [*Lost in Thailand*].

NAEN MAHA TRI: Oh, you know about the movie! Yes, the Chinese, they come to my temple, they make it dirty. They don't take off their shoes, and I am sorry. The bathroom, they make it so dirty. I see them [in the temple building] and I have to tell them, "Take off your shoes."

AUTHOR: What do you think about this fee, as a novice monk living in this temple?

NAEN MAHA TRI: Nowadays, the temple seems like a business or company. I don't like that. Look at the old days. We don't have much, but we can maintain without the fee. We don't need it [the fee]. Money is dangerous for people who take care of the temple. It can make one monk [who controls the money] become a bad person. Look at the money corruption and laundering in Bangkok—you know about this, right? The fee has been for two to three years now—it should be enough. It is the opposite of the teaching of the Buddha. He teaches people what is enough. The building is enough. Why do we have to keep building?

In contrast to monks who espouse the rhetoric of deprivation, others like Naen Maha Tri have taken up what I term the "rhetoric of enough." Naen Maha Tri believes that the temple has enough and does not need to generate more money. The ticket collector I spoke with, Khun Ou, clarified that the temple must charge a fee in order to have someone clean the toilets and maintain the grounds of the temple (*prap prung wat*). He also stated that Thai people know how to make merit and how to act in the temple, and therefore they do not have to pay. The temple committee (*khana kammakan*), consisting of Thai laypeople and senior monks, decided to charge a fee of twenty Thai baht (US$0.70) beginning in April 2016.[28]

On July 1, 2016, Wat Chedi Luang began instituting a fee of forty Thai baht (US$1.40). A few months before, an announcement printed on three billboards in Thai, English, and Chinese explained that the fee is necessary in order to cover the costs of the care, repair, and renovation of the temple due to the increased number of tourists. In an article about this development at Wat Chedi Luang, the Thai website Chiangmai News justified the fee in several ways. First, it is a typical practice in many countries today, as Vietnam, Burma, and Japan are also charging a fee to enter popular temples. Second, because money from donations and the government are not enough [displaying a rhetoric of deprivation], the temple had two choices: institute a fee or rent space in the temple for restaurants and coffee shops. Since the temple has a traditional and historical feel, it should not be filled with modern amenities. Third, Chiang Mai tour companies told Wat Chedi Luang there would be no negative effect because tourists will understand [the necessity of the fee].[29]

Concerning this fee, one of the monastic assistants to the abbot at Wat Chedi Luang, Phrakru Winay, emphasized to me in an interview that, in the history of this temple, there was no collection of money before July 2016. In describing the decision to collect money, he said, "The tourists started coming a lot, and the temple committee decided, especially since the Chinese came in large numbers, they have to manage this with a fee." Further validations of the fee were that the government does not contribute much to the budget of Wat Chedi Luang; it is an old place (*sathan boran*) that deserves to be preserved; other temples around Chiang Mai are also collecting money; and the temple needs a larger budget to hire staff to clean bathrooms, take care of the buildings, and serve as security guards and gardeners. He argued that tourist money was necessary to pay both for costs incurred by tourists' visits and for temple expenses not covered by government subsidies or donations. The rhetoric of deprivation leads to more engagement with the tourist and capitalist economy.

The assistant to the abbot also felt it was important to mention that since the money is used to preserve the temple and hire staff to care for the temple, the fee is not for profit. In reference to the higher numbers of tourists, he stated, "The Chinese are loud in the bathroom and other places. The security guard can check and tell them to be quieter. There is no problem with other groups, but I am not looking down on [*du thuk*] Chinese." When asked why Thai people do not have to pay, he explained, "The temple committee decided they are part of the community. They are Buddhists. They just held the *kathin* where they offered much more than forty Thai baht. They will never be charged. They are Thai people [*pen khon Thai*]." Because they participate in the economy of merit, Thai people do not also have to participate in the capitalist economy in order to enter the temple.

However, as at Wat Buppharam, there have been some unenthusiastic responses among the student monks. The temple has a Monk Chat program where tourists come to learn about Buddhism from monks. Former president of Wat Chedi Luang's Monk Chat, Phra Ruang, a student from Thailand, believes that paying to enter a temple does not allow easy access to Buddhism. Instead, he thought a temple should be welcoming, showing that Buddhists are open to all. He has seen a 30 percent decrease in Monk Chat attendance since the institution of the fee.

At Wat Phra Singh, there is a fee to enter the main Buddha image hall of the temple. I spoke with Khun Nat, a middle-aged Thai woman who collects the fee and checks that foreign tourists are wearing appropriate clothing. While I spoke to her, she was busy collecting money for tickets and handing out sarongs to the many foreigners who arrived in short shorts and skirts. I asked if there were any issues with tourists paying the fee. At first, she found there were some problems with the Chinese groups not wanting to pay, but it is starting to be accepted now that the tour guides are helping them to understand the fee structure at popular temples around Chiang Mai. As I observed this scene on a busy Saturday afternoon, I heard a young woman say to her travel companion, "Oh, you have to pay money to go in here. Let's leave." If any tourists have an issue, Khun Nat insisted that this is fine because they can see the rest of the temple for free. There is no notice outside the temple about the fee, so most tourists are surprised when they get to the top of the stairs of the main hall and are asked to pay a fee. As I was about to hand my twenty Thai baht fee to enter the hall, Khun Nat explained that I did not have to pay since I was a Thai person (*pen khon Thai laeo*). Although I am not Thai, and do not have Thai heritage, Khun Nat was referring to the fact that I speak Thai and was wearing clothing similar to a Thai person, not a tourist. At this superficial level, it is easy to be regarded as part of Thai Buddhism.

Phra Daeng, a student monk at Wat Phra Singh, commented on the tourist fee:

PHRA DAENG: The fee in the temple makes it seem like the temple should be a museum, but this is not a museum. It's not a business. The fee is not a lot of money, but inside it's not a good feeling for the monk or, I think, for the tourist.

AUTHOR: But some monks say the fee is necessary for cleaning and maintenance.

PHRA DAENG: Well the toilet is not free. You have to make a donation
for the toilet, and the temple has its own money from the Thai people
from the annual ceremonies [*kathin*].

I also heard from a number of student monks this rhetoric of enough, that
the temple must have sufficient funds from donations alone. These student
monks have their basic living needs met, so it is difficult to understand why
the fee is necessary.

In contrast, senior teacher monks have a more practical view of the balance between deprivation and enough that allows some mixing of the
sacred and the profane, the existence of both types of economies, and a
wider range of acceptance of various practices. The Buddhist monk professor Phra Ajahn Jong reasoned: "We need to take care of the temple, so it's
okay [to use the temple fee] to pay for water, electricity, [the] toilet and . . .
to maintain the buildings and clean the temple. It is not like a business,
because it's not much—twenty to thirty baht. One hundred to two hundred
baht would be too much. That makes it like a business." Here, business
(*thurakit*) has similar connotations to the profane that should remain outside of Buddhism and the temple sphere.

Other senior monks I spoke to were not happy about the fee but saw its
necessity. They tried to think of ways the system could work better for Buddhism and the tourists. When I told Phra Maha Insorn Khunawuttho,
principal of Wat Nong Bua Pariyattitham, that more city temples have
recently begun to charge a fee, he stated:

The government should have one big budget, collecting money from all
the tourists. Then the temple can count how many tourists they receive
each year and the government would give the temple the amount of
money based on how many tourists come. I think that would be better
than [the] temple charging [a] fee. This is how other countries do it, with
a fee for the visa. Sure, the temple needs money for renovation and to
maintain the area, but it's not right to charge a fee unless they explain
that. They have to explain what the money is for to the people. That is
what is right.

A solution I heard from Phra Vin, a monk who recently graduated from
MCU at Wat Suan Dok, was to "make a big signboard and let the people
know that they are building something. That there is a purpose for using

this money and explain to show to foreigners how they might help." Buddhists and Buddhist temples rely on signs for communication with the public. Because there is often no monk or staff available to communicate directly with visitors, information needs to be delivered through promotional posters and signs indicating proper behavior and ways to support this sacred space. Another alternative I heard from a lay Thai Buddhist professor at MCU was to educate the foreign tourists coming to the temple about donations. In that way, the temple could survive on donations and not appear like a business, or part of the commercial, material world. Information could be shared by tour guides and posted on signs at the temple indicating how much money is appropriate to give. Here again, what is at issue is not only the sacred and profane distinction but the economy of merit. Tourists need to be educated about the nature of sacred space as well as the economy of merit in order for their behavior and actions to be considered appropriate and similar to that of Thai Buddhists.

But the general opinion of Thai laypeople about tourist fees in temples is difficult to locate. Many of them do not notice the fee since they do not have to pay. When I searched online for representative opinions, it was difficult to find any discussion about this topic. If the issue of temples and money is raised, then the topic often turns to Wat Dhammakaya, but not specifically to tourist fees in temples. One monk at Wat Doi Saket, Phra Maha Mitra, formerly a student at MCU, Wat Suan Dok, explained: "In my opinion, Thai people are okay about [there being a] tourist economy in Buddhism because they understand the expenses of the temple, or they may think [of the tourist entrance fee] as donating, or maybe this thing is even not [on] their mind. Even Thai people parking at some temple [in] Bangkok and in Chiang Mai, the temple charges a fee for that and they [Thai Buddhists] are okay with that."

However, this relationship between the tourist economy and temples is an important issue for Buddhist monks, as they have expressed, and foreign tourists to Chiang Mai. Although these temples are using the popularity of Buddhism to bring in tourist revenue for necessary maintenance, the mixture of what is perceived to be sacred and profane is upsetting to some foreign tourists and residents, who discern a clearer separation between these two categories than exists within Thai Buddhism.

There are multiple Internet forums dedicated to complaining about the fee to enter Wat Doi Suthep, the most famous temple, located on a mountain above Chiang Mai City. This temple was the first to charge a fee, of thirty Thai baht (US$1), due to its location with beautiful views.[30] This comment from a traveler on TripAdvisor's website is representative: "There's a fee to enter the temple and it's weird to pay to enter a temple (a place of worship). I think this truly eradicates any spiritual sense to the place."[31] And there is this remark on the ThaiVisa Forum: "Doi Suthep, along with Wat Phra Singh, charge[s] foreigners entrance fees for entering their temples. I'm not a Buddhist scholar but I know this is wrong. Buddhism is about donations and intentions."[32] About Wat Chedi Luang, one commentator writes, "Personally I done [sic] appreciate it when religion and money are mixed together."[33] In these comments the strict separation of sacred and profane, rather than a pragmatic alignment, is apparent. Foreigners can become upset at what appears to them to be a commodified aspect of Buddhist tourism in northern Thailand. Some tourists would rather offer a donation, so they could make an offering "from the heart, not from force."[34] The lack of equality in the pricing and the lack of perceived sacredness of a temple that has an entrance fee are the major factors causing this resistance.

Fees have been controversial in many religious tourist sites. A main source of tension is that those who have come to worship wonder why they have to "pay to pray" (Olsen 2006, 105). In Luang Prabang, Laos, visitors expressed dissatisfaction with the fee system. Similar to the student monks of Chiang Mai, they wanted to know where the money was going and wished for more information about the temples in exchange for the fee (Lenaerts 2015, 73). However, the amount of the fee, important in the discussions of some senior monks in reconciling its necessity, is also used in discussions by tourists, who note that it is a cheap, trifling amount to pay for the ability to photograph and view the temple spaces.[35] These tourists felt that the exchange value was worth the amount charged. In this way, some tourists do not consider the dynamic of sacred and profane or the economy of merit but see only a commercial exchange.

However, if foreigners treat the temple fees as payment for visiting a tourist site, rather than as a way of participating in the economy of merit, Thai Buddhists can logically in turn treat these foreigners like tourists, not Buddhists, and ask them to pay a fee. But that does not mean that some monks and foreigners do not find the fee questionable. Monks who believe the temple has enough are more upset by the profane presence of the capitalist economy, while those who perceive the temple as deprived see the necessity of locating funds outside of donations and the economy of merit. The monks in charge of these fees have not fully accommodated to tourist uses of the space, but are not resisting their presence either.

SHOPS AND COMMERCE IN THE TEMPLE SPACE

Temple entrance fees are not the only way to fundraise for a temple. Shops selling souvenirs and even coffee shops have also become popular recently in Chiang Mai's city temples. The sale of food, drink, and devotional items on temple grounds, along with stalls offering massage, lottery tickets, fortune-telling services, and flea markets, can be found inside a number of temples. An attraction of some temples is the presence of a wish-granting Buddha called Phrajao Tanjai. An advertisement at one temple famous for its statue of this kind, Wat Doi Kham, states that one can ask Phrajao Tanjai about matters relating to business success. The removal of bad luck or a wish for prosperity and long life can be facilitated by purchasing and burning candles associated with one's day of birth or by a ceremony performed by monks, available at a number of temples, such as Wat Lok Moli and Wat Srisuphan. These intersections with the capitalist economy do not often concern tourism but relate to the ways temples connect the urban landscape, economy, and visitors' aspirations. With a density of people and temples in Chiang Mai, services and commodities are a way to attract Thai Buddhists or anyone wishing for wealth, health, and happiness.

When I discussed the general issue of selling commodities in temples, however, most student monks felt this did not align with the intention of the temple space. One novice monk, Naen Pong, in a discussion about commerce at temples, remarked: "The shops are all bad. It does not seem like a temple anymore. You should feel relaxed in a temple, but now you feel [like] everything is changed." Naen Pong posits a strong binary between the sacred space of the temple and the mundane world of commerce. Other monks as well felt that the temple should not be a place for shopping but should be a place to feel calm in order to learn about the Buddhist teachings. Phra Akara believed that the recent development of commerce in the temples changed their nature and purpose:

> The temple now is like a shopping mall. I don't want to show this to
> people. Now people, Thai people and Chinese people, they come to get
> holy water and amulets. That is the news that goes to China, and now
> Buddhism is changed a little bit by a little bit. Instead, we should care
> to start teaching Buddhism and spread the teaching of Buddha. But now
> the temple is for traveling. It's for the beautiful thing. Just to come by
> and look for shopping. It makes people think the temple is about money,
> but it's for practicing and meditation.

Phra Sarit agreed: "The people come and they think, 'We are looking at an old place,' and take a photo and then go back [to their home or hotel]. This makes people change the priority. The temple should be a quiet place where people feel peace, relax the mind. If they just come and shop and then go back, they don't have any teaching to remind them to purify and improve the mind."

For these two Thai monks, studying in their fourth year at Mahamakut Buddhist University (MBU), commerce does not honor the purpose of the temple. Rather, the shops lessen the temple's value because they cause the people who enter the temple to think more about what they can buy than about the Buddhist teachings. But some student monks agreed that some forms of consumerism in the temple were acceptable if they helped the temple community and created a space for laypeople to relax in the temple. Phra Sonalin, who is from Laos and lives at Wat Palad, explained: "Every big temple, royal temple, they have a big tourist attraction. They have coffee shop[s], [they offer] shops, for both Thai laypeople and foreigners. I don't disagree with business. I care about the budget and where it goes. If the temple has a Pali school or they need food for the monks, it [the money] should go there. But the activities in the temple sometimes look like a business, especially coffee shops. But at least this gives support to the people, and the people that come to the temple can stay longer." He points out, from his perspective, the positive and negative aspects of small business enterprises on temple premises—that they can be useful and necessary but can also change the look and feel of the temple space.

As Phra Sonalin discussed, one way to attract tourists and Thai Buddhist laity to enter and spend more time in the temple is with a coffee shop on the premises. A similar trend has begun in Korea, where Korean Buddhist temples are replacing traditional tea shops with cafés in an attempt to stay relevant in modern Korean society (Kaplan 2017). This kind of creativity has been observed in the economic activity surrounding the recently deceased monk Luang Por Khun and his embrace of capitalism to help those around him, from villagers peddling their wares at his temple to devotees selling amulets blessed by him (Pattana 2012). However, not all monks can reach the level of charisma and fame that Luang Por Khun did. The examples described here are more local and practical ways to generate income for a temple, discussed by its purveyors as a necessary compromise. The following two case studies provide a snapshot of the reasons and the stories behind the establishment and use of coffee shops to generate income for Buddhist temples.

The first case study is Wat Palad, which established a coffee shop in 2016. It happened by coincidence (*doy bang oen*), as the abbot, Phrakru Tirasuttapot, explained in an interview. This temple, situated in a scenic spot on the way up Suthep Mountain, is well known to hikers and foreigners looking for exercise as well as Buddhist aesthetics. Monks at this temple remarked that they usually see the same foreigners everyday making the climb from Wat Palad to Wat Doi Suthep. Using Buddhist temples as stops on workout routines could be seen as antithetical to these spaces, with exercise being a profane activity and visiting temples considered sacred. However, the monks I spoke with did not hold this stark binary, asserting that some of the foreign hikers are very interested in Buddhism, and they often stop to talk to them for a long time about Buddhist teachings and meditation. Because of this population, it would seem that the coffee shop was set up to capitalize on the morning influx of foreign hikers. However, the abbot of Wat Palad did not mention tourists at all when narrating the establishment of his temple's coffee shop.

The abbot created the coffee shop for an unexpected reason—to support a dental fund for monks at his temple. When a dentist came to ordain temporarily at the temple, he asked the abbot about the best ways to make merit (*rueang tham bun*).[36] The abbot responded that one does not have to go to the temple to make merit. Giving to the poor and helping make people happy are also important merit-making activities. After considering ways the dentist could help the temple with his skills, they decided that the dentist would offer monks at Wat Palad free annual checkups and cleanings. However, there was no fund established for those monks who might need more costly dental surgery or braces. Soon afterward, another man, who had experience with hospitality, came to ordain, again temporarily, and they came up with the idea of Bun Coffee. This name is important to the abbot—the coffee shop is about making merit, not about business (*thurakit*). It was also significant for the abbot to point out that the coffee shop is the only commerce in the temple. Unlike other temples, it does not have any stalls selling lottery tickets or worship items (*khong bucha*). Anyone can have the coffee for free if they do not have money, and when there is an event (*ngan wat*), the drinks are available for everyone. In order to create the dental fund, the coffee shop is set up so that nine Thai baht (US$0.30) of some drinks go toward this fund (figure 2.2). The aim of the coffee shop, as Phrakru Tirasuttapot stated, is to support the dental fund while maintaining the temple as a place where one can calm down the mind (*chitchai lotlong*) in nature, not a place for business. The abbot made clear that he did

2.2. The coffee shop at scenic Wat Palad supports a dental fund for monks. Photograph by the author.

not decide (*tatsinchai*) to establish this coffee shop, and it was not his plan (*mai mi wang phaen*), but it just happened (*koet khuen*).

Not all the monks at this temple totally agreed that the coffee shop is beneficial. One monk living at Wat Palad, Phra On, contended, "The temple is supposed to be clean, beautiful, tidy, easy, quiet and peaceful, but the coffee shop changes this atmosphere. When people come to look at the beauty of the temple, the coffee shop can conflict with this." However, he continued, "Some big temples need to charge a fee for the staff they need to employ to manage the temple space. We have to look at the context of the temple and what they need to maintain themselves." Phra On asserted that at Wat Palad "we don't need any staff to maintain the temple, so it doesn't work for us to charge, even for the hikers." The abbot of Wat Palad, Phrakru Tirasuttapot, does not like the idea of an entrance fee and thinks the temple should be a public place, open to everyone, to see the beauty and unique architectural style.

The abbot also felt that tourists only cause a few problems (*mi panha noi*). Some of the hikers come prepared with clothes ready to wrap around themselves in the temple, but others are not aware of the dress code, so the temple provides loose skirts and pants for them to wear. As elsewhere, the monks rely on signs to communicate with visitors. The abbot explained,

"We don't need to tell them [about the correct clothing for the temple] because there is a sign when they enter from the hiking trail. The sign will tell them [pai bok]." I have seen inappropriately dressed hikers, some of them my students, attempt to enter the temple space. When a monk sees a female in shorts, he points to them and then to the box of clothing at the temple's front entrance. For the monks I spoke to, the tourists and hikers do not detract from the sacredness of the space. At Wat Palad, the abbot is careful to point out that the purpose of the coffee shop is to benefit the monastic community. Because it is not used as a business, it can fit within the temple environment. Despite this population and the modern commodity of coffee, Phrakru Tirasuttapot finds no trace of the profane.

The second case study is Wat Phan Sao, located on a main road close to, but not inside, the old city of Chiang Mai. With no special reason to visit this temple—no famous murals, no important Buddha statues, and no natural mountain beauty—Wat Phan Sao has no easy way to attract income and donations. As Phra Maha HaOrn, abbot of Wat Phan Sao, explained, "There is nothing here!" (Mai mi arai ti ni). For that reason, in contrast to the situation at Wat Palad, he intentionally opened a coffee shop. Phra Maha HaOrn conducted research around Chiang Mai to discover ways for the temple to generate income, concluding that coffee shops were very popular (dang mak). So he decided to make a coffee shop in the style of a temple, where on one side visitors can see the view of the temple and on the other side they can look out to the city.[37] He looked to start a franchise coffee shop but found they were very expensive, so instead he created his own brand called Boon Raksa, using local coffee beans. According to Phra Maha HaOrn, the coffee shop has several benefits: (1) it helps the student supporters of the temple, who can work there while studying; (2) it pays for all of the costs of the temple (chai chai nai wat thang mot) through the shop's profits; and (3) it allows people to make merit at the same time they are buying drinks. At first the coffee shop received criticism. But after the abbot posted a sign explaining the shop's purpose to maintain the temple (bamrung khong wat), the Thai Buddhist community accepted the shop.

Phra Bunma, a monk living at Wat Phan Sao, concurred with the abbot: "Money from the donation box is not enough. So this is the good way to get income and give a chance for [the] temple boy [dek wat] to have work." He continued: "Not only coffee shops, but every temple [has some kind of] shop to help [with] expenses in [the] temple. My abbot told me that in [the] future, if he dies, the temple can't stand by itself because our temple is little and not famous. So, he decided the shop will help the temple. And the government, they don't care about [the] expenses of [this] temple, so we should help ourselves."

Although Wat Phan Sao is concerned about separating the temple from business, the sacred from the profane, what matters most to this temple is survival. When asked about the introduction of fees and shops at temples, some Buddhist monks display the rhetoric of deprivation, while others perceive that the temple has enough. These disparate perceptions illustrate the lack of transparency about temple budgets. However, one way to survive in Chiang Mai City is to utilize the urban space and the tourist industry. With ancient temples finding themselves situated within prime locations or in areas becoming newly popular with tourists, they are participating in some of these resources. Temple fees and commerce show the agency of monks within the urban and tourist landscapes as they create ways to draw from these new revenue streams. They use the money to benefit and maintain the temple; although coffee shops and fees are not without complaint by some of the student monks, for many they are seen as a necessary compromise.

THE AGENCY OF CULTURAL EXCHANGE PROGRAMS

In addition to temple space and its relationship to money, cultural exchange programs have their own reasons for engaging with tourism and the resources from the urban environment. Other advantages that Thai Buddhists derive from tourism, besides money, include spreading Buddhism and making English practice available to underprivileged monks and novice monks. The Wat Sri Boen Ruang Temple Stay and Retreat program takes advantage of tourism for spreading Buddhism. As part of this program, "foreign guests," as the organizers refer to tourists who come to stay at this temple, experiment with Buddhism on a short- or long-term basis, from as little as a week to up to several months. Guests have the opportunity to participate in Buddhist rituals and practice meditation, with male participants having the option to ordain as novices. Some of the male guests have a dream to ordain, but it is intimidating and difficult to do so in Thailand for foreigners today. Currently, the Temple Stay and Retreat program is the only program that offers to foreigners who do not have any relationships in Thailand the opportunity to ordain temporarily as a novice monk.[38]

This program demonstrates agency over tourism in its approach to the guests. Although the temple is open to whoever wants to come, guests must follow the rules of the temple—either the Eight Precepts of a Buddhist layperson staying in a temple or the Ten Precepts of a novice monk—and they must understand the value of merit making in Thai Buddhism. Male guests who seek ordination must show that they are sincere and not just "ticking wearing monastic robes off their traveling checklist," as a program coordinator told me. As soon as foreign guests arrive, they have a conversation about the importance of generosity within Buddhism. Instead of marking their difference and lack of participation in the economy of merit with a fee, this program brings the foreigners into the culture of merit making. If foreign guests are interested in joining a Buddhist community, they must follow lay Buddhists' and novice monks' rules along with the Buddhist practice of donation. This demonstrates that the temple program is not resisting the wishes of tourists but not fully accommodating them either. Besides offering male guests the unique opportunity to ordain, another aim is to benefit the young Thai novices who live or study at the temple. When first encountering foreigners, novices are usually shy to speak English. For the novices at Wat Sri Boen Ruang, it is natural to greet new guests in English. When I first arrived at this temple, I was surprised when the monk who met me asked in confident English, "What is your name? Where are you from?" The Temple Stay and Retreat program is able to run on a donation basis through the efforts of the program coordinator and the foreign monks who take care of the visitors.

Volunteer tourism is another way in which Buddhist monks express their agency over tourism and where monastic leadership maintains a balance between accommodation and resistance. Temple abbots and principals of temple schools are in charge of allowing volunteer teachers of English into their classrooms. They also choose whether or not they want to affiliate with volunteer tourism companies to receive volunteers. Volunteers who enter the classroom through these companies have received a background check in their home countries, an orientation to Thai Buddhist temple behavior, and English-teaching strategies. This connection between monastic schools and volunteer tourism companies allows monastic leaders to benefit their communities of novice monk students.

Novice monks enjoy the volunteer teachers, who have fun activities for them, such as competitive games in which students race to the board and write in the correct letter or word to complete a sentence in English. More importantly, the volunteer teachers open up a completely new social space for the monks. In the novice monk classroom, the students clearly view this time as a chance to joke around, tease each other, and play with both English and Thai language in new ways that they would not and could not within a Thai social space. Once, when a volunteer teacher asked me to explain the somewhat complex homework assignment to the novice monks in Thai, so they could understand it, the novice monks immediately changed their demeanor. Their jocular energy was depleted as they stiffened their bodies and responded with a uniform "Krab"—the equivalent of "Yes, ma'am." English, although they were not proficient at it, provided a new social space for the monks, one that involved freedom and playfulness. Thai language in the classroom setting, in contrast, signaled obedience, respect, and physical contractions of one's body, demonstrating that language comes laden with culture and values. The novice monks may not learn a large amount of English given the limited time frame and the continuous change of international participants; however, the constant exposure to foreigners helps novices feel more comfortable conversing in English and opens these possibilities of existing in different social spaces. Two case studies exemplify the varying ways that leaders of Buddhist communities have agency over the volunteer tourism program at their temples.

The first case study involves Wat Nong Bua Pariyattitham, a monastic school about forty minutes outside of Chiang Mai City that services novice monks aged twelve to eighteen, and where Phra Maha Insorn Khunawuttho is the principal. At Wat Nong Bua, novices learn both secular and Buddhist subjects. Phra Maha Insorn is committed to this type of education, where boys can learn skills to become either monks or laypersons. Phra Maha Insorn was interested in volunteer tourists teaching English because he has found from Thai teachers that novices can read and understand English grammar but not speak well in English. He has seen the results of the volunteer tourists' presence, as now his novice monks are brave to speak with foreigners, they have motivation to study, and some former students are now studying in the English department at Chiang Mai University. Phra Maha Insorn is happy with the volunteer organizations that he has affiliated with, most recently the FutureSense Foundation, and their outreach, which has brought the temple school more than one hundred volunteers every year from some seventeen countries.

The foreigners also benefit the school through their ability to attract donations. Usually when there is a large group of foreign volunteers, the temple sponsors a big activity, such as an English camp, with all local schools from the area invited. The lay Buddhists in the community are aware of such activities through the temple's advertising on billboards and posters placed throughout the main street of this small town. Phra Maha Insorn reported that when Thai lay Buddhists see the good work the school is doing to educate the youth in the community and bring in foreigners from all over the world to teach, they want to donate by offering money for electricity and food. Because of this support, Phra Maha Insorn asserted, his monastic school does not have to worry about funding. In this way the foreign volunteers not only motivate the novice monks to learn English but also motivate the lay community to donate.

There is clearly a respect for Buddhism among the volunteers and a benefit to the community and school because of their presence. With this ability to regulate the volunteers, educate them about Buddhism, and attract donations through their presence, Buddhist monks maintain agency in their temples. However, in 2017, the volunteer tourism company moved in order to focus on other projects in another area of northern Thailand. I went back to Wat Nong Bua in June 2018 to discuss the effects of this departure. Phra Maha Insorn stated that the volunteers did help the laypeople to think the temple has a good school, and thus had a good effect (*mi phon*). But there are other ways to raise funds, which are needed to maintain and complete construction of the school. Wat Nong Bua has an affiliated temple in California, and according to Phra Maha Insorn, the people there "feel good [*ruseuk chai di*] to give. The money for them is only a little, but for us it's a lot." The school also has supporters in many provinces, especially in Bangkok, and on Facebook's live video streaming they can see their donations and offerings being received.

As part of the temple's long-term plans for the school, four or five rooms will be built for volunteers. Phra Maha Aat, another teacher at the school, reports, "We are waiting and ready for the volunteers. If they come, they can learn about Buddhism here, whatever they want, I can answer their questions and teach them meditation." It was clear that although the temple is set up to accommodate volunteers, it is not able to locate them. This is one area where the temple is lacking in agency. The monastic school is open to the volunteers and knows their value for the temple community, but the temple is currently missing the support of a volunteer tourism organization.

The second case study involves Phra Ajahn Dr. Thani Jitawiriyo, the founder of Plik Wiwek Dhamma Center, built in 2011. He usually has around twenty novice monks at his center, but these numbers can swell during special camps and religious seasons. He envisions his Dhamma center as a place of development for the novice monks where they can learn how to live their lives as good citizens and Buddhists. Beyond this aim, Ajahn Thani has a goal for his novices to learn English skills in order to be able to exchange with and learn new things from different kinds of people.

Ajahn Thani spoke warmly of many volunteers whom he thinks of as members of the center's family. The volunteers who became family, for the most part, did not come through the volunteer tourism organizations. He has noticed that the volunteers who do come through organizations have to report to or speak with the staff there. As a result, it seemed to him that their volunteering was not as heartfelt, as they could just leave and go teach at another temple, village, or school. But the foreign volunteers can adapt better and integrate into the community when they arrive through the networks of Ajahn Thani and Plik Wiwek. He sees these foreigners as volunteering from the heart (*chitasa ma jak huachai*). He can observe this when volunteers play with the novices and open up to them, when they join the novices' football game every night, or when the novice monks make a special meal of pancakes on the last day a volunteer stays at the temple.

Because of this difference he sees between volunteers who come on their own and volunteers who come through a company, he has chosen to stop his affiliation with volunteer tourism agencies and instead exclusively use his own international networks to find volunteers who will be dedicated and stay for long periods of time (at least three months). Although managing this process himself means he will receive fewer volunteers, Ajahn Thani would rather have quality foreign teachers. These types of foreign volunteers, Ajahn Thani finds, are good for the novice monks. The novices' English improves, they are more considerate, and they know there are people who care about them. But unlike Phra Maha Insorn, Ajahn Thani asserts that the foreigners do not motivate the laypeople to offer donations. Donations only come to this center because of the population of novice monks. The donors are happy that novices have opportunities to speak English, but if the volunteers did not come, the donors would still offer the same amount. In this center, Ajahn Thani exhibits agency over the volunteer tourist program by choosing whether to affiliate with a volunteer tourism company and selecting the volunteers who will most benefit his community.[39] He does not resist volunteer tourists coming to his temple but also does not accommodate all persons who are interested.

The Buddhist relationship with tourism and the urban environment in Chiang Mai does not lead to an alteration of Buddhist practices but instead demonstrates agency. Although some student monks would rather no commerce take place in the temple, and there is a diversity of opinion, the consensus is that some kind of fund-raising needs to be done by the monastic leadership of temples. For city temples, it is not feasible to simply reject the association of Buddhism with all commercial activity and funds. Entrance fees for foreigners and shops within the temples exist in the capitalist economy. Because foreigners, for the most part, do not participate in the economy of merit, but do contribute to the wear and tear of the temple through their presence, Buddhist monks have reasoned, they must give back to the temple in a more direct and enforced way than the culturally specific, donation-based economy of merit. The urban environment of city temples allows them to draw from the resources of a broad facet of Thai society, especially with coffee drinks and other commodities for sale at the temple. Although cultural exchange programs sometimes partner with foreign individuals or companies in order to manage the flow of volunteers and foreign guests to the temple, the temple leadership has not handed over responsibility to a third party. Monastic leaders align with people they trust, create the conditions necessary for volunteers to enter into their classrooms and temple spaces, and have control over whether the temple continues to affiliate with these foreign individuals or companies. The main value of tourist encounters, for Thai temples, is the ability to educate the population of novice monks and take part in some of the resources tourism brings to pay monthly expenses and maintain temple structures. This is accomplished through neither completely resisting tourist demands nor accommodating them fully. The agency of monastics is thus located within the temple space.

Many monks stated that in order to maintain the temple some commerce is regrettably necessary. So, the sacred and the profane can mix in the temple space, but as many senior monks stated, not too much—not too many shops or high entrance fees. Other student monks posited a stricter dichotomy between the sacred and the profane, finding that no money outside of donation within the temple space should be allowed. These monks viewed the temple as exclusively a sacred place that is degraded by the presence of commodities and tickets. When a monk perceives the temple as deprived, he has a more flexible relationship to the capitalist economy and is more inclined toward taking part in the resources of tourism and the urban environment.

Tourists had mixed ideas about the nature of the temple space and questioned whether sacred and profane could exist together. Some found charging a small fee worthwhile for the experience of viewing the beauty and culture of the temple. Others found the profane mixed inappropriately with the sacred temple space, especially because of the entrance fees. But all of these perspectives, in their consideration of what is appropriate for the nature of this space, posited some binary between the sacred and the profane. These categories are thus significant in considering the nature of contemporary Buddhist space. However, for the most part, the Buddhist monastic thinking about the sacred does not reflect complete separation. From the varying opinions about what belongs in the temple space and what does not, it is clear that the relationship between the sacred and the profane is not straightforward, but ambiguous and dependent on different contexts.

The perspectives of both senior and student city monks express the diversity of Buddhist monastic relationships with money. Comparing the lifestyles and activities of city monks with those of forest monks and Krubas allows for a further understanding of the balance city monks must enact. Forest monks distance themselves from money as much as possible, maintaining what they would call the "monastic ideal." They live an ascetic, renunciant life that is more remote from Buddhist laity than that of other types of monks. The Kruba saints of northern Thailand, although also ascetic and renunciant, maintain close ties with a range of lay Buddhist communities. Their relationship with money is directed toward improving the material conditions of their followers. City monks are less involved in asceticism or building projects than they are with education. Because of this focus, city monks' relationship with money is based on compromise, which they deem necessary to maintain their temple spaces and educational institutions. The friction of global tourism and increasing urban environments has necessarily had an effect on Buddhist temple economic practices. Another outcome of Buddhist encounters in Chiang Mai is the formation of particular attitudes toward religious others.

CHAPTER 3

RELIGIOUS OTHERS IN THE BUDDHIST EYE

EVERY WEEKDAY AT 5:00 P.M. ABOUT TEN MONKS ARRIVE AT WAT Suan Dok eager to discuss Buddhism with the thirty to forty curious tourists who filter through the space for the next two hours as part of the Monk Chat program. In 2016, at Wat Doi Suthep, the most famous temple in Chiang Mai, a Chinese tourist was suspected of kicking a temple bell, a sacred object, which should not be touched with one's feet.[1] In 2015, a monk from Wat Benjamobophit, a royal temple in Bangkok, called on his Facebook page for the Thai government to burn a mosque for every Buddhist monk killed in southern Thailand.[2] These are all aspects of social friction involving Buddhist attitudes toward religious and cultural others. Such attitudes are shaped within wider state, regional, and transnational influences and by multiple, historically situated factors.

In recent decades, Buddhist studies scholars' increased attention to lived practice has opened up a variety of topic avenues, such as how contemporary Buddhists view religious others. For example, scholarship has investigated the effects of Thai Buddhist nationalism toward groups of Muslims. However, broader attitudes and responses to religious and cultural others have not been explored, particularly toward tourists. Limitations persist in conceptualizing tourism as superficial or irrelevant to the study of religion; yet, tourism continues to be significant for understanding attitudes toward religious and cultural others. Buddhist monks within Chiang Mai temples that host Monk Chat programs are making strategic decisions to enhance the ways that tourists understand Buddhism. Furthermore, they are taking advantage of the curiosity of tourists and the popular and positive image of Buddhism internationally.

Monk Chat monks typically encounter four groups of non-Buddhist visitors—Westerners, Chinese, Muslims, and Christian missionaries—and have distinct attitudes toward each of these religious others. Of the four groups, I use labels of nationality for Western and Chinese groups and religion for Muslims and Christian missionaries because these are the ways the monks I interviewed differentiated these groups. Westerners in particular are thought to embody the modern, as they bring with them advanced technologies and represent an opportunity to practice the global language of English. Asian, especially Chinese, and Muslim tourists do not offer these benefits and therefore are not viewed as positively as Western tourists. Christian missionaries are distinguished from Western tourists because their interest is in debate and conversion. Because of these dynamics, in order to characterize relations with these groups, Westerners might be considered "the beneficial other," Chinese "the familiar other," Muslims "the distant other," and Christian missionaries "the competitive other." Although monks in Chiang Mai encounter Westerners more frequently than other groups, including other groups allows for an understanding of the complexity and comparisons involved in determining attitudes toward religious others.

Why are certain attitudes toward religious and cultural others chosen out of a range of responses? Which factors determine attitudes toward particular others? It is impossible to locate one unified mode of Buddhist relations toward the religious and cultural other, as the tradition is situated within particular times and places and within specific historical and economic circumstances. A useful way to answer these questions in a nuanced way is to investigate the "rearticulation of religion in specific contemporary settings," through religious expressions and practices (Meyer 2009, 1). This rearticulation includes the shape of the religious message, its relation to the state and market, structures of authority, and modes of belonging (10). When religions assert themselves within the presence of other religious or nonreligious persons, specific presentations and repertoires are used.

Buddhist monks who interact with tourists as part of the Monk Chat program assert their religion to others and perceive these others in particular ways, relative to their position in the monastic system. The monastic participants in this program are all affiliated with one of two Buddhist universities in Chiang Mai. Because Monk Chat monks are college students, their ideas and responses to the religious other are part of "ascendant doctrinalism" as opposed to "resurgent magic" (Jackson 2014). The doctrinalist position is text-based and orthodox, upholding a disenchantment of rational modernity. The "resurgent magic" position is more interested in eclectic practices, such as magically empowered amulets, Chinese and Hindu ritual and symbols, cults of national figures, and spirit mediums (4).[3] Because of these student monks' location within the Buddhist education system, they fall much more closely into the doctrinalist position, rather than one inclined toward magic. Subsequently, they have a particular view of the "good" Buddhist that contributes to their attitudes toward religious others. Crucial factors shaping these attitudes concern not only individual Buddhists and their sociocultural affiliation but also the particular religious other—their power dynamic in relation to the Buddhist majority nation-state of Thailand, as well as their demonstrated curiosity and interest in the beliefs and practices of Buddhism.

Theravada Buddhist Attitudes toward the Religious Other

The Buddhist attitude to other religions has been characterized as "critical tolerance" based on an overview of selected texts from the Pali Canon (Jayatilleke 1975, 2), as well as by more qualified characteristics that are situated within varying times and places. Religious studies scholar Elizabeth J. Harris (2013, 89) articulates five attitudes of the Buddha toward religious others: "adherence to a code of conduct predicated on respectful, non-violent yet rigorous debate; robust teaching of ideas that opposed or challenged those taught by other groups; ridicule of the practices/beliefs of the 'other'; the demotion or subordination of these practices/beliefs; the appropriation and modification of practices/symbols from the religious 'other.'"

Harris (2013) argues that all five were present throughout early Buddhist history; however, which became dominant in a specific time and place and which were sublimated "was conditioned by socio-economic factors and power relations" (93). Regarding historical Buddhist attitudes beyond the Buddha's lifetime, Harris produces a sixth attitude, that of "peaceful coexistence between religions through mutual respect in the interests of societal harmony" (94), and under colonial rule the attitude of "skilled pragmatic decision-making about survival under imperialism" can also be seen (102). Reactions to Christian missionaries evident in Sri Lankan Buddhist works from the seventeenth to the twenty-first century have been characterized as displaying parody and contempt (Berkwitz 2013). Some of this writing creates a hybrid between Christian and Buddhist cultural forms; other writing pokes fun at Christianity and its missionaries, painting them and their practices in a negative light; and some labels Christian missionaries as disingenuous and concerned only with conversion rather than actually providing aid. These writings illustrate the range of possible Buddhist responses to Christian conversion efforts (Berkwitz 2013, 101).

Historian of religion David W. Chappell (1990, 443–44) identifies six positions of Buddhists expressed in a diversity of Buddhist writing, from the Pali Canon to that of contemporary Buddhist teachers, regarding religious differences:

1. separate and superior to other religions
2. compassionately engaged with other religions
3. other religions are early stages of development
4. Buddhism and other religions are complementary
5. all religions are historically relative and limited
6. Buddhism and other religions share the same essence

This suggests the breadth of possibilities for Buddhists in Thailand to draw from in understanding and expressing their religion in comparison with others.

In studying Theravada Buddhist encounters with religious others, many studies focus on philosophical and historical or theological approaches.[4] Among the few anthropological approaches are studies of Theravada Buddhists' relations with Muslims in southern Thailand (Jerryson 2011); Buddhist-Muslim relations in the Songkhla region, bordering the deep south of Thailand (Horstmann 2004, 2011); contemporary Thai Buddhist-Christian relations (Fleming 2014); and relations between central Thai Buddhism and its peripheries, including upland peoples (Keyes 1993b; Ashley 2013). These accounts, for the most part, depict these Buddhist-other relations as marked by processes of exclusion through discourses of a particular kind of Thai national identity that distinguishes starkly between upland and valley, Buddhist and Muslim, Buddhist and Christian. There have been even fewer ethnographic accounts regarding Buddhist relations with English-speaking temporary visitors to mainland Southeast Asian countries. One examination of novice monks' encounters with tourists in Luang Prabang, Laos, is concerned more with how Lao Buddhists are responding to changes in their social environment than with Buddhist attitudes toward international visitors (Holt 2009, chap. 4).[5] These anthropological perspectives have started to open up new possibilities to characterize Theravada Buddhism in relation to religious and cultural others. Yet, in contemporary Thailand there is much more to analyze within these encounters. Monk Chat monks draw on this broad context of comparison with religious others within Thailand, their experiences discussing religion with tourists, advice and ideas from their university teachers, and their own research into how best to explain Buddhism to religious others.

Religious Attitudes toward Tourists in Chiang Mai

Phra Saneh Dhammavaro, one of the founders of Monk Chat, along with foreign teachers at Mahachulalongkorn University (MCU), began this program in 2000 based on a perceived need. According to Phra Kyo, adviser to Monk Chat, the founders observed that many foreigners curious about Buddhism were coming to Chiang Mai, while at around the same time MCU had begun to receive international monks studying in English.[6] The factors of tourism within the city of Chiang Mai, international interest in Buddhism, and Buddhist universities that offer monks the possibility of obtaining their bachelor's degrees in English all facilitate the perfect conditions for this program.[7]

International and Thai monks come to Chiang Mai to study because they see educational opportunities and support for Buddhism that they cannot access in their hometowns and countries. International monks make up the majority of monastic participants in the Monk Chat program at MCU, as they are the group that most often studies English. Some of these student monks from MCU manage the Monk Chat program at Wat Srisuphan. Also known as "the Silver Temple," Wat Srisuphan is a highlight of the tourist-populated Saturday Walking Street on Wualai Road. Because the temple is very close to this road and it contains unique architecture, including a silver ordination hall, this tourist attraction is a place where monks can engage with foreigners about Buddhism. Although there is no university associated with this temple, the tourism intersection there generated another branch of the program. While international monks from MCU are the majority of Monk Chat participants at Wat Suan Dok and Wat Srisuphan, at Wat Chedi Luang's Mahamakut Buddhist University (MBU), there is no English track. Because of that, the student monks from MBU who participate in Monk Chat at this temple are from Thailand, many of them studying in the teaching English major.

Monk Chat is a program unique to Chiang Mai, and some monks come to study in this city specifically because of it. One of the reasons Phra Vin, a Thai monk from Chiang Rai, chose to study at the Wat Suan Dok campus of MCU was the Monk Chat program and the opportunity to learn about the lives and religions of foreign tourists. Indeed, other international monks I have spoken with who originally began their study in MCU's Ayutthaya Wangnoi campus transferred to Chiang Mai in order to participate in this program. Although they are not all Thai, international monks are operating within the Thai Buddhist sangha and have spent many years living in a Thai Buddhist setting. That does not make them Thai Buddhist monks, but certainly the environment has affected their responses and attitudes toward the religious and cultural others they interact with in their daily lives in Chiang Mai.

Monks who live or study at temples popular with tourists feel they have a responsibility to meet the needs of those interested in learning about their tradition. A significant way they do that is through answering tourists' questions in the Monk Chat program. The monks represented in this study have participated regularly in the Monk Chat program for two or more years. The encounters of these monks with Western, Chinese, Muslim, and Christian missionary visitors take place in relation to the economic, social, and political power structures that are part of Thai society.

Even though most monks see Westerners as Christian and Chinese as Mahayana Buddhist, they primarily understand them as Westerners (*farang*) and Chinese people (*khon chin*). The monks I interviewed identify Muslims (*khon musalim*) not by nationality or ethnicity but primarily by their religion. Although the Christian missionaries appear similar to Western tourists, the Monk Chat monks place them in a separate category. Important factors in the range of attitudes toward tourists include their openness to learning about Buddhism, the particular aspects of Buddhism they are interested in, and the broader global and societal perception of each group.

ATTITUDES TOWARD WESTERN TOURISTS
(THE BENEFICIAL OTHER)

Monks in the Monk Chat program, over time, become comfortable conversing in English and speaking with international visitors. Because the majority of these international visitors are English-speaking Westerners from North America, Europe, and Australia, they are part of "the allure of the West as a charismatic and appealing cultural site" (Harrison 2010, 3).[8] This group can be regarded as the "beneficial other" because their presence is seen to bring not only possibilities of English conversational practice but also prestige to a temple community that foreigners would choose to visit.

Whiteness is favored in Thailand as a consequence of imperialism and racial ideologies that derive from both national and international sources.[9] The explicit connection to the European colonizer has a significant impact on how intercultural exchanges in the postcolonial period are contextualized (Chakrabarty 2010, viii, xii). However, at the same time, Thais of all ideological statuses and backgrounds have criticized blind imitation of the West. In this way, the West is viewed as a "superior but suspicious Other" (Pattana 2010a, 58), with the *farang* perceived as lighting the path toward modernity and civilization as well as being cultural signifiers of cosmopolitanism (61). These ideas inform the context of the encounter between monks taking part in Monk Chat and the Western tourists.

The Monk Chat monks I interviewed all agreed that Westerners make up the majority of international tourists who take part in their program. Their impression is that most of the Western tourists they meet are Christian, and that they benefit from being able to compare their tradition with Buddhism. Monk Chat monks see their main task as explaining Buddhism to curious tourists. The monks characterize most Western participants as friendly, but some are more interested than others in learning about Buddhism. When a foreigner or group of tourists sits down, the monk introduces himself and asks them where they are from. The tourists then usually ask questions about the monk's background and how he chose to become a monk. Monks typically divided the Western tourists into two groups: those who do not know anything about Buddhism and those who have some knowledge. The first group of Western tourists is mostly curious about what they see around them in the temple, including the Buddha statues and other structures within the space, and ask about their meaning and significance. They are also curious about monastic life and its symbols, including the monks' robes and shaved heads, and compare this way of life to their own in North America, Europe, or Australia. Phra Udom, from Laos, commented, "Mostly the people who come are interested, but some don't care and look here and there." The second group of Western tourists, who know something about Buddhism, usually ask the monks to explain more about Buddhist doctrines, specifically asking about rebirth and karma, and the relationship of Buddhism to science. Phra Trilok, from India, has participated in Monk Chat at Wat Chedi Luang for two years and would rather have a conversation about these doctrines, as he finds they are "rational" concepts.[10] This was a word I encountered often in interviews, always used in a positive connotation and in reference to the Western tourists, demonstrating

3.1. Monk Chat at Wat Suan Dok with a monk and students from the United States conversing about Buddhism. Photograph by the author.

this group of monks' preference for discussions of Buddhist doctrine and meditation over what they consider to be "irrational" ideas of magic.

Indeed, most of the monks are primarily interested in discussing the Buddha's teachings in English with knowledgeable Western tourists for several reasons. First, these Buddhist teachings are something that the tourists can continue to think and learn about. Second, these monks are studying Buddhist concepts in their college classrooms and are happy to practice their grasp of these ideas in English. Third, they are proud of the Buddhist doctrines, characterizing them as unique and deep (figure 3.1).

A number of the monks, including Phra Thach, a Khmer Krom monk from southern Vietnam who has joined Monk Chat at Wat Srisuphan for three years, were excited to talk about their strategies for memorizing English words for Buddhist concepts and their increasingly skillful abilities to explain the Buddhist teachings. Phra Thach showed me his cheat sheet of Buddhist terms and lists in English, containing the Three Defilements (greed, anger, delusion) and the Three Marks of Existence (suffering, nonself, impermanence), which he practiced writing many times while waiting for the next foreign participant to arrive.[11] He explained, "When I wait for the next tourist, I practice and remember what I want to share with them." Phra Maha Mitra, from Nepal, recounted how, during his first year with the program, he would begin conversations with the most complex Buddhist ideas, such as non-self, in order to impress the Westerners, assuming they would automatically become Buddhist once they heard these teachings. But he soon found they were not ready. With a laugh, he continued:

> As I was trying to explain these Buddhist ideas, the foreigners just looked at me like they were so confused. I think many Monk Chat monks start like this, with the highest teaching. But they [the foreigners] cannot understand *nibbana* [enlightenment]. . . . Some ideas are better not spoken about . . . stick with the basics that relate to their lives and the level the foreigner is at. Then they can gradually increase [their] understanding. We have to teach basic[s] first. Otherwise, it's useless. We have to start with an easy topic, step-by-step, and put [the teachings] in the right order.

Instead, Phra Maha Mitra now begins to talk about Buddhist teachings with more basic ideas of morality for laypeople, such as the Five Precepts.[12] Although these monks most enjoy discussing these deep topics, they believe that making the teachings understandable is the main priority. In this way Westerners are "beneficial others" because they are interested in learning about the Buddhist religion, and the monks enjoy discussing Buddhist doctrines with this curious population. However, that was not always the case when the monks spoke of the relatively few Chinese and Muslim tourists who visit these temples popular with tourists.

ENCOUNTERS WITH CHINESE TOURISTS (THE FAMILIAR OTHER)

In contrast to their positive attitudes toward curious Westerners, monks who interact with tourists in Monk Chat have less enthusiasm for Asian tourists, especially Chinese, the "familiar other." This group has some knowledge of Thailand and Buddhism; however, it is this familiarity that puts them at a disadvantage vis-à-vis the curiosity the Western tourists display. While ethnic Chinese tourists from Malaysia, Singapore, Taiwan, and Hong Kong have seen Thailand as a tourist destination for many decades, only recently have tourists from mainland China visited Thailand in large numbers.[13] Following the huge success in China of the 2012 blockbuster comedy *Lost in Thailand*, coupled with eased visa restrictions between Thailand and China, Chiang Mai has seen a rapid increase in Chinese tourism.[14] Temple visits, however, can be a point of tension, as when the alleged Chinese man was recorded kicking a temple bell at Wat Doi Suthep to much consternation of Thai authorities,[15] and Chinese were nearly banned from the architecturally stunning Wat Rong Khun in Chiang Rai after the artist and owner, Chalermchai Kositpipat, complained about the state of the bathrooms after a visit by a Chinese group.[16] An article on the news website *Asian Correspondent* argues that these Thai reactions amount to racism, as Westerners also commit cultural crimes daily that do not become viral videos discussed through social media.[17] Whether these reactions can be considered racist or not, the perceptions of Chinese and Western tourists are starkly different.[18]

Monks participating in Monk Chat, for the most part, do not see Asian tourists, especially Chinese, as being curious or interested in learning about Buddhism. Monks noted traits similar to those that Chinese have been criticized for as tourists in Thailand generally, such as staying with their big tour group, not engaging with the culture, and being most interested in shopping and taking photos.[19] Most Chinese, remarked Phra Jaya, a Khmer Krom monk who has joined Monk Chat at Wat Srisuphan for four years, "visit the temple not to pay respect to the Buddha, but to take a picture with the Ganesh statue or [the] silver ordination hall in the temple." The Chinese come to sit and chat on rare occasions, but they mostly walk by in a big group, leaving them fewer opportunities to discuss and engage.

The monks at Monk Chat recalled a few times when Chinese men came to consult one of them about a problem in their lives. They also ask questions about the difference between Theravada Buddhism in Thailand and Mahayana Buddhism in China. Part of the monks' responses to these questions includes a perceived superiority of Theravada over Mahayana. Phra Aakash, from Nepal, who has lived in Thailand for four years and regularly participates in Monk Chat at Wat Suan Dok, explained that "the Theravada tradition is from the time of the Buddha, but the Mahayana Buddhists have added their own new rules and scriptures," and he believes this has resulted in decreased purity. However, by and large, Monk Chat monks see other Asians as those who already practice one form of Buddhism and consequently are not interested in learning more. Phra Thet, from Myanmar, came to the conclusion that "when Chinese people come to Thailand they are not interested in Buddhism because they see monks every day and are used to it." Phra Kai, from Laos, compared the Western and Chinese tourists, saying, "Buddhism in China is something they know about already. For Westerners it's really a different culture, and they always have a purpose when they travel. It's a part of European and American culture to be curious. It's part of their education and habit." Phra Sonalin, also from Laos, took issue with this, stating, "There is a lot to compare between Chinese and Thai Buddhism, so maybe they should come if they are interested in religion. Maybe they are not interested. Look at their activities. They are more interested in photographs and vacation." Besides the difference in activities and some familiarity with Buddhism among Chinese tourists, other Monk Chat monks pointed to the fact that most do not speak English very well and they are not interested in dialogue or practice. Phra Daeng observed that when the Chinese tourists see that the Monk Chat sign is not in Chinese, they walk away.

Monk Chat monks find that, when Chinese do venture beyond their tour group, they seem to be most interested in devotional activities. Unlike Western tourists, for whom devotion is typically not important, the Chinese tourists participate in chanting, circumambulating the pagoda, and bowing. Phra Dipankara, a Bangladeshi monk who has been involved in Monk Chat at Wat Suan Dok for four years, finds that "Chinese sometimes give donations and bow in their way to pay respect." In contrast, he said, very few Westerners practice any kind of worship with the Thais, but often ask about meditation centers. Because Western tourists want to know about meditation and are curious about Buddhist teachings, from the Monk Chat monks' points of view, even though they do not involve themselves in merit making or Buddha worship, Western tourists still display more interest in Buddhism. These student monks' hierarchy of Buddhist practices places meditation at the top, as part of their orientation toward "ascendant doctrinalism" over "resurgent magic" (Jackson 2014).

Parts of the Thai Buddhist religious complex, which involves receiving blessings and obtaining powerful objects, such as amulets, are not foreign to Chinese. For Chinese Singaporeans, Thai magical paraphernalia are often used as methods for business success (Johnson 2016, 446). Specifically, Thai objects are seen as powerful by Chinese Singaporeans because they are considered older than Chinese objects, and their foreignness allows businesspeople to discover and conquer an unknown realm (Johnson 2016, 449). This magical orientation toward Thai religion is part of Malaysian and Chinese Singaporean tourism in southern Thailand. These religious tourists are very interested in large Buddha images, which they visit to ask for worldly favors or to thank for good luck received (Askew 2008, 89). Unlike the more doctrinally oriented student monks, monks located in southern Thai temples and especially monks who are known for their powers or protective tattoos are following resurgent magical practices, along with the Chinese tourists.[20]

While Thai tourism officials do not mind the Chinese orientation that seeks holy objects for protection and blessings at religious sites (Askew 2008,

97), monks studying for a bachelor's degree in a Buddhist university express a preference for "rational" interpretations of the teachings. Phra Trilok stated that the Chinese tourists, if they do interact, ask for an amulet or blessing, which he explained is a preoccupation of the Chinese he does not agree with. Phra Day and Phra Jor, Thai monks at Wat Chedi Luang's Monk Chat, believe that an interest in amulets "can help to remind [*chuai tuean chai*] people of a monk or the Buddha." In addition, they believe that amulets "do not help [if owners] do not maintain their morality [*mai chuai raksa sinlatham*]." These ideas support an understanding of Buddhist teachings learned in their college classes that places the importance of doctrine above the so-called magical practices. The monks have a particular idea of the good Buddhist, a rational person interested in meditation and Buddhist doctrine, one who is open to new ideas and curious about Buddhist teachings. The monks who participate in Monk Chat did not characterize this "familiar other" as having any of these qualities. Western tourists, then, seem to fulfill this ideal more than Chinese do.

ENCOUNTERS WITH MUSLIM TOURISTS (THE DISTANT OTHER)

Monk Chat monks are eager to interact with international non-Buddhist tourists who participate in cultural exchange programs. However, a different attitude can be displayed toward those of other religions living in the same region or nation-state, who some Theravada Buddhist leaders feel pose a threat to their religion. Although Monk Chat monks do not appear to follow these extremes, because they have less interaction with Muslims and view Islam as more divergent from Theravada Buddhism than Christianity or Mahayana Buddhism, Muslim tourists can be thought of as "distant others."

The Theravada Buddhist doctrine of impermanence and continued decline of the Buddha's teachings create a discourse of the religion as in constant need of protection against signs of decay.[21] Historically, these ideas have become central during threats of colonial subjugation.[22] In the case of Muslims in southern Thailand, this rhetoric of protecting Buddhism from decline is again invoked. In an article for the Buddhist magazine *Lion's Roar*, religious studies scholar Michael K. Jerryson quotes a southern Thai monk he interviewed on the presence of military monks on duty in temples located in conflict zones: "Military monks in the three southern provinces of Thailand [Yala, Pattani, and Narathiwat] are like guardians that protect Buddhism from deterioration."[23] This need to protect the Buddha's teachings from decline is still felt, as both internal and external threats are real and possible for some Thai Buddhists. Because of that, Thai Buddhist monks and laity have formed groups to spread their message of Buddhist nationalism.

Buddhist nationalist groups such as the Buddhism Protection Center of Thailand have existed since 2001. This group of about three thousand Buddhists, comprising laity and monks, devote their time to "defending Buddhism," mostly through political means and dispensing information to people about threats to Buddhism (Katewadee 2013, 122). They are most interested in lobbying for increased representation of Buddhism in the government and naming Buddhism as the national religion in the constitution (126). This group understands Buddhism to be in a state of decline, descending in influence, and in need of restoration, especially in response to the growing presence of foreign religions in Thai society (145).[24] In particular, the Buddhism Protection Center of Thailand is concerned with what it perceives to be increased Muslim influence combined with the relative weakness of Buddhism in Thai society (Katewadee 2013, 172). The center portrays Islam as a violent religion with a long history of aggression toward Buddhism. The perceived domestic decline in reverence to Buddhist institutions is imagined as a major part of the problem (Fleming 2014, 74).

In Thailand, where the dominant ethnic group's religion has been closely connected to the state, the presence of minority religious populations has led to reactions affirming Buddhism as a religion. This setting has stimulated the response of defensive opposition (Harris 2013, 97). The reification of Thai Buddhist identity with the Thai nation-state has caused alienation among Malay Muslims (Jerryson 2011). Martial law in the three southernmost provinces since 2004 and several violent attacks that have ended in the deaths of both Buddhists and Muslims illustrate the extremes of this intolerance of the religious other. In order to maintain a strong Buddhist national and religious identity, there must be a clear distinction between those inside the dominant group and those outside of the imagined community (Jerryson 2013, 42). Although Thai Buddhists are victims of violence, they are also privileged members of the power structure within the Thai nation (McCargo 2009, 3). Interactions with religious others living in the same nation-state (in contrast to those with tourists) carry sources of tension, including rights to claim religious and national identities and political and economic competition for resources.

Muslim populations in Thailand do not have the cachet of a powerful religious or cultural other. Instead, they are distinguished and displaced from the majority population through their non-Buddhist identities. For the most part, Monks who participate in Monk Chat do not discuss Muslim tourists as a threat to Buddhism, but do acknowledge their differences from other kinds of tourists. Monks relate that they rarely encountered any Muslims at their temples, which contributes to their feeling of distance and otherness. The few Muslims who stated their identity did not make a good impression on Phra Sonalin and Phra Kai, fourth-year Lao students at MCU, who recounted, "One time there was a Muslim imam, and we had to take turns to talk to him because he wanted to make problems and ask us questions to show Buddhism was not right." But that, I was told, is rare, and more often Muslims do not identify themselves as such. There is no way to know the actual number of Muslims who attend Monk Chat, as the programs in all three temples record the participants' names and countries, but not religious affiliation. Therefore, as Phra Chandra, from Nepal, told me at the Wat Suan Dok Monk Chat, if the foreign participant does not reveal his or her religion, only by identifying factors such as a man who has a name like Muhammad or a headscarf on a woman would monks know they were talking to a Muslim. Anthropologist Amporn Marddent (2007, 52) found a similar situation while conducting research in southern Thailand, stating that her headscarf marked her as "the other" and a suspicious outsider for local Buddhists. In addition, Phra Kyo, a Bangladeshi monk and adviser to Monk Chat at Wat Suan Dok, reports, "There are very few Muslims who come to Monk Chat that we know about. Maybe some Muslims are also afraid and keep secret their religion? The majority who come are American Muslims, British Muslims, Canadian Muslims, like this, and a very little from Indonesia or Malaysia." When I asked about Muslims attending Monk Chat at Wat Chedi Luang, the Thai monks there stated that none attend these programs as other groups of tourists do. The president of Monk Chat at Wat Chedi Luang, Thai monk Phra Ruang, confirmed, "I have never seen Muslims come to Monk Chat."

When I asked why they thought that was the case, many of the monks explained that Muslims already have a religion they are committed to. Phra Daeng, a Thai fourth-year monk at MCU, said, "The Muslims, they believe themsel[ves]. They have their own belief. They think I believe myself and that the other is wrong." For these monks who participate in Monk Chat, Muslims are not interested in learning about Buddhism, unlike Western tourists who are assumed to have a Christian background. These Christians are seen as less committed to their religion or at least interested in applying some aspects of Buddhism to their lives. The baseline of comparison is always the most populous group, the Western tourists. Phra Kai asserted by way of comparison: "For Islam, maybe they have rules like don't learn about another religion. I don't know, but maybe. There is some conflict for them, but for Christians, they are more open and as part of their education learn about religion as another subject."

Phra Jiu, a Thai monk at Wat Chedi Luang who has participated in Monk Chat for three years, demonstrated the most extreme view when he stated that Muslims do not come to the temples because "they are dangerous [antarai]," and "their parents told them not to enter the Buddhist temple [mai hai khao wat]." This suspicion of Muslims extends beyond the conflict zone in southern Thailand. The incident of a Buddhist man shouting at a young Muslim woman on a Bangkok bus was labeled by Amporn Marddent (2007, 58) as "a case of affectation of an ongoing conflict," located in southern Thailand, coupled with news stories concerning global Muslim terrorists. The effect of the violence in the south can be seen in reactions to Muslims in central and northern Thailand. In contrast, Phra Jor, a Thai monk at Wat Chedi Luang who has taken part in Monk Chat for two years, notes that domestic and regional Muslims of high school age occasionally come to learn about Buddhism, but adults do not come. In addition, Indonesian Muslims have been known to attend the Monk Chat at Wat Srisuphan. Phra Thach described an enjoyable conversation comparing Buddhism and Islam, calling Muslims "very gentle people." Phra Chandra told about a recent conversation with two Muslims, a brother and sister from England, whose parents were from Pakistan:

> They asked totally normal questions like other Western people. They asked about our monk life and what we can do. In our understanding, Muslims are fighting and don't like to talk to other religions. But these two were not like that. I could learn about Islam too, what they can eat and drink. They also told me only a few Muslims are like terrorists and think killing is okay if they are saving many people. It was a good exchange. I did not know this about Muslims. I am grateful. Now I can also have a good experience the next time Muslims join.

This exchange was positive and resulted in increased understanding. A similarly positive experience occurred for Phra Akara, a fourth-year Thai monk at MBU: "Muslims [who come to Monk Chat] are also scared of death and love peace. If I didn't meet them, I wouldn't know this just based on the news. Maybe the religion it looks dangerous, but not all of the people are. Sometimes we [the Muslim tourists and I] talk about southern Thailand. And we think the religions are friends, but politics makes everyone scared. When I ask them about Islam, I learn about how they pray and how they pay respect. Before, I think I'm scared to go to the mosque, but now I know Muslims are okay."

Although Muslims themselves can impress and change the views of individual monks, many of these monks are still cautious about the religion of Islam. Naen Maha Tri, a participant in Wat Chedi Luang's Monk Chat, differentiated between Islam and Muslims, finding that individual Muslims can be good people, but he is not as sure about the religion itself. He remarked that Muslims who came to Monk Chat are different and better than Christian missionaries.

> NAEN MAHA TRI: They did not even try to compare religion, just asked about Buddhism, didn't try to tell me about Islam. They came twice from England.
> AUTHOR: How did you know they are Muslim?
> NAEN MAHA TRI: They were wearing [makes a gesture over his face].
> AUTHOR: Did you ask them about the hijab and their religion?
> NAEN MAHA TRI: No, I am afraid to ask about it. Just like Thai people, we do not know about this, so are afraid to talk about it.

In the novice monk's encounter there is respect but not a deep exchange because the discourses of wider Thai society make some Buddhists fearful to speak directly to Muslims to learn more about Islam.

There exists a range of attitudes toward Muslims, from indifference and avoidance, on one end, to interest in learning about and comparing religions, on the other. Because this group does not often enter temples, there are fewer experiences to draw from and fewer opportunities to create any generalizations about this group, based on experiences in Monk Chat conversations. However, the Monk Chat monks' characterizations revealed a feeling of distance partly because Muslims are perceived to be so committed to their religion that they are not interested in discussion about or comparison with Buddhism. As well, local media from southern Thailand affects Monk Chat monks' views and willingness to engage with this particular group of non-Buddhists.

ENCOUNTERS WITH CHRISTIAN MISSIONARIES (THE COMPETITIVE OTHER)

The monks of the Monk Chat programs were most animated when discussing the topic of Christian missionaries. All of these student monks had encountered this group, whom they characterized as very different from the usual Western tourists. As well, they all recounted a similar story about their first encounters with Christian missionaries, represented here as a composite narrative of several monks' descriptions:

> They [the Christian missionaries] come up to us and seem like normal tourists. At first, they ask normal questions about the monks' life. But then they ask more deep questions like "How did the world begin, if in Buddhism there is no God?" At first, I think it is a friendly conversation, so I try to answer a little. But they keep pushing about how there is no God in Buddhism, so how can there be a beginning to the world? They are not satisfied when I say it doesn't matter for Buddhists. I feel like I am being attacked and have to defend Buddhism, but it's not fair. I'm not prepared, but they have prepared their questions and for their debate with me. And I don't know English as well as they do. I would like to do this debate in my language. But I keep trying and practice. So, the next time they come, I know who they are, and I can be prepared.

Along with feeling unprepared and attacked by Christian missionaries, what disturbs these student monks the most is the certainty and rigidity of this population. Phra Maha Mitra, a fourth-year student at MCU from Nepal, remarked, "They say they have the right way and want other people to come to the right way. It became an argument with monks sometimes. Their main thing is believing in God. One missionary was so stubborn, he just kept saying, 'You are wrong, I am right.'" He continued, "When I said that Buddhism has no God, one missionary stood up like he wanted to fight. The other hit the table. They were very angry." Phra Tummarat, a fourth-year student at MBU, concurred and contextualized the Christian missionaries' strategy: "They always ask, 'What is the origin of the world? What does Buddhism tell you about [the] origination of this world?' Then they ask directly, 'Who created the world?' They say God created [it], and they have absolute understanding on this, and Buddhism cannot give a satisfactory understanding." Because of these carefully chosen questions and debates, the student monks are left feeling defensive and not sure how to respond.[25]

After feeling attacked by the missionaries the first time around, some monks prepared their own questions for the next visit. Naen Maha Tri, for example, asked whether, if God created nature, he also created natural disasters, like earthquakes and tsunamis that kill people. He then said to them, "Your God kills people. I cannot accept that if God is killing people."

Phra Canda, a fourth-year MCU student from Thailand, asked the missionaries, "'If there is one person who believes in God but does some bad things and confesses and then another person who doesn't know God but does good all the time, which one will go to heaven?' They couldn't answer."

In addition to anticipating and combating their debate techniques, the Monk Chat monks have also learned how to spot the Christian missionaries. They do not know the differences between the various types of Christian missionaries, they said, having never heard of categories like Mormon or Jehovah's Witness. The student monks discovered that if a big group of young people show up to Monk Chat, wearing modest clothing and sometimes little hats, they could guess the group is composed of Christian missionaries. Most of the time, at the end of a conversation, the Christian missionaries pray aloud. Not knowing what to do and not wanting to participate, the student monks just look away.

Although the majority opinion is quite negative toward Christian missionaries, whose conversations were described as attacks the monks were not ready for, a few monks saw an opportunity for edification and deeper understanding. Phra Ajahn Kaew, a teacher of English from Thailand at MBU but also a participant at Monk Chat, was amazed at the missionaries' faith and their certainty about God. Because of his fascination, he has had conversations with Christian missionaries lasting for over three hours. The idea of God is so strange to him that he finds it difficult to comprehend the world from that point of view. Phra Ajahn Kaew believes it is possible to compare sin and suffering, God and karma, but finds this comparison would only be "like a frame." "The details are very different. It's like a language where the basic frame is the subject and verbs are the same but the grammar is very different." He continues to reflect on this topic, explaining, "Missionaries offer a chance for monks to learn something new. The [student] monks usually run away when they see them, but they can learn from them. In Thailand it's a mono-religion. They [the student monks] are taught that Thai culture, language, and Buddhism are the best. [Because of that] they have a bad interpretation of other religions." Thai society is thus part of this encounter, as the nation's essential connection to Buddhism makes engagement with Muslims and Christian missionaries especially fraught.

Another monk, Phra Kyo, from Bangladesh, an adviser to Monk Chat at MCU, explained that he is open to dialogue, learning, and understanding from the Christian missionaries. He has kept in touch with many of them and occasionally attends one Protestant missionary's church events outside of Chiang Mai City. However, in comparison with Muslim tourists, Phra Kyo thinks there is more of a problem with Christian missionaries: "I want to know about God, but they want to have something like a debate and don't want to listen. Instead, I tell the monks to think about how to explain so there is no debate and then forgive, forget—don't show anger but remember loving-kindness and compassion." In this way, Phra Kyo focuses on his Buddhist practice in talks with the Christian missionaries and urges the other Monk Chat monks to do the same. He said, "I do not want to debate with them. I just tell them about Buddhism, and if they question, I go to another topic. I never say no to them when they mention God. I never say I don't believe. Usually, I can have a good time to talk to them." Phra Kyo finds Christian missionaries offer the opportunity to consider another point of view and to explain about Buddhism to a new group. After his many discussions with the Christian missionaries, he has been given several Bibles, which he keeps on a shelf in his room. He relates, "The Traipidok [Pali Canon] and the Bible are on my table in my room. They are never fighting."

AUTHOR: You don't mind learning about God when you are a Buddhist monk?

PHRA KYO: No, I want to always learn more. I don't know about God. I want to learn things I do not know yet.

Phra Sek, a third-year student at MCU from Cambodia, took the Christian missionary discussions as an opportunity for learning and challenging himself. He explained, "It's hard for me to understand heaven and hell, so I try to ask them about it. They have many interesting questions to ask and I like to think about them. Talking to them gives me homework to research more and read more topics." He continued that because it can get tedious to discuss the monastic life all the time with more typical Western tourists, he appreciates the opportunity to think deeply about Buddhism and ask questions about the Christian God and the nature of prayer with Christian missionaries. But other monks would rather talk to tourists, because it is more relaxing. Phra Myo, a fourth-year student at MCU from Myanmar, commented: "Speaking with general tourists almost makes me feel more comfortable, less pressure[d], and happy because they are not very crazy about God. Tourists come to monks like to find the key to open the door, but missionaries approach monks like to give a lock to close the door. I feel like more pressure I have when I speak with missionaries. Sometimes, it happens in my mind like, 'What is the point? What do you want from me?'"

Phra Neyya, a fourth-year Burmese monk at MCU, compared the Christian missionaries with other tourists. He praised the friendly relations he has with tourists, thinking of them as relatives and friends. He continued, "On the other hand, some [of the Christian missionaries] were very competitive to us Buddhist monks because they had strong faith in Jesus Christ. When I asked questions about the Bible, I was told that Christianity is the best religion." In this way, most monks prefer to talk to the less stressful, less competitive tourists, but a few find Christian missionaries more interesting because of their unusual questions and the opportunity to learn about an alternative point of view.

This ambivalent attitude toward Christian missionaries is not surprising. This group comes laden with the history of colonialism throughout mainland Southeast Asia. Buddhist studies scholar José Cabezón (2012, 205) writes, "When Buddhists, especially in South and Southeast Asia, truly began to learn about Christianity (and about Jesus), this knowledge was in many instances mediated by the fact of colonialism." Jesus was seen by Theravada Buddhists in mainland Southeast Asia as a foreign god, who, although seemingly powerful, was brought from a culture that was subjugating their own. This complex relationship has resulted in Christianity representing both an appealing modernity and a source of opposition, much like Westerners, or *farang*, themselves. Although more recent Buddhist teachers, such as Thich Nhat Hanh from Vietnam and Buddhadasa Bhikkhu from Thailand, have praised and sought dialogue with Christianity, for many the idea of a Christian missionary's work of conversion seems to be in competition with Buddhism. In the nineteenth century, Protestant missionaries in Sri Lanka enlivened within Buddhism a competitive paradigm (Harris 2013), which continues today, wherein one maverick monk situates the figure of Maitreya Bodhisattva similarly to the savior figure of Jesus Christ, who is accessible in the near future (Mahadev 2015). Although Western tourists in general, who appear to be Christian to Monk Chat monks, are praised for their interest in Buddhism, Christian missionaries have been seen in Thailand—and other countries with a majority Theravada population—as competitors.

One dominant representation of converts to Christianity in colonial Sri Lanka was that they were bribed with worldly gains. For Sri Lankan Buddhists, this is not a legitimate religious reason for turning to Christianity over Buddhism (Berkwitz 2013, 102). I heard similar reasoning from MBU monks while eating lunch in the university's cafeteria after teaching the "Buddhist English" class. When I asked about some of the lay students in the class, Phra Ruang responded that some of them are Christian and mostly from the indigenous hill tribes. When I remarked on the strangeness of Christians attending a Buddhist university located in a Buddhist temple, he gave his opinion that these students do not really practice Christianity. Phra Ruang believed they converted because the Christian missionaries gave them money, education, or medicine, and, as he noted, "they know how to chant, make offerings, and bow to the Buddha statue."[26] Phra Ruang brought these Christians into the Thai Buddhist orbit by essentially claiming that they were really Buddhists who had to maintain a Christian veneer for the material benefits they were provided. Competition in Thailand between Thai Buddhists and Christian missionaries has been attributed to vestiges of the past when missionaries openly criticized Buddhism. Buddhist nationalist groups today still feel victimized and threatened by Christianity (Fleming 2014, 34). Although Islam is the main focus of the Buddhism Protection Center of Thailand, the group also views Christianity as an untrustworthy religion, seen as a possible danger to Buddhism and a contributor to its decline in Thailand (79).

Thailand has a particular relationship with Christian missionaries that contributes to this feeling of ambivalence and competition, dating back to the nineteenth century. During the reign of King Mongkut (1851–1868), American missionaries were able to insert themselves into relationships with the Bangkok elite, offering their contributions of medicine, science, and technology (Thanet 2009, 407).[27] The best parts of the missionary encounter, then, were the modern and secular benefits. King Mongkut hired Anna Leonowens as an English tutor for children in the royal court, to teach subjects such as language, science, and literature, but not Christianity (Thanet 2009, 413). This bifurcation of knowledge is similar to the attitudes displayed toward Western tourists and Christian missionaries. The Western tourists are beneficial because they can cordially compare religions, and offer new knowledge. In contrast, Christian missionaries present conflict and the assertion of a foreign religion, something not of interest to either King Mongkut or most of the Monk Chat monks.

Other Thai Buddhist monks have stated more overtly their distrust of Christianity, Catholicism in particular. Phra Sobhon-Ganabhorn (1984, 6) details his many grievances with the ways that Catholics in Thailand treat Buddhism, writing that he wants Catholics "to stop insulting the Triple Gem (including the Buddha, his Dhamma and his Order of noble disciples) by distorting facts without evidences in history, in the Buddhist scripture and the Christian Bible itself." He continues that although Christian missionaries have been aggressive, brutal, and focused singularly on conversion "without letting any obstacle stand in the way," Buddhists have been tolerant and broad-minded (19). Buddhists are thus positioned as victims in their relationships with other religions.

Buddhism scholar and author from Thailand Sunthorn Plamintr, in his overview of Buddhism and Thai society, follows a similar argument. He writes, "Buddhists are generally tolerant and accommodating, which is why religious persecution at Buddhist hands is unheard of in the long history of the religion. This has emboldened people of other religions to take advantage of Buddhist hospitality and tolerance by engaging in activities that are detrimental to Buddhism."[28] Although some Thai Buddhists find Christians to be hostile aggressors preying on the tolerant Buddhists, others have engaged in textual study with the aim of finding similarities between the two religions.

The internationally known monk Buddhadasa Bhikkhu (1906–1993) undertook the most serious theological comparison of Buddhism and Christianity in Thailand. He gave the Sinclair Thompson Memorial Lecture on Christianity and Buddhism in 1967 in Chiang Mai. This series of three lectures focused on different aspects of comparison between the two religions, documented in the book *Christianity and Buddhism* (Buddhadasa Bhikkhu 2006). In the first lecture, he discusses Christianity from the standpoint of Buddhists. For the most part, in this lecture, Buddhadasa Bhikkhu reinterprets Christianity to fit into Buddhist frames of reference, such as karma and Buddhist enlightenment (*nibbana*). He places Jesus and Buddha on the same level as enlightened beings leading others on the path to absolute and universal truth (27). Buddhadasa Bhikkhu does this by separating conventional language from Dhamma language, or ordinary speech from the viewpoint of absolute truth. Conventionally, it seems that Christianity is based on the other-power of God and Buddhism is based on the actions of the self, under the law of karma. However, in Dhamma language, as Buddhadasa Bhikkhu interprets it, this other-power of God actually falls under the framework of karma. He writes, "As the Law of Karma is absolute and unbiased we can name it God as well. To see this with reference to Christianity we may say that God, through whom we harvest the fruits of our actions, undoubtedly is no other than the 'All Mighty—Law of Karma' of Buddhism" (33). He continues, "We feel that Christianity is a religion of Karma (action), Wisdom, love (Mettā), and self-help" (38).

Professor of Thai Buddhism Saeng Chandra-ngarm finds many similarities between Buddhism, Christianity, and Islam, in a small booklet called *A*

Buddhist Looks at Christianity. From his perspective, Christianity, Islam, and Buddhism originated from suffering, and each man—Jesus, Muhammad, Buddha—sought a path to alleviate the suffering of humanity (Saeng, n.d., 2–3). He argues that the central core of Christianity is purity of heart, which he locates in Buddhism as freedom from mental defilements of greed, hatred, and delusion (7). Yet, viewing Christianity through this Buddhist lens does have barriers. Saeng admits that as a Buddhist he must understand Jesus as a human being, not the son of God (11).

Although the monks at Monk Chat do not always place other religions within a Buddhist framework, they do hope to show Buddhism's compatibility and complementarity with Western theistic traditions. In the Monk Chat booklet *Thai Buddhism*, author Phra Saneh Dhammavaro (2009, 1) offers this comparison implicitly in his definition of Buddhism: "Buddhism is a religion of man by man for mankind. It is introduced from a direct individual experience. It is not a revealed religion as the founder did not get any divine message." The booklet continues to stress that Buddhism follows rational reasoning and focuses on self-development (2). Dhammavaro highlights Buddhism's difference from Abrahamic religions, but at the same time creates space for those identifying with a theistic religion to take part in Buddhist practices. This compatibility is important to Monk Chat monks in their discussions with Western tourists. They highlight Buddhism as a practice to complement other religious beliefs. However, discussions with Christian missionaries are usually not so flexible. Instead of compatibility, competition is the dominant attitude that Monk Chat monks connect with Christian missionaries. But, drilling deeper, the attitudes range from understanding them as aggressors to locating complementarities and appreciating an alternative religious view.

One result of the friction of Buddhist encounters is the formation of responses and attitudes toward groups of people within Chiang Mai's global orbit. Thus, Westerners function as the "beneficial other," Chinese as the "familiar other," Muslims as the "distant other," and Christian missionaries as the "competitive other," within a context of broader Thai societal dialogues concerning these groups. These attitudes reveal mostly positive responses to Western tourists, from the perspective of student monks who value Buddhist doctrine over magical elements, and who are most impressed by those who demonstrate curiosity, rationality, intelligence, and an interest in meditation. Reflecting Orientalist dichotomies of East and West, Siamese rulers have maintained that *farang* (Westerners) are superior in secular and worldly matters but Siamese (Thai people) are superior in religious and moral matters (Pattana 2010a, 70). Westerners are seen to be intelligent and interested in Buddhism, but they need the East for wisdom and spirituality. In contemporary Thailand, however, instead of wisdom and spirituality located in "Eastern" religious texts, the agency is located with Asian teachers as representatives of Buddhism.

In contrast, Chinese are characterized as lacking curiosity about Thai Buddhism and disinclined toward meditation. Instead, the Chinese are seen as focused on superficial tourism, along with magical and devotional practices. Muslims are not seen to be interested or curious about Buddhism at all, contributing to the feeling of distance. Although these monks do not take on the Thai Buddhist nationalist perspective, Islam is seen as too different to compare or be in dialogue with about Buddhist practices. Christian missionaries are viewed separately from Western tourists. They do not ask "normal" questions about the monastic life and meditation, but instead attempt to debate the logic of Buddhism. Student monks feel defensive about Buddhism and worry that Buddhist teachings are in competition with Christianity. Monks who frequently interact with tourists display attitudes toward religious and cultural others that are informed by their own observations of interactions with these groups as well as by experiences in Thailand and broader global discourses about each population.

In order to understand what determines these various responses, it is important to analyze the conjunctures in which they are employed as well as the factors that are most significant in producing particular responses. Scholars' observations of Theravada Buddhism have not sufficiently interpreted contemporary Theravada Buddhist attitudes and responses to the religious and cultural other. Buddhist cultural exchange programs, such as Monk Chat, offer a lens through which to view Buddhism in the global sphere. When a Buddhist monk meets a tourist in Monk Chat, he is considering the particular person as well as how he or she fits into the monk's own past conversations with similar types of tourists and the national and global perceptions surrounding the individual on the other side of the table. A history of colonialism, missionizing, and modernization lies in the background of each encounter with Western tourists and Christian missionaries. The decades-long Buddhist-Muslim struggles with violence in southern Thailand shape opinions and meetings with Muslims. With the recent influx of Chinese tourists, their documented habits of staying in a large group and interest in taking photos rather than engaging with Thai Buddhism have colored the ways student monks approach this group.

The extremes of Buddhists either being in dialogue with religious others or inciting violence against them are not the only options for Buddhists. Global developments, such as Buddhist nationalism, are significant for Buddhists worldwide, and certainly influence how student monks perceive religious others. The effects of these global discourses and opinions of religious and cultural groups can be seen in student monks' responses to their encounters with the various groups of tourists who attend the Monk Chat program. There is friction within these global connections, but there are also opportunities. Buddhist encounters in Chiang Mai produce a chance for Buddhist monks to spread Buddhism among a curious population of tourists.

CHAPTER 4

BUDDHIST SPACES OF MISSIONIZATION

I ENTERED THE MONK CHAT SEMINAR ROOM EXPECTING TO SEE students, travelers, and monks, all arranged in separate small groups, but instead I found Phra Kyo, the adviser to Monk Chat at Wat Suan Dok, as the lone monk in a circle of about fifteen students and travelers. Not many monks showed up that day, even though a group of study abroad students from the United States were expected to attend. Although the students would not experience more intimate conversations, they were able to listen to a monk with personality, one who knew his audience and how to engage them. For the next forty-five minutes, Phra Kyo discussed the peaceful and universal nature of Buddhism and how it contrasts with Christianity, the religion that most in the crowd presumably were familiar with. His words proved to be a touchstone for me in clarifying many of my ideas on the Buddhist missionaries whom I had observed in my investigations of Buddhist encounters.

Buddhists in northern Thailand, as the cultural exchange program opportunities available show, seek to facilitate religious encounters between Buddhist monks and non-Buddhist tourists. From a Theravada Buddhist perspective, an important aspect of such encounters is the ability to spread the dhamma, or teachings of Buddhism. Religious encounters are an opportunity for Buddhist monks to missionize and develop strategies for spreading their teachings to international tourists. When Thai Buddhists interact with the international community, they respond to interest from outsiders and also actively help to shape the international appeal of their religion.

Buddhist cultural exchange programs become sites of missionization, shedding light on how Thai Buddhism works in practice to develop strategies of action that will attract a modern international audience while being rooted in the history and teachings of the tradition. Throughout its history, Buddhist missionaries have spread Buddhism within Asia, but missionization outside of Asia became more common only in the nineteenth century. Scholarship on Buddhist missionization has mostly characterized modern Buddhist missions as monastic networks connected to diasporic and non-Buddhist populations outside of Asia (Cheah 2011; Pattana 2010b; Van Esterik 1992), as civilizing and nationalist movements within a Buddhist nation-state (Ashley 2013; Keyes 1993b; Kamala 1997; Sanit 1988) or toward another Buddhist nation-state (H. Kim 2012). With these examples one can see that Buddhism has not been exempt from missions with the goal of conversion within contexts of globalization, nationalism, and colonialism.

However, due to the scholarly focus on missionizing in new and different contexts, knowledge of Asian Buddhist monastics' central role in creating and maintaining the global popular image of Buddhism has been obscured. Historically, missionization projects included building stupas and powerful Buddha images, along with printing scriptures for distribution. Today, in addition to establishing temples abroad in major cities like London and Los Angeles, Thai Buddhists have established a new context for missionizing in Thailand that takes advantage of tourism. Because of globalization, paradoxically, monks do not have to travel in order to missionize. Buddhists have an international platform in their homelands through foreign audiences interacting with the tradition while traveling. In the same way that definitions of religion had to be expanded to include Buddhism, ideas of missionization do as well, so that this religious practice does not have to include the goal of conversion or even travel to a foreign country. These new strategies create opportunities for non-Buddhist travelers to Thailand to join a Buddhist cultural exchange program, demonstrating that missionization continues to be a dynamic force shaping modern Thai Buddhism.

Mission within Theravada Buddhism

Buddhism is considered to be one of three missionary religions, along with Christianity and Islam. However, rarely in Buddhist studies scholarship is this part of the tradition analyzed or considered. For example, only a few works of scholarship engage theoretically with the category of Buddhist mission: Jonathan S. Walters's (1992, 2005) dissertation and entry on "Buddhist missions" in the *Encyclopedia of Religion*, as well as Linda Learman's (2005a) edited volume *Buddhist Missionaries in the Era of Globalization*. These authors analyze mission within Buddhism by comparing this practice with Christianity. Walters (1992, 108) argues that the term "missionary" should be reserved for those religions in which proselytization and conversion are defining characteristics; preaching and spreading the teachings are not missionizing. He applies similar criteria for "missionary" in his encyclopedia entry, stating that the term "Buddhist mission" "was invented in the 1830s to explain the religion's diffusion throughout Asia, and 'missionary spirit' has been treated as an essential dimension of Buddhist spirituality in virtually all English-language works about Buddhism composed since" (Walters 2005, 6077). For that reason, he argues, the category of mission, drawn from Christianity, does not fit Buddhist practices. Although a distinction between the two religions is necessary, this does not mean that Buddhists cannot correctly be called missionaries or that proper missionary practices are exclusive to Christianity. The definition of missionary need not be so limiting (Learman 2005b, 6), and instead of imposing these etic criteria from Christianity, one can look to the ways the Buddhist tradition has internally discussed its practice of spreading the teachings.

As Walters (2005, 6078) notes about the premodern Buddhist tradition, there existed limited specialized vocabulary for missionizing activities, and explicit missionizing was never mentioned in any of the Buddhist lists of practices and virtues. However, searching for a kind of formal missionary program in continuity with the modern tradition in canonical Buddhist texts places too much emphasis on these writings as part of a reified "original" Buddhism. This focus on texts assumes that the religion should not adapt to new circumstances and implies that any change to the religion necessarily comes from outside forces (Schedneck 2019). Factors such as Christian missionary practices, colonialism, print media, international travel, nationalism, technology, and mass communications certainly pushed Buddhist missionizing enterprises from being unofficial and ad hoc in early Buddhist missionary efforts before the nineteenth century to official and substantial in the contemporary period (Learman 2005b, 10). However, Buddhists have used the resources and vocabulary from their own tradition in order to missionize, whether informally before the nineteenth century or more formally afterward. Distinguishing not only Buddhism from Christianity but also between Buddhist missionizing within formal and informal circumstances opens up the category of mission to include a diverse group of practices.

Buddhism has distinct practices of missionization, which have developed along with Buddhist communities. From an emic perspective, Thai Buddhists discuss missionizing activities, for the most part, as the duty to spread the teachings (*phoei phrae satsana*). But this sense of duty to help others through the Buddhist teachings does not follow in the same mold as Christianity, as there is no active proselytization or conversion. This could be part of the reason why Buddhist studies scholars have not substantially reckoned with Buddhist missionizing.[1] In comparison to Christianity, the stakes for Buddhists to spread their religion are much lower. Within the Buddhist cosmological view of karma and rebirth, there are many more chances to learn and apply Buddhist teachings than in the single lifetime of a Christian, who, without hearing the Gospel, could fall into hell for eternity (Eddy 2015, 96).

For Buddhists, conversion to a Buddhist identity or becoming a member of a Buddhist community is not the goal. Because studying the teachings and practicing meditation is the typical path to the goal of enlightenment, or *nibbana*, many Buddhist monks I have spoken to state that becoming a Buddhist, although it might be helpful, is totally unnecessary. Buddhists make a distinction between Christian mission, which is proselytizing, and Buddhist mission, which is interested more in the welfare of individuals and society than in conversion to a Buddhist identity (Fleming 2014, 181). Religious studies scholar Glenys Eddy (2015, 102) writes that the gulf between the scholarly etic view of Buddhist mission as "an Anglo-American construction and not representative of the tradition" and the Buddhist emic view as "transmission of knowledge of the dharma, for the compassionate purpose of liberating people from suffering caused by ignorance" remains to be reconciled.

There is also a gulf between the Buddhist view of a missionary and Buddhist ideas of spreading the teachings. Many Buddhists attempt to distance themselves from the word "missionary" and hesitate to call Buddhism a missionary religion. That is because they do not want to associate themselves with what seem to be aggressive proselytizing efforts (Thelle 2004, 540). A similar dynamic is demonstrated by Buddhist monks involved in Buddhist cultural exchange programs. They are interested in teaching anyone who demonstrates curiosity about Buddhism by visiting their temples, rather than seeking out people to missionize to. Although Buddhists may not subscribe to the proselytizing practices of Christianity, they missionize in ways that make use of practices and ideas from their own tradition. Their faith in the dhamma has led many Buddhist monks in Chiang Mai to contemplate the best ways to explain and show Buddhism to the foreigners they encounter. They believe helping all people who come to their temples is their duty, to reduce suffering. These global encounters allow Buddhists to missionize in their own way, demonstrating that spreading the dhamma is an important part of their roles as ordained persons.

Buddhists themselves have discussed missionizing through metaphors of spreading out, sharing, building compassion, and hoping to make Buddhism present in the world, rather than looking at similarities and differences with Christian missionary ideologies. The student monks within Chiang Mai's Buddhist cultural exchange programs are part of an informal missionizing process. These Buddhist missions are not formal societies cast in the image of Christian missionaries but rather seek to spread the Buddha's teachings to curious tourists in an unofficial capacity. In this way, bringing tourists into the temple even for an informal chat or to teach English can serve as part of the missionization process.

Textual Examples of Missionization

Although authoritative early Buddhist texts located in the Pali Canon are believed to contain the words of the Buddha, they do not represent any kind of standard or original Buddhism from which to evaluate contemporary Buddhist practices. However, these early texts do provide evidence for the values of the early tradition. The most important passage from early Buddhist texts that depicts Buddhism as a missionary religion is, "Walk, monks, on tour for the blessings of the manyfolk, for the happiness of the manyfolk, out of compassion for the world, for the welfare, the blessing, and the happiness of *devas* and men. Let not two (of you) go by one (way). Monks, teach dhamma that is lovely at the beginning, lovely at the middle, and lovely at the end. . . . There are beings with little dust in their eyes, who, not hearing Dhamma, are decaying, (but) if they are learners of dhamma, they will grow" (*Great Division of the Vinaya* [Mahāvagga], translated in Horner 1971, 28).[2]

This passage appears three times in the Pali Canon, but the translation above is from the most quoted version, the Mahāvagga of the Vinaya. This has been called "the Buddha's great commission," in which the Buddha directed his disciples to spread the teachings to those with little dust in their eyes, or those who have some understanding already and will likely be able to hear the teachings and reach the final goal of enlightenment quickly. In this passage, Buddhism seems similar to the other religions considered to have missionaries, Christianity and Islam, as Buddhism also sends missionaries out to find people to teach about their religion.

Another aspect of Buddhism's missionary motivation, the Buddha's teachings' eventual decline, puts the tradition's distinct expression of mission into sharper focus. Within Theravada Buddhism the idea of decline of the Buddha's teachings is pervasive. It is thought that the Buddha's teachings will eventually disappear, as everything is subject to impermanence within Buddhism, except for the final goal of enlightenment. Within Pali texts there are numerous narratives addressing this point. A three-part decline within the *Commentary on the Connected Discourses* (Saṃyutta Nikāya) delineates the disappearance of the possibility of enlightenment and precept-observance, followed by the final loss of scriptural knowledge (Strong 2004, 222).[3] One of the most detailed views of this decline is found in Buddhaghosa's *Commentary on the Gradual Collection* (Aṅguttara Nikāya) (Turner 2014, 27).[4] This commentary describes a 5,000-year scheme in which every 1,000 years one of the five aspects of Buddhism will gradually disappear: (1) the ability to reach attainments toward enlightenment; (2) the existence of monks who are able to maintain their precepts; (3) textual knowledge and knowledge of the life of the Buddha; (4) signs of Buddhism and the monastic life, such as robes and alms bowls; and, finally, (5) the Buddha's relics (Strong 2004, 223–24).[5]

These decline narratives are not definite. The exact timing of this decline could be hastened or abated depending on the ways individuals, communities, and institutions enact Buddhist religiosity in their behavior and learning (Braun 2013, 70). Ways to slow this decline include studying the scriptures; maintaining proper monastic practices, rituals, and ordinations; and teaching and spreading Buddhism beyond the boundaries of one's community. In Burma, this idea of decline was significant during colonialism and the loss of the king, the protector of Buddhism (Turner 2014). In Thailand, it is the sexual and financial scandals of Buddhist monks reported widely in the media since the 1970s that have signaled a decline for some (Keyes 2007). This aspect of the tradition indicates the motivation for missionization. If Buddhism is spread to non-Buddhist communities, the tradition might not decline in the present time, but further in the future. Buddhist monks in Chiang Mai, who notice foreigners interested in their religion, feel proud and happy that the immediate future of a global Buddhism will be secure.

A chant from the Pali Canon is used by lay Buddhists to formally ask for a preaching or a dhamma talk in Theravada Buddhism:

> The Brahma god Sahampati, Lord of the world,
> With palms joined in reverence, requested a favor,
> Beings are here with but little dust in their eyes,
> Pray, teach the Dhamma out of compassion for them.
> (Chant based on *The Request* [Ayacana Sutta] [*Connected Discourses* (Samyutta Nikāya), 6.1].)[6]

When the Buddha was still deciding whether he should teach after his enlightenment, the god Sahampati attempted to convince him to do so. If he did not teach, the dispensation (*sasana*) would not continue. The Buddha, like monks today, needed to be reminded that teaching is valued and necessary for others on the path. After a monk hears a layperson in the community recite this chant, he knows the laity is ready to hear the dhamma. This chant reveals two important points: (1) the Buddha's teachings are closely connected to the modern-day interactions between laypeople and monastics, and (2) Buddhists follow a missionization strategy of teaching those who are already curious and interested, or those with "little dust in their eyes." Of course, this ideal is not always followed, but this rhetoric can be seen at work in Thailand's Buddhist cultural exchange programs.

King Aśoka, one of the most important figures in early Buddhist history, is credited with Buddhism's spread throughout Asia and its historical missionizing tendencies. The early legend of Aśoka's life tells of the Buddhist conversion of a cruel king who killed his own brothers. These atrocities are reversed with Aśoka's subsequent remorse and his zeal for spreading Buddhism (Nikam and McKeon 1959, 4). The legends of Aśoka appear in the *Legend of King Aśoka* (Aśokāvadāna) and the *Great Chronicle* (Mahāvamsa), which include Aśoka's dispatch of missionaries to spread the Buddhist faith. Buddhist studies scholar John Strong (1983) points out missionary activities in these texts: "The elder Majjhantika, we are told, is sent to Kashmir and Gandhara, the elder Majjhima to the Himālayas, Mahādhammarakkhita to Mahārastra, and Sona and Uttara to Suvannabhumi in Southeast Asia. Finally, and most importantly for the *Mahāvamsa*, Aśoka's own son, the elder Mahinda, is sent to Sri Lanka" (25). These stories represent an opportunity for their authors to missionize, using "their literary skills actively to promote and to reinforce the spread of Buddhism" and "to attract potential converts or maintain the faith of previous converts" (32). Besides sending physical missionaries, Aśoka is also most well known for spreading Buddhism through the construction of eighty-four thousand stupas containing the relics of the Buddha (109). Scholars discuss the example of King Aśoka in relation to missionizing but tend to ignore the contemporary work of Buddhists in spreading the teachings, which are significant to Theravada Buddhists today. Missionizing explains the spread of Buddhism within premodern Asia, but it is not only a historical phenomenon. Buddhist ideas of mission continue to explain the ways Buddhists act in the world today.

Given these historical examples of Buddhist missionary activity, how should the category of missionary be rethought? When Buddhism is not properly acknowledged as a contemporary missionary religion, Christianity becomes the default model for mission, and an important component of Buddhist motivation is obscured. What are the criteria for someone to be called a Buddhist missionary? Previous to the nineteenth century, much of the missionary activity of Buddhists was informal, but missionary projects became more formalized after the colonial period. In order to understand these two modes of formal and informal missionization, the sociopolitical conditions of missionaries and their projects need to be taken into account. In Thailand in the 1960s, formal programs for nation-state building and promoting Buddhism abroad were created. Buddhists seized opportunities to utilize Buddhism as a symbol of the Thai nation. Thai Buddhists have also established formal programs and networks to send missionaries outside of Thailand. In contrast to these formal programs, Buddhist cultural exchanges represent a new version of informal missionizing through their student monk participants. Cultural exchange programs are not part of official missionary discourse, but are not resistant to it. Their work is not centrifugal, like the historical examples of King Aśoka and Buddhist missionaries who move out of Buddhist centers, but centripetal, from the peripheries to the center as the foreign visitors come to their temples to take part in Buddhist encounters.[7]

Buddhist Missionizing Projects in Thailand

There are two broad categories of Thai Buddhist mission: (1) formal state-sponsored and (2) informal international monastic networks. In the late nineteenth and early twentieth centuries, the royal government sponsored reformist monks of the Thammayutnikai from central Thailand to missionize to the peripheries in the north and northeast. The goal of this mission was to homogenize Thai Buddhism and secure power over monks in these outer regions (Taylor 1993). The Thai state created formal missionary projects in the 1960s with the *thammacarik* (dhamma wanderers) and *thammathut* (dhamma ambassadors) programs. The *thammacarik* program is an internal nation-building effort utilizing Buddhist monks to strengthen ties between indigenous hill tribe groups and the central Thai government. *Thammathut*, managed by the Department of Religious Affairs, was originally conceived as a way for monks to take part in community development, but today it is the formal missionary arm of Thai Buddhism, sending Buddhist monks to locations throughout the world, especially North America and Europe. The second area of Thai Buddhist mission is not connected to the state but rather occurs through informal Buddhist monastic international networks. Significant examples of this type of missionizing include the Thai forest tradition and the Dhammakaya meditation technique from Wat Paknam and Wat Dhammakaya in Bangkok, which have all created connections with communities interested in Buddhism outside of Thailand.[8] These diverse areas of Thai Buddhism illustrate the characteristics of Buddhist missionizing within national and international contexts.

In Thailand, the formal, centrifugal Buddhist missionary exists in state missionary programs. The *thammacarik* program was created to propagate Buddhism among indigenous groups within the nation-state boundaries (Hayami 1999, 53). The aims of this program included conversion of indigenous groups to central Thai Buddhism as a way to instill national loyalty (Keyes 1971, 564). The *thammacarik* monks' roles were to encourage ordination and merit making but also to teach Thai language and a sense of obligation toward the government (Hayami 1999, 54). The headquarters for this activity was Wat Sri Soda, a temple at the base of Suthep Mountain in Chiang Mai. Prawit Tantalanukul, author and translator of northern Thai temple histories, in a bilingual (Thai-English) history of the *thammacarik* program he wrote at this temple, states that Buddhist monks can "teach the hill tribes and remote people about the Buddhist teaching" in order for them to realize "they should pay loyalty to the king and the nation as their refuge, and worship Buddhism" (2002, 35). Wat Sri Soda continues to be the headquarters for the *thammacarik* program due to its location near the hill tribe people of northern Thailand and the education centers for hill tribe monks established there (45).[9] In this way the *thammacarik* program was a missionizing propagation tool that served the needs of the Buddhist tradition as well as the Thai state.

The *thammathut* program, which began in 1965, is currently the official international missionary activity abroad for the Thai sangha, with both sects of Mahanikai and Thammayutnikai participating.[10] Spreading Buddhism abroad is one of the core aims of the Thai Sangha Supreme Council, dating back to the 1970s (Pattana 2010b, 110). Instead of "missionary spirit," Pattana Kitiarsa (2010b) uses the term "missionary intent." He defines this as "the Sangha's assiduous efforts to send personnel to engage in evangelical or humanitarian missions abroad" (115). Mirroring what many monks have told me, Pattana writes: "All monks are by definition and practice Buddhist missionary monks" (115). This is true at the informal level for the broad population of monks; however, for *thammathut* monks, spreading the teachings to non-Buddhists is not the only objective. Part of the Thai Buddhist missionary program's aims is to serve and support Thai Buddhists abroad, in order for them to maintain their Thai and Buddhist identity (121). The *thammacarik* and *thammathut* programs are interested in spreading the Buddhist teachings, but not only for the sake of reducing suffering. There is a clear element of nationalism within these programs with the intention to spread Thai identity to hill tribe groups, Thais living abroad, and non-Thais. These programs are focused on Thai Buddhism's close relationship to the nation-state. However, the second type of missionary project, which includes informal monastic international networks, focuses more exclusively on spreading the Buddhist religion to non-Buddhists, especially through meditation.

Luang Por Wat Paknam, also commonly known as Luang Por Sot (1884–1959), was a prominent Thai monk who hoped to create networks abroad in order to propagate his meditation technique, called Dhammakaya, out of Wat Paknam in Bangkok. William Purfurst (1906–1971), a British convert, became an unlikely Buddhist missionary of Dhammakaya meditation. As Bhikkhu Kapilavaddho, Purfurst was the first foreigner ordained in Thailand. Less than a year after his ordination, Kapilavaddho was sent by Wat Paknam's abbot, Luang Por Sot, to spread Dhammakaya meditation in England as well as gather British monastic candidates (Skilton 2013; Randall 1990). Luang Por Sot directed Kapilavaddho to leave Wat Paknam and missionize, stating:

> Now you go back to your people, Tan William. Face whatever has to be faced. Teach what you have learned, no harm will come to you. There may be some who wish to do as you have done. If that be so, bring them back here and we will arrange to support them. You will have to work

hard because you will have to gain the support of your own people, so
that their passages are paid for. You will succeed, I know. I will see you
again at the end of one year. Blessings and wishes go with you. (Randall
1990, 190)

Bhikkhu Kapilavaddho was shocked by this statement. He had never
thought to go back to England, because he was living happily in Thailand
and felt accepted by Thai society. Luang Por Sot replied that Kapilavaddho
must return, as he had already arranged and paid for everything:

He told me that he knew that I had many friends in England and that
there were groups and societies of people who were trying to study and
practise Buddhism. I had a duty to these and to myself, for was it not
these people in England who made it possible for me to come to Thailand? I had to return, he said, to repay my debt by way of service and
instruction to them. I also owed a debt to my past, and I must return to
the country of that past to test my way of life, to see if in true fact what I
had learned would sustain me in any circumstance. (Randall 1990, 178)

It was the goal not of this British monk but of the Thai monk abbot,
Luang Por Sot, to spread Buddhism. Luang Por Sot had the idea to spread
his meditation practice outside of Thailand, and that is why he sent one of
his English-speaking Thai monks to London in 1953 (Skilton 2010). This
monk, Phra Thitavedho, located Purfurst and brought him back to Thailand
as part of Luang Por Sot's plan (150–51). Therefore, while Kapilavaddho was
most interested in learning meditation in a Buddhist environment, it was
Luang Por Sot's ultimate intention to use his new disciple to spread the
Dhammakaya meditation technique outside of Thailand. In 1955, Kapilavaddho came back to Thailand with three English candidates for ordination. However, in the end, this group of monastics did not successfully take
root in Thailand, and Bhikkhu Kapilavaddho disrobed in 1957, citing ill
health, and subsequently changed his name to Richard Randall.[11] The main
task of this Western monk missionary was to spread Dhammakaya meditation in England, and preferably create a large enough group of Western men
to ordain and sustain a monastic sangha outside of Asia. Although this
particular mission did not succeed, this example establishes the importance
and interest in missionizing through international monastic networks.

Wat Dhammakaya is another temple that teaches Dhammakaya meditation, seeking to propagate its version of this technique throughout the world

by adapting its message to global audiences. Its Thai connections abroad have led to propagation efforts toward non-Buddhists and non-Thais alike. Religious studies scholar Rachelle M. Scott (2014), in her investigation of Wat Dhammakaya, finds that the temple's activities fit within the idea of proselytization, which she defines as a "pro-active missionary campaign whose primary aim is to invoke a significant change in the religious thought, practice, and identity of others" (233). Wat Dhammakaya follows this through its promotion of the Dhammakaya meditation method throughout the world. The temple markets itself as modern, in contrast to traditional Thai temples, which, Dhammakaya followers assert, are out of touch with today's society. Wat Dhammakaya brands itself as modern through the emphasis on meditation as the principle religious practice engaged in by all members of and visitors to the temple (Scott 2014, 239). The first aim of the Dhammakaya Foundation, the global arm of the temple, is the promotion of its method of meditation to the general public. While the promotion of Wat Dhammakaya in Thailand references amulets and merit making within Thai Buddhist culture, the foundation has set up international centers where the principal practice is Dhammakaya meditation divorced from the activities of Thai Buddhism generally (Scott 2014, 244–45). Scott concludes that this exclusive focus on one technique and the belief that it will lead to transformation for all constitutes proselytization (246). The Dhammakaya Foundation does not need partners or sponsors abroad, but completes this task without state sponsorship, Western monks, or Western lay Buddhists. Its missionizing, although not official, is generated through the efforts of its many volunteers, followers, and supporters.

Luang Por Sot ultimately did not succeed in creating a monastic sangha in England. The Thai forest lineage of Luangpu Ajahn Chah (1918–1992), however, through the English Sangha Trust, was able to establish an international community of monks, which took root in England and eventually in many parts of the world.[12] The English Sangha Trust, a charitable organization established to create a Buddhist monastic community in England, purchased land for a temple in Hampstead, London.[13] However, with Bhikkhu Kapilavaddho's failed attempts at missionizing, the Hampstead Vihara remained without a regular monastic sangha until 1977. In that year, the English Sangha Trust reached out to Ajahn Chah. After spending several months in England, Ajahn Chah was able to establish a community of some of his Western monks there, appointing his senior Western disciple, Ajahn Sumedho (b. 1934), as abbot. In contrast to Randall, Ajahn Sumedho stayed with Ajahn Chah for ten years, before being asked to establish a forest monastery in Thailand just for Westerners. Ajahn Chah told him that he had confidence in his practice and encouraged him, and Sumedho listened.[14] Both of these monks, Bhikkhu Kapilavaddho and Ajahn Sumedho, had the initial idea and encouragement from their Thai teachers to missionize in England. This collaboration shows the reluctance of some Westerners and the eagerness of some Asian teachers. It portrays the confidence of their teachers that their students can missionize the teachings in their own countries. It is also clear that Thai Buddhist monks seek to create new communities through international monastic networks.

Ajahn Chah's missionizing strategy was to walk daily collecting alms in order to create the connections between monks and laypeople necessary for a successful monastic sangha (Bell 2000, 13). Ajahn Sumedho and his Western monks continued to walk on alms-rounds, which were perceived by the wider community as impressive, tenacious, and a sign of devotion to their teacher (14). This practice aligns with Thai Buddhist monastic strategies today, which emphasize showing Buddhism. Instead of telling others who may not be interested in Buddhism, the monks demonstrate their lifestyle in public through their demeanor, behavior, and actions. In addition to maintaining the traditions and purity of Thai monastic practices, Ajahn Chah was part of the "'revival' of Buddhist meditation practice in the Thai forest monastic tradition" (Mellor 1991, 82). This appealing combination of authority, tradition, and the practice of meditation ultimately resulted in successfully rooting the Thai forest tradition in England.

Before the English Sangha Trust connected with Ajahn Chah and established its monastic sangha, a group of Thai lay Buddhists had heard about the Hampstead Vihara and the interest in Buddhism among the English, as part of the Vipassana Foundation committee at Wat Mahathat in Bangkok, the head temple of the Mahanikai. Eventually, this group decided to establish its own Thai temple, the first official Thai monastery abroad, Wat Buddhadipa, in 1964 (Cate 2003, 24). The purpose of this temple was explicitly to promote Buddhism in England, teach people in advanced nations about meditation, and enhance the Thai sangha (22–23). During this time, two monks from Wat Mahathat were invited to teach meditation at the Hampstead Vihara.[15] Through this experience, one of these monks, Phra Raja Sittimuni Chodok (1918–1988), strategized some of the best practices for presenting Buddhism to foreigners.

Phra Raja Sittimuni was the abbot of Wat Mahathat during this period. He was also an expert in *vipassana* meditation, having learned the practice in Burma, and held the highest meditation rank in Thailand (Cate 2003, 22).

He wrote the booklet *Dhamma of Interest for Foreigners* when he served as the head of the missionaries of London in 1966.[16] In it he advocates beginning with the rational, practical, meditation technique of *vipassana*, as he finds this training is the most important (*wipatsana pen lak yai lae samkhan thisut*) to begin presenting Buddhism to non-Buddhists. Only after the foreigner can practice well should the teacher missionary introduce the study of the Pali Canon (Chodok 1966, 1). And the last step for his students is to learn rituals like bowing, prostrating to Buddha statues and monks, reciting the Five Precepts, chanting in Pali, and delivering protective blessings (1). This Buddhist missionary agrees that practice is the most important for non-Buddhists and only after this understanding can the non-Buddhist move on to more devotional and committed activities. The leadership of Wat Dhammakaya—Luang Por Sot, Ajahn Chah, and Phra Raja Sittimuni—all thought that non-Buddhists would be most interested in meditation, so they led with this practice with the hope of establishing Buddhism in England.

Thai monks who pursued missionary projects drew from the characteristics of modern Buddhism in their recommendations for initial missionizing strategies. In North America, modern Buddhism has manifested as a reinterpretation of Buddhism focusing on reason, meditation, and the canonical texts, while decentering ritual, image worship, and local beliefs and practices (McMahan 2008, 7). In colonial Cambodia, the Buddhist modernist movement emphasized rationalism, authenticity, purification, new methods for Buddhist education, and new versions of Buddhist texts as a way to modernize Buddhist understanding in Cambodian society (Hansen 2007, 3). The concept of modern Buddhism has dominated much scholarship within Buddhist studies during the past two decades. Because of that, Buddhist leaders are more commonly labeled as modern Buddhists than as missionaries.[17] The focus on this label within Buddhist studies scholarship has contributed to the eclipsing of Buddhists as missionaries of their own tradition. Well-known Buddhist monks are often modern in their approach, but a significant underlying goal of the selected content of their messages is spreading the teachings. Buddhist modernism aims to persuade diverse audiences that Buddhism is applicable to their lives. The rational aspects of Buddhism are not only meant to prove Buddhism's status as a modern religion, but are also, at least partially in many cases, in the service of Buddhist missionary activity.[18] As a way to spread their teachings, Buddhists argue that their tradition is modern and relevant to the world. And as seen above with Phra Raja Sittimuni, the practice of meditation is the first step leading to the full tradition, which includes devotion and chanting.

The monks participating in Chiang Mai's cultural exchange programs do not think of themselves as official missionaries because they are not part of the formal *thammathut* program and are not being sent to Thai temples abroad. Instead, they consider their work as missionaries to be indirect and informal. Some of the monks think of themselves as spreading Buddhism among tourists but also note that they cannot see the effects of their efforts in the same way that they might if they were living long-term among Thai temple community members abroad. But in some ways, student monks in Chiang Mai can be more effective than *thammathut* monks. The formal missionary monks must adapt to a new lifestyle and environment with different people and culture, distinct laws for their temple, and expectations of increased labor (Bao 2015). As well, some Thai temples abroad serve Thai people only, with little opportunity to interact with non-Thais (Cadge and Sidhorn 2005; Pattana 2010b).

In an article on a Buddhist missionary monk in Indonesia in the national newspaper *Thai Rath*, the author defines *thammathut* as a monk who has the duty "to announce and spread [*prakat lae phoei phae*]" Buddhism along with "showing the teachings of Buddhism [*sadaeng tham kham son thang phra phutthasatsana*]" for Buddhists and the general population and leading to Buddhist practice both in the country and abroad."[19] Student monks, who are not part of the formal *thammathut* program but take part in cultural exchange programs, fit the category of missionary monks with this definition. For this reason, more flexibility is needed for the category of Buddhist missionaries. Thai Buddhist missionaries carry out their duties through the Thai government, international monastic networks, and cultural exchange programs. They do this in formal and informal, structured and semi-structured, and centrifugal and centripetal ways.

Informal Buddhist Missionaries in Monk Chat

Student monks involved in Chiang Mai's Monk Chat programs see their participation as an opportunity to spread Buddhism and show how it is practiced and lived in Thailand. They understand their monastic position as part of their duty to meet the needs of those who are interested in learning Buddhist practice. However, it was difficult to talk to the student monks about the idea of missionization. There is not a direct translation of the word "missionary." In Thai, the words *thammathut* and *thammacarik* are the closest to "missionary." Since the monks I spoke with were not part of these formal programs, they felt they could not use these titles for themselves.

When asked specifically about the term "missionary," in English, they equated the term with Christians and stated that they were not missionaries because they were not trying to make anyone a Buddhist. Their response demonstrates the ways monks have also been affected by the limiting ideal of missionizing as a Christian practice focusing solely on conversion.

The monks I spoke to did not claim any formal missionary status. To this effect, Phra Maha Mitra explained: "We feel we are not real missionaries because we are not part of *thammathut* program to go out somewhere—we feel this is missionary, the one who goes abroad. Monk Chat is not effective as missionary because it's too short and people come and go. It's not a place where many foreigners can come back to, that would be more effective, like a temple in your home. Monk Chat is more effective to give foreigners an idea of Buddhism for future and for monk to practice English."

But there was definitely the sense of an informal duty to spread the teachings. As Phra Ravi, a fourth-year monk at Mahachulalongkorn University (MCU) from Nepal stated: "It is the social duty of monk to spread Buddhism, to tell foreigner about Buddhism. I came to study here [in Chiang Mai] because I can practice English [in Monk Chat], so that I can spread Buddhism. I can tell many people about Buddhism and Buddhist teachings. I can study English here and get a chance to apply my knowledge with the foreigners who come to Chiang Mai." Learning English is part of the goal for many of these monks. Another goal of practicing English is their intention to spread Buddhism to non-Buddhists. Some of these monks may continue to missionize in more formal settings, such as the *thammathut* program, later in their careers. They may also disrobe and teach English in their home countries. However, while in their position as monks, they speak clearly of the good that spreading Buddhism would do.

In the small book *Thai Buddhism*, published by the Monk Chat program at Wat Suan Dok, the main author, Phra Saneh Dhammavaro, writes in the foreword: "I hope that this booklet will be benefit [*sic*] to the foreigners and the beginners of Buddhism and encourage them in their pursuit of the essential teachings of the Buddha and lead them to achieve real peace, enjoyment, and happiness" (2009, n.p.). Here he encapsulates some of the ways monks approach teaching Buddhism to foreigners. They want to make it available so that the teachings can lead to less suffering in each individual. Like much of the framing of Buddhist missionaries, the rhetoric is not interested in commitment or religious identity. The booklet describes the Buddha as using "new rational reasoning which can be practiced, understood and proved by everyone here and now" (2). Phra

Dhammavaro's espoused ideas of a rational Buddhism are used not only in the service of aligning with modern discourses, but for the purpose of missionizing.

Monk Chat monks, in their tourist encounters, also focus on practice and the practical applications of Buddhism. Although they are open to any question the foreigner has about Buddhism, many of the monks have a preference for discussing Buddhist teachings and practices. The monks distinguish between discussing important Buddhist teachings, such as the Five Precepts and the Four Noble Truths, and Buddhist practice, such as meditation, and teaching about the monastic life. Most questions these monks receive are concerned with leading the monastic life: What are the rules you have to live by? What happens if you break one? What is your daily life like? Why do you have to wear robes? Can you have a girlfriend? Although the monks will answer these questions from curious tourists who find it difficult to imagine such an alternative lifestyle from their own, the monks do not find this line of questioning useful because not many of these tourists are considering ordination. As Phra Thet, a fourth-year student at MCU from Myanmar put it: "Very few of these tourists will be ordained, so this kind of talk has little benefit for them." The monks reason that if the foreign visitors can learn about Buddhist teachings and meditation, then they will be closer to understanding and reducing suffering.

Phra Bunmi has a similar strategy for presenting Buddhism to foreigners: "I present Buddhism as like nature—it is accessible to everyone, whether you believe in religion. I tell them it is universal—everyone can come and learn the way to practice. It's not about belief or study. I invite them to practice to understand clearly." This kind of broad description of Buddhism shifts the conversation away from the unfamiliar nature of the monastic life. Through considering how to explain Buddhist teachings in an accessible way that will allow foreigners to continue to seek out knowledge about Buddhist teachings and practices, the Monk Chat monks are hoping to spread Buddhism. In this way, their preferences, although through informal channels, match the strategies of formal Buddhist missionaries.

These monks also use negative ideas surrounding Christianity and Christian mission to their advantage. In the Monk Chat discussion with groups of American students referenced in the beginning of this chapter, Monk Chat adviser Phra Kyo stated: "Buddhism is not really a religion but a philosophy. There is no relationship between Buddha and me, just as teacher and student. Have you ever seen a Buddhist monk knocking on doors telling the Buddha's teaching? Some of you have been here for a few weeks, a few months already. Have you ever seen a monk outside of the Buddhist temple waving people in with pamphlets talking about Buddhism?"[20] The audience laughed and nodded. The image of a Buddhist monk actively converting non-Buddhists in this way is laughable because it is so dissonant with expectations of Buddhism. Phra Kyo, obviously knowledgeable about the ways Christians missionize and the negative attitudes that many Westerners have toward it, uses Buddhist difference to his advantage. He continues by asking the crowd, "Who does not know suffering? Who has never suffered? Hello? Anyone? Who wants to remove suffering? See, everyone. When I look at you, I don't see other religions, I only see human[s]—we have the same blood." Here Phra Kyo characterizes Buddhism as free and open, so much so that it is not even a religion.

In the same discussion, Phra Kyo also used recent news of religious conflict to position Buddhism above other religions. He stated: "We all suffer in the same ways. Do Buddhists wish loving-kindness only to Buddhists? No, to all living beings." Buddhism's inclusivity is emphasized with the implication that if other religions were like Buddhism, there would be less religious conflict in the world. Going back to his discussion of Buddhism as a non-religion, Phra Kyo continued: "It's not a religion because there is no creator. If a Christian asks who created the world to a Buddhist, the Christian will be happy to respond, 'God.' But the Buddhist says, 'I don't care who created the world, but I want to be happy now and relieve suffering.'" The audience nodded enthusiastically in response to his rhetoric, although they did not realize that this is the exact question Christian missionaries have asked Phra Kyo many times (as discussed in chapter 3). He went on: "I tell you, don't become a Buddhist. Because Buddhism is not exactly a religion, so anyone can become a monk. You can stay believe in God, no problem. . . . Anyone can ordain, Catholic, Jewish, no problem." Through sentiments like these, religious people are positioned as concerned with unimportant, superficial things, while Buddhism, as a non-religion, is focused on something much more significant—happiness in the present moment.

Other monks within the Monk Chat program echo Phra Kyo's statements in their conversations with foreigners. When Phra Jor, a twenty-year-old monk in the Monk Chat program, meets visitors participating for the first time, he begins by saying that Buddha is not a god and that Buddhism is not a religion, it is a way of living. He wants to emphasize this as he compares Buddhism with Christianity. He believes that most of the foreign tourists participating in Monk Chat are Christian, and he wants them to know Buddhism's differences from and similarities with their religion. He is especially interested in separating Buddhist monks from Christian missionaries: "[Christian] missionaries try to talk and try to convert them [non-Christians]. This is not good or useful. Monk Chat has spread the Buddha's teachings for twenty years now and we have taught many people. But Buddhists aren't missionaries like Christians, because we don't try to convert, we just tell you what you want to know, but you don't have to do it, and it is up to you to follow."

Phra Kai and Phra Sonalin also distinguished between Monk Chat, the *thammathut* program, and Christian missionaries. When I asked if Monk Chat was a kind of missionary project, Phra Kai responded: "The missionary is a leader of that religion, they promote the religion, but we just only are in the temple giving information to those interested in Buddhism. But the missionary is one who promotes, we just supply." Instead of active missionaries promoting Buddhism, they consider themselves to be passive but available resources. Phra Sonalin hesitated to use the term "missionary" for the Monk Chat program as well, distinguishing their activities from Christian missionaries and centripetal missionaries, who travel to new places. "The Monk Chat monks are not the people who are going out to convert. It's just waiting for foreigners here, we just share our experience, but not like a missionary. It is not important for Buddhist monks to make other people become Buddhist. It's more important to bring people together. The missionary [in contrast] promotes, like selling." Because of the negative characteristics he associates with Christian missionaries, and profane activities like selling, Monk Chat monks do not fit under this category for Phra Sonalin. He also distinguished between the *thammathut* program and Christian missionaries: "The *thammathut* learn how to live abroad and answer foreigners' questions and how to live life not in a Buddhist country. The *thammathut* monks teach people who are curious, but it doesn't mean to teach everyone. This is the meaning of a missionary for Buddhist[s]. When I think about Christian missionary, I think there is no word for 'missionary' in Buddhism. Instead, we use 'spreading the teachings.'"

For Phra Sonalin, Christian missionaries, through their dominance, have captured the word "missionary" to the extent that he feels he cannot use it to describe even the formal *thammathut* program. Because conversion is so important for the Christian missionaries Phra Sonalin has met, he feels Buddhists cannot be included in this term. Many of these monks do not view Christian missionaries favorably, so to call themselves missionaries would be saying that they are forceful and aggressive. Instead, Monk Chat monks understand their approach as giving information about Buddhism and sharing their experience in a gentle way to those who come to them out of their own curiosity.

Another group of monks studying in their fourth year at Mahamakut Buddhist University (MBU) at Wat Chedi Luang debated how or whether the term "missionary" can apply to Buddhism. Phra Akara said: "You can say we are like missionaries because we spread Buddhism, but we don't convert." However, Phra Atid felt that the activity of Monk Chat, just sharing about the monks' life and Buddhist philosophy, means they are not missionaries. Because he never encourages the foreign visitors to be Buddhist, and the Christian missionaries he is familiar with invite the other person to become part of their religion, he finds Buddhism is drastically different. At this point in the conversation, I asked, "So maybe 'missionary' has different meanings for different religions, but can you use the same word of 'missionary' for both Christianity and Buddhism?" A novice monk, Naen Samrin, replied: "It depends on your definition of 'missionary.' If it includes conversion, then no. If not, then yes. It's the same for religion. If your definition of religion is about a god, then no, [Buddhism isn't a religion]. But if it does not include a god, then Buddhism is a religion." Naen Samrin here clarified for the other monks one way to understand the term "missionary" as it relates to Buddhism and Monk Chat. While Phra Akara and Phra Atid struggled to reconcile the model of Christian missionary conversion with Buddhists, Naen Samrin asserted both could be true. Buddhists could be missionaries if one does not have the Christian model in mind.

Phra Daeng and Naen Maha Tri, in another conversation at Wat Chedi Luang, agreed that it is difficult to consider Buddhists fitting into the category of missionary because of the necessary comparison with Christian missionaries.

> AUTHOR: What is the definition of a missionary?
> PHRA DAENG: The definition of missionary is they say you have to believe what I believe.
> AUTHOR: Is this definition influenced by Christian missionaries?
> PHRA DAENG AND NAEN MAHA TRI: Yes.
> NAEN MAHA TRI: The definition of missionary is they try to make their religion be better than the other. Their mind-set is so strong, and they ignore other ideas. They are a person who tries to sell religion and convince people to believe in their way but never listen to the other and argue and then try to be the winner and never give up.

This definition is influenced by my discussions with Christian
missionaries.

PHRA DAENG: For Buddhists it's different because the purpose is not
believing but showing and knowing. They [Buddhist missionaries]
know this is the way and then let others know. They don't believe.
They know. So, this is the kind of Buddhist missionary like the Buddha,
the one who knows can show.

This is another strategy monks use to distinguish themselves from
Christian missionaries. They emphasize that their way is showing Buddhism, not telling. Phra Maha Mitra from Nepal stated: "[The Buddhist]
monk is not like Christian missionary because it is not our way to go talk
to people. We just show our practice, learning and understanding, and
people will see and it [their faith] will happen automatically. The monks'
practice inspires people. Yes, that is how we do. Practice first and then
people will follow." This connects well with the historical and textual
examples of Buddhist missionizing discussed above where the Buddhist
monk will only preach after being invited by the people.

Only one monk, Phra Ruang, at Wat Chedi Luang's Monk Chat, felt
unequivocally that he was a missionary: "I am a Buddhist missionary monk
who loves teaching and sharing with the people and children, and I just
want to do this for training myself to be wiser, to be smart, and to be better."
When I asked him, "What is a Buddhist missionary?," he replied: "Buddhist
missionary means practicing so we can share Buddha's teaching. It means
sharing with the people from your direct experience."[21] Phra Ruang does
not compare himself with Christian missionaries or the *thammathut*
program but instead considers sharing with others, spreading the Buddha's
teachings, as enough of a qualifier to be considered a missionary. However,
for most Monk Chat monks, there was some debate and consideration about
how and whether to apply the term "missionary" to their activity or even to
Buddhists at all. It was clear that Christian missionaries had affected their
ability to consider how "missionary" could apply to their religion. They
distinguished themselves from Christians by describing their actions as
showing Buddhism, not being interested in conversion, and only answering
questions and sharing their experiences with those who are curious. In this
way, they represent an informal kind of Buddhist missionizing. But the
Monk Chat activity is set up to facilitate the duty that all monks agree is
their role—spreading the Buddha's teachings.

Missionizing Possibilities

Factors that contribute to Buddhist monks' positive responses to religious and cultural others include level of commitment to religion and interest in Buddhist doctrines. But another important factor is the potential to practice Buddhism. To understand how these monks see their roles as informal missionaries, I asked them where they would most like to travel. Anthropologist Peter van der Veer points to this technique in his work on urban aspirations: "By paying attention to the aspirations of people, communities, classes, experts, and institutions, one can get away from the static connotations of the concept of identity that tends to fix people to what and where they are rather than to what and where they aspire to be" (2015, 4). The monks' answers to my question about imagined travel destinations reveal their aspirations to see developed countries as well as missionize Buddhism. When monks imagine traveling abroad, their destinations mostly include countries where spreading Buddhism would be beneficial. In these imagined scenarios, there was less ambiguity about the term "missionary" and more focus on their perceptions of where Buddhism would be best received.

Phra Day, a Thai monk studying and living at Wat Chedi Luang, wants to travel to Europe in order to observe advanced technology and be able to watch football. He is intrigued by this region because he does not know about Europeans' rules or way of life. Besides expressing fascination with visiting what he considers to be a developed area, he spoke about Buddhism: "I want to teach Buddhism in Europe, because I can help spread teachings [*phoei phae satsana*] there more than in Thailand or Mahayana Buddhist countries." To indicate that, Phra Day motioned vaguely to the Thai people on the street, stating that they do not appreciate all the opportunities to learn about Buddhism around them: "In Buddhist countries, laypeople already know the basic [*phuen than*] Buddhist teachings and are not interested in learning more. However, for Europeans, even the basic teachings of the Five Precepts are interesting. Europeans are interested more than Thais because many of them don't have a religion and so are more open [*poet chai*] and have many questions."

For these monks, the time is ripe for Buddhism in the West. Naen Samrin concurred: "I [would] love to be a part of Buddhism going to the West. Here in Southeast Asia, Buddhism is going away. Westerners have an open mind and I can really teach them. They really listen to us. You cannot teach the real teaching to Thai people or people from my country [Vietnam]." The West is seen as an open missionary field ripe for spreading the Buddhist teachings. In reflecting about the locations they would like to travel to, Monk Chat monks imagined themselves as effective and formal Buddhist missionaries.

Phra Jor, another Thai monk living and studying at Wat Chedi Luang, said he "wants to go to England to spread teachings because they have a community of Buddhist people, but it is not too big." There is potential in England for Buddhism to spread, and much missionary work can be done there. Phra Jiu, a Thai monk, would go to New Zealand to share the Buddha's teachings because of its good environment as well as its Western population. He described Westerners as "not knowing much about Buddhism, but they are curious to learn more and want to practice [*patibat tham*]" and noted that "when they think of the Buddha, they think of meditation." He thinks this is a good start but that there is much more to teach them. Phra Jaya, a Khmer Krom monk from Wat Srisuphan, stated: "Europe is a good place to travel to spread Buddhism because their governments will welcome new ideas, unlike Asian governments." These monks see Western countries as an important and emerging area for missionizing Buddhism not only because they are developed countries but because Western people have been observed to be curious and receptive to learning more about Buddhism.

Westerners are thus deemed an important field for sowing the seeds of Buddhist teachings. In contrast, Thai and other Asian Buddhists represent fields that have already been harvested. Although Monk Chat monks do not see themselves as formal missionaries, when asked where they would want to travel they imagined themselves as part of formal Buddhist missions in Western countries. They agreed that Buddhism could spread easily in Western countries and revealed that they would like to be a part of the official missionary activity there. The informal missionary work of Monk Chat gives way to more interest in spreading Buddhism. Therefore, not only tourists plant seeds for their own further understanding of Buddhism, but also monks in Monk Chat plant seeds for their further work as formal missionaries. The significance of spreading Buddhism for monastics can also be seen in other types of Buddhist cultural exchange programs.

Spreading Buddhism through Volunteer, Gap Year, and Temple Stay Tourism

Researchers of the anthropology of tourism have found that Thai village host communities are not sure why foreign groups have come to their particular settings (Conran 2006, 278). By contrast, novice monks, who receive volunteer tourists as English teachers in their classrooms, are sure that Buddhism is the main attraction. They believe that foreigners have heard about Buddhism and how it can solve their problems, so they come to see for themselves. The monastic teachers and principals have an even clearer idea. Phra Maha Insorn, when asked why he thinks volunteers come to his temple school, Wat Nong Bua Pariyattitham, pointed to his robes, saying, "This, this, they want to see something they have never seen before. Being in a classroom filled with robes is very different for them." Ajahn Thani, of the Plik Wiwek Dhamma Center, explained that the volunteers come for the "culture and exchange": "They don't want to help so much as learn." In perceptive ways, these monks, who have observed many volunteers teaching English to their novice monks, understood the appeal of their monastic classroom for a foreign audience.

Phra Maha Insorn spoke of Wat Nong Bua's affiliation with volunteer tourism organizations: "It is not the aim of this program to spread Buddhism. We do not compel [bangkhap] [the volunteers] to learn anything about Buddhism, not ordain and not spread [Buddhism]. The first aim [for the temple] is to study English." However, at the same time, he was clearly excited to talk about the secondary aim—the ways that volunteer tourism created opportunities to spread Buddhism to an interested population. Phra Maha Insorn feels it is his duty to supply volunteer tourists with experiences and information about Buddhism if they are curious: "If they [the volunteers] are interested, they can do anything—there is no limit. They are welcome to speak and learn about any aspect of Buddhism, from practice to beliefs to ordination." He found that there are not many opportunities to spread Buddhism if the volunteers teach for only a short time, but if they stay for some months, they can learn a lot about Buddhism. Being open to the volunteers' questions and allowing them to experience further is part of Phra Maha Insorn's way of spreading Buddhism. He has facilitated, for some of his more curious volunteers, opportunities to attend nearby meditation retreats. One of his volunteers even ordained for a few months. The monks at the school remember fondly the volunteers who became engaged with Buddhist practice.

At Plik Wiwek, monks have observed and interacted with students on gap year and study abroad programs. Phra Jing, a twenty-four-year-old monk, said of the foreigners he has encountered: "They often don't have a religion, but every religion can practice [Buddhism]. They can change to be Buddhist, and two to three [students] have ordained here. This center can help to spread Buddhism, but we don't compel anyone to worship. The religion is in the heart." Because Phra Jing believes Buddhism is inclusive and open to different levels of practice, he finds that the teachings and practices are easy to spread and get into the "hearts" of the foreigners. Phra Bong, also a twenty-four-year-old monk, added that the longer the foreigners stay, the more they realize the effects of Buddhist practice. He said of the foreign visitors he has encountered: "They become part of the community—they talk and play with the novices, they practice Buddhism, they have good thoughts about Buddhism, they become peaceful and start to calm down. This environment, the people, and the practice help them do this." Phra Bong sees the benefits of living in a Buddhist environment and Buddhist practice for the foreigners.

Beyond simple curiosity, foreigners are perceived to be genuinely intrigued by the practice of the religion, which is valued by the monks here. Phra Sukkasem explained: "The foreigners turn to be interested in Buddhism because it is called the 'religion of philosophy' and they want to know about meditation. . . . The foreigners have many conflicts in their lives and want to solve through knowing about themselves in meditation. Some of them are Christian but can practice with no problem with their religion. The foreigners do not truly believe in Buddhism but believe in practice and that meditation can calm the mind. They are only interested in philosophy because then they don't have to believe, but they can over time."

Although the monks at Plik Wiwek are happy that the foreigners are interested in meditation, they hope that eventually they will embrace the entirety of the religion. The monks typically foresee a trajectory where foreigners come to Buddhism through the door of meditation and grow in their understanding and interest from there.[22] Phra Jing agreed and continued with his thoughts on this theme: "The foreigners don't worship but are focused to do it [meditation] well, as opposed to Thais, who are not interested and play on their phones or talk. The foreigners aren't Buddhist, but they can practice. They don't want to worship but want to practice because it can help calm down their hearts [chitchai lotlong] and they want to know because science has found proof and benefits. They want to see if it's real. . . . They don't know about merit, devotion, offering. This is the next step for them."

As seen above, Monk Chat monks also contrast Thai and Asian Buddhists with the new field of Western visitors. Like formal Buddhist missionaries who advocate for meditation as the foundational entry for non-Buddhists, the monks in Chiang Mai observing foreigners have come to the same conclusion. Although informal and formal missionaries have different official roles, their understandings of their audience and activities are similar.

At Plik Wiwek, Ajahn Thani considers it his and all monks' and novices' duty and responsibility to spread Buddhism to all people. For Ajahn Thani, the goal of spreading Buddhism is not conversion to Buddhism. The aim of monks and novices instead should be to help everyone find happiness and freedom from defilements (*kilet*). He encourages all foreigners who stay at Plik Wiwek to try Buddhist practice but emphasizes that it is up to them to choose to continue after they leave the center. His interest in facilitating Buddhist practice for foreigners, he explains, is "not about worshipping the Buddha, and it's not about tricking [*lok*] someone into being Buddhist through magic [*saiyasat*], but showing them the teachings, benefit, and effect. And they can see it helps them become peaceful and not selfish—they can let go of everything [*ploi thukyang*]." He stresses that Buddhist teachings are effective for all people—they are based in reality, and the teachings are not trying to force someone into following a religion or teacher. In discussing his relationship with foreigners who stay at his center, he describes the characteristics of informal Buddhist missionizing—open, flexible, and oriented toward non-Buddhists' curiosity and interests.

At the Wat Sri Boen Ruang Temple Stay and Retreat program, Naen Pairat is happy that foreign participants come to stay at the temple:

> AUTHOR: Do you like having foreigners come to this temple?
> NAEN PAIRAT: Yes, I like it.
> AUTHOR: Why do you like it?
> NAEN PAIRAT: It is a good opportunity for them to learn the Buddhist way and practice [*patibat tham*].
> AUTHOR: Does this temple help to spread Buddhism?
> NAEN PAIRAT: Yes, it helps to spread the method [*withi*] of Buddhist practice and Buddhist ideas.

Naen Pairat feels glad that these guests will be able to understand Buddhism and experience the peacefulness of living in a temple surrounded by a Buddhist community. When the guests in this program go back home, he does not think that they will become Buddhist, but he hopes that they will "be able to continue to practice aspects of the Buddhist life they learned" and that "if there is a Buddhist temple near their home, they can visit and support it." However, Naen Somchai explained that the most important way for Buddhism to remain in their ordinary lives is if they choose to ordain.

When the foreign male participants ordain, "they can change their heart [*plian chai*] easily and really know the Buddhist way of life." These novice monks see value in spreading Buddhism to non-Buddhists because they believe Buddhist teachings and practices will benefit these non-Buddhists' lives, penetrating deep into their hearts. The monks involved with these programs are clearly excited to be in dialogue with an international non-Buddhist audience. Besides the excitement of gaining new skills, such as learning about foreign countries and studying English with native speakers, this is also an opportunity to spread Buddhism. Although the monks who participate in these cultural exchange programs do not see themselves as formal missionaries, the idea of an informal missionary resonates because their efforts and activities are directed toward Buddhist ways of spreading their religion—allowing those curious to come to them with no pressure of conversion.

Missionizing is a dynamic force motivating Thai Buddhism's interaction with the international community. Missionization is grounded in the history and textual tradition of Buddhism, but creative new opportunities are emerging to engage curious travelers in understanding the teachings and practices of Buddhists. Buddhist missionizing is a major factor in student monks' motivations and actions during their encounters with international communities in their local spaces. The monks who are part of Buddhist cultural exchange programs, although not formal missionaries, do consider their role as informally spreading the teachings. Student monk participants in the Temple Stay and Retreat program as well as in temples that host gap year and study abroad programs recognize the global appeal of Buddhism. They notice the willingness of foreigners to listen and sincerely practice, and they are impressed, especially when compared to their perceptions of Thai Buddhists. Because Buddhism is new and different for foreigners, these monks view Western countries as fertile places to continue to spread Buddhism.

Monk Chat monks, as college students, distinguish themselves carefully when considering the category of missionary. They do not see themselves as part of something like the *thammathut* program of Thailand, where monks travel abroad to maintain Thai Buddhist communities and make Thai Buddhism available to others. But the most important reason that student monks would not call themselves missionaries is because of the model of Christian missionaries. They are aware of these Christians' emphasis on conversion and agree that Buddhism does not include such proselytizing in any way. These student monk informal missionaries find it difficult to label themselves as missionaries even as they agree they are spreading the teachings and showing their practice to foreigners.

Just as monks have been influenced by the Christian missionary model, so too have scholars. Buddhist studies scholars rarely take the category of missionary into account for understanding the motivations of Buddhist monks. As the examples from Thailand demonstrate, from modern history through today, Buddhists are engaging in missionary activities. They are spreading Buddhism to North America, Europe, and other parts of Asia through the official *thammathut* program. There have been formal programs for missionizing in Thailand through the Thai government as well as Thai Buddhist integration into the fertile missionary fields of the West through international monastic networks. Informal missionary activities, such as Buddhist cultural exchange programs in Chiang Mai, are more difficult to identify. Scholarly labels for contemporary Buddhists have been dominated by the category of "modern Buddhism." Many of the efforts to present Buddhism as modern have roots in missionizing. This modern label, although important, has obscured an important motivating action for Buddhists. The definition of missionary needs to be expanded to include religious traditions that do not follow the model of Christianity and should take into account the actors' motivations, not only the content of their messages.

CHAPTER 5

SELF-TRANSFORMATION AND BUDDHIST AUTHENTICITY THROUGH VOLUNTEER TOURISM

VISITING ANCIENT TEMPLES IS A MAJOR TOURIST ACTIVITY IN the old city of Chiang Mai. The first thing international tourists notice is the difference of this religious space from familiar landscapes at home. Architectural details, from the mythical creature guardians at the gated entrances to the curved roof finials shaped like flames, provide aesthetic beauty and sensory stimulation. Some tourists merely take in the atmosphere, not attempting to fully understand the meaning behind each of these details. But others feel lucky that they will be able to consider these deeper meanings by volunteering their time to teach English in a Buddhist temple with Buddhist novices and monks as their students.

Volunteers' reflections on their experiences teaching Buddhist monks in temple schools reveal perceptions about difference, authenticity, and possibilities of transforming the self within Buddhist contexts. Their initial understandings of "Buddhist authenticity" include images of peaceful temple settings and implacably calm Buddhist monks—something that would be very different from home. However, volunteers highlight their own transformation not only when encountering difference and experiencing this expected form of Buddhist authenticity, but also when their expectations of the other are challenged. Their narratives show that although the familiar and unexpectedly modern lives of novice monks is disorienting for volunteers at first, this encounter can lead not only to a revision of their understanding of authenticity in a Buddhist setting but also to a transformation of the self. The number of volunteers is fairly small in comparison to that of student monks. Additionally, volunteers typically have not had years to process their understanding of Buddhist encounters as many student monks have, and their time volunteering is limited, usually around two weeks. Yet, their views represent another side of the cultural encounter, in which both expected difference and unexpected familiarity can lead to self-transformation, even in small ways, during visitors' volunteering experiences.

Volunteer Tourism in Thailand

Due to the postcolonial economy of volunteer tourism from the global North to the global South, the promise of difference creates unique cultural experiences (Parreñas 2012, 673).[1] In volunteer tourism, unskilled workers who are traveling temporarily assist with projects designed to alleviate poverty.[2] Volunteer tourism attracts those in search of authentic tourism, which involves participating in social and educational projects while living in a country different from their own (Wickens 2011, 43). Projects include assisting in orphanages, building homes, taking care of endangered animals, and, more commonly, teaching English (Jakubiak 2016, 93). Young travelers see a need for volunteerism as stimulating a sense of purpose and facilitating meaningful encounters with locals. Travel is increasingly linked by tourists and the tourism industry to ethical concerns, with the goal of creating a new kind of moral tourist (Butcher 2003). This is one of the reasons volunteer tourism has become the fastest growing niche tourism market (Mostafanezhad and Kontogeorgopoulos 2014, 264). Volunteer tourism combines travel with service and appeals to participants who are interested in their own personal development while helping others socially or environmentally at the same time (Wearing 2001, 1).

Although there is an element of neocolonialism present in the predominantly global North coming to the assistance of the global South, volunteer tourism does not have to imply a colonialist agenda. That is because, by and large, volunteer tourists do not want to bring Westernization to their service localities. On the contrary, they want to learn from different lifestyles and support a preexisting way of life, often rejecting signs of modernity (Butcher and Smith 2010, 33). There might not be the civilizing project of colonialism, but there is still something of the romantic nature of Orientalism within the volunteer tourism project. When volunteer tourists encounter poverty, they are often struck by how happy the local people are, in comparison to the depressed but materially wealthy people in their own developed countries. This idea of "poor-but-happy" can lead volunteer tourists to claim that "the locals did not mind being materially poor, thereby romanticizing and trivializing poverty" (Crossley 2012, 249).

Other important critiques of volunteer tourism target its neoliberal agenda (Vrasti 2013; Mostafanezhad 2014) and its limited value for host communities (Bernstein and Shih 2014, 434). Clearly, volunteer tourism benefits volunteers, and this is part of its appeal. The tourist gains social capital, engages in cosmopolitan experiences, and is able to encounter an "authentic" lifestyle. As a result, during the search for the authentic, the host community must remain static, untouched by development or Westernization, in order for volunteer tourists to meet their expectations and feel that they will be able to make an impact. This, of course, "absolves volunteer tourists of any responsibility to reflect upon, and attempt to alter, the structural inequalities that lead to this poverty" and "promotes an apolitical response to underdevelopment" (Kontogeorgopoulos 2016, 460).[3]

Despite the critiques, I find that volunteer tourism in Chiang Mai's Buddhist temples can create meaningful encounters between visitors and members of local communities. Volunteer tourists in Chiang Mai are not interested in development work or effecting long-lasting social change, and volunteer tourism companies working with Buddhist temples do not claim this is their goal.[4] My intention here is not to evaluate volunteer tourism as a social project. It is clear from my interviews that volunteer tourists choosing to teach English to novice monks in Buddhist temples not only hope to give to their host country but also to receive new ideas and experiences. In Buddhist volunteer tourism, difference, authenticity, and transforming the self work together in these unique kinds of encounters.

Since the 2004 Indian Ocean tsunami, which devastated parts of Thailand's southern islands, the country has been a key player with organizations that send volunteers, distinguishing itself as the second most popular destination in Asia, after India (Tomazos and Butler 2009, cited in Kontogeorgopoulos 2016, 455). Chiang Mai is also the top volunteer tourism location in Thailand, receiving one-third of all volunteers in the country (Keese 2011, 265, cited in Kontogeorgopoulos 2016, 456).[5] This is because of Chiang Mai's combination of tourism facilities and attractions along with a vibrant NGO community. Unlike the big city of Bangkok, Chiang Mai offers natural, religious, and village settings in which to search for authenticity.

Buddhist Volunteer Tourism in Chiang Mai

Within Chiang Mai, there are numerous opportunities to teach novice monks in temple schools.[6] During the course of my research, much has changed in the Buddhist volunteer tourism scene. Since its inception in 2009, the Wat Doi Saket Project has hosted hundreds of volunteers arriving in groups or individually.[7] They stay for varying lengths of time in temple accommodation, teaching English and even helping with temple building projects.[8] In 2014, the FutureSense Foundation took over the project. This did not concern the temple school because the volunteer company staff members remained the same and the change came with added benefits of support from a multinational organization. However, in 2017, the FutureSense Foundation decided to focus on the indigenous groups of Mae Sariang, in Mae Hong Son Province, in northern Thailand.[9] As a result, the temple school that was supported by the FutureSense Foundation, Wat Nong Bua, does not currently have any connection to foreign English-teaching volunteers.[10] This case displays the vulnerability of the monastic school in relationship with the volunteer tourism company. The school had a partnership with various iterations of volunteer tourism, but with similar and overlapping staff whom the monks knew and trusted, for almost ten years. The monastic school leadership would like consistent volunteers who can teach regularly and reliably, but it would be difficult and possibly seen as inappropriate for the monks to seek out these relationships on their own. When the volunteer tourism company approaches the temple school and maintains a good relationship, then the temple does not have to be concerned with finding and training volunteers. It can simply receive the free labor of English teachers as long as the relationship with the volunteer tourism company can be maintained.

Since 2008, Friends for Asia has offered opportunities to teach monks in temple schools. The director of Friends for Asia, Todd Cikraji, started the organization with the Teaching English to Monks program, with its first volunteer arriving in February 2008.[11] Currently, fifty to sixty volunteers participate in this program annually. When Cikraji created this program, he wanted to locate the neediest school that could benefit from volunteer teachers, but at the same time he hoped to provide a unique cultural experience for the volunteers. As a resident and teacher in Chiang Mai, he knew that temple schools would uniquely fit these criteria. With his idea, he visited one temple school in 2007 and soon was able to connect with a number of temple school principals. The leadership of the schools liked the fact that the foreign teachers came at no cost to the temples. Friends for Asia currently sends volunteers to seven schools in the city of Chiang Mai. Cikraji does not send volunteers to temples where the school leadership is not interested in their services or to temple schools that will not be able to provide support for the volunteers. But he has found that each school varies in its level of conservatism regarding novice monk interaction with foreigners, with one school stating that it did not want to participate because its novices were so naughty they would create a negative picture of Thai Buddhism for the international community.

As of 2018, Friends for Asia was the only volunteer organization able to place foreign volunteers in Buddhist classroom settings in Chiang Mai City. Volunteer organizations are also in vulnerable positions relative to their temple school partners. Friends for Asia's temple affiliations depend on good relationships with the English teachers at each school, and each temple school principal must see the value of having volunteers. The Thai English teacher, employed by the temple school, must be able to speak English well in order for the volunteer to have a good experience. If the temple school has a skilled English teacher and the novice monk students are learning well with the volunteers, then Friends for Asia can send more volunteers. But if the English teacher cannot speak English well, goes abroad, or moves to another job, then the relationship between the school and the volunteer tourism organization might end for a period, until personnel changes.

Volunteers, as tourists and newcomers to Chiang Mai, also have particular needs that must be met by the volunteer organization. It is easiest to place volunteers in temple schools located in the old city, because they can walk to these schools within five to ten minutes. But placing them in rural schools, accessible by public transportation, or even in schools slightly outside the city, a fifteen- to twenty-minute bike ride away, is more difficult. A delicate balance is necessary to keep all of the components in place to maintain volunteer tourism in temple schools. Nonetheless, the Teaching English to Monks program is one of Friends for Asia's most popular and longest-running volunteer programs in Thailand. The volunteers I interviewed chose this program over other possibilities, such as teaching in Thai public schools, caring for elephants, or working with orphans. Volunteers within these organizations can teach for as little as one week but are encouraged to stay for at least four weeks.

Volunteers express their attraction to Thailand as a context in which they can immerse themselves in an interesting culture, see something new, feel useful while traveling, learn about Buddhism, or experiment with teaching as a career. The comments of one college-aged American volunteer, Jen, are representative of those seeking these experiences: "Teaching the novice monks was definitely challenging, as I am not an educator and do not have a knack for it. However, I am grateful for all that I learned from the monks and my time in Thailand. I believe my experience opened my eyes towards other cultures and people. I realized that there is so much to learn from other people and cultures. I also realized how much I wanted to actively focus on trying to help others."[12]

Because of these various motivations—encountering authenticity and difference in a Buddhist community, learning about Buddhism, and gaining teaching experience—volunteer tourism organizations' advertising must assure potential participants of their role and impact. The Wat Doi Saket Project website offers background on the socioeconomic status of most novice monks, explaining that they are often poor boys from rural villages who are seeking an education. Not only will volunteers be offering this important service, but the novices and monks will reciprocate by helping their teachers understand Buddhism and Thai culture. Therefore, volunteers are assured by their sending organizations that they are making a valuable contribution and are "giving back" to a worthy cause.

The costs for these programs vary depending on how long one stays and which volunteer tourism organization one works with. Typically, there is an application fee of US$250, and the initial two-week cost is around US$700. Each additional week costs approximately another US$100–$200. These organizations offer English-teaching support as well as airport transfer, accommodation, some food subsidy, excursions to temples or other tourist attractions, and twenty-four-hour assistance for any emergencies or concerns. The volunteer fee does not cover a donation to the temple. Some organizations suggest volunteers bring souvenirs from their home country or items such as notebooks, books, and pencils to donate to monks or the school library.

Most volunteers are native English speakers from England, the United States, and Australia. However, non-native English speakers from Europe and East Asia also volunteer. Program coordinators acknowledged that the latter present a challenge for temple placements, as most abbots of temple schools prefer that volunteers be native speakers. East Asian volunteers can sometimes be placed in a classroom teaching Chinese or Japanese. This minority of volunteers from East Asia also have a different experience because they are usually familiar with temples and the monastic life.

However, the Thai Buddhist codes of behavior are often new and provide a basis for comparison.[13]

Both Teaching English to Monks programs, as run by the Wat Doi Saket Project and currently by Friends for Asia, emphasize that each individual determines the extent that he or she will learn about the religion. The Friends for Asia website states clearly that Buddhist practice and learning is not compulsory. If a volunteer is not interested and wants to concentrate solely on teaching, no one will be offended. The director of Friends for Asia said that some volunteers think they will learn about Buddhism more directly and may be disappointed that it is not "a full-on Buddhist experience." No one sits down and teaches the volunteers about meditation and Buddhist philosophy. Volunteers sometimes do not take away as much about Buddhism as they would have liked because this is not part of the structure of the program, but it depends on the initiative of the volunteer.

The Wat Doi Saket Project also advertises that through volunteering there are limitless opportunities to learn about Buddhism and meditation, if one chooses. The main appeal of the program comes from the cultural exchange one is able to experience by teaching the monks and experiencing a different life at the temple. According to the Wat Doi Saket Project website:

> Buddhist ceremonies and events like funerals, house blessings, local fundraisers, etc., will occasionally take precedence over a planned class, and volunteers are always invited along. We view this as a great benefit of the program and a unique opportunity for the volunteers to experience Buddhism, life in Thailand, and life at a temple. As a volunteer living at a Wat you have several unique opportunities. You can observe daily life and how monks actually live and what they think and feel. While living with and teaching novice monks, you are able to interact with them (and the older ordained monks) on a daily basis. Although there are no scheduled classes or seminars, the monks are eager to teach what they know about Buddhism and the potential to gain knowledge and insight is endless.[14]

For these volunteer tourism organizations, religion becomes something optional to experiment with or to be curious about in a pluralistic manner.

Because of these programs' focus on the difference of the Buddhist way of life, novice monks become an essential component of the experience. When I spoke with the novice monks about why they thought the volunteers came to their classrooms, they had not yet developed a way to explain this phenomenon. For example, Naen Win, a novice monk at Wat Phra Singh's Thammaraj School, responded that he did not know why the volunteers chose to come to teach in his school. But upon further reflection, he said, "The volunteers are probably Christians interested to study and learn about Buddhism. Probably they don't have any Buddhism in their countries. They can get to know the life of the novice monk. They can experience something different and new [Mi prasopkan mai lae taek tang duai]." Naen Supakorn, also studying at Thammaraj School, stated simply: "The volunteers come here because they want to help novice monks. They want to teach us because they want to know about Thailand. They want to know about Buddhism because this is the foundation [chut raek] of Thailand." From this, one can see that novice monks understand the appeal of difference for the volunteers and how Buddhism is part of the brand and identity of Thailand. But they do not have the language for comparison between East and West that volunteer tourists, volunteer tourism organizations, or student monks in the Buddhist universities have. From the novices, one does not hear about how Western countries have more stress and how Thailand can help with that through meditation and the Buddhist ways of life. They do not yet know how to compare religions, nor can they relate arguments about how Buddhism fits nicely into modern life the way that many of the college monks involved in the Monk Chat program can.

Temple school leadership—principals of the temple school and abbots of the temple connected with the school—is a crucial component of the Buddhist volunteer tourism program. Through relationships with temple school principals, volunteer tourist organizations provide the connections necessary for volunteers to experience teaching and living in a Buddhist temple while traveling the region. It is important to note that although the abbots and temples remain in charge of allowing volunteers to come into their classrooms, the volunteer organizations function to administer the volunteer program by advertising, screening potential volunteers, and helping to orient and acclimate new volunteers. With monastic principals and teachers focusing on education and maintaining the temple and school, it is much easier to affiliate with these professional organizations because of their expertise in attracting and locating volunteers. But the orientation volunteer tourism organizations provide, of course, cannot fully prepare the volunteers for all of the experiences and possibilities they will meet when teaching novices and living in a Buddhist temple. While encountering the other in these Buddhist temples and their classrooms, volunteers have their ideas of difference and authentic Asian Buddhism both confirmed and challenged.

Expectations of Difference and Authenticity

For international tourists, the promise of difference and authenticity through encountering "the other" during travel creates unique cultural experiences. In contrast to tourists' inauthentic, modern, and busy lives, the cultural others' static and simple lives have the potential to provide authenticity through "geographic and cultural *difference*" (Jakubiak 2016, 99). It is clear that tourists are interested in authenticity, but they do not always have the tools to discuss why it matters to them (Rickly and Vidon 2018). The volunteer tourists I have spoken with have had a chance to think about their experiences in Thailand but have not reflected on authenticity or, for them, the meaning of Buddhist teachings and practices as much as the student monks in Monk Chat have. Authenticity is a slippery concept, which can beg the question: Does authenticity still matter in tourist settings? Tourism geographers Jillian M. Rickly and Elizabeth S. Vidon believe that it does, "but in ways no one has been able to fully pin down, not even the tourists who are out there searching for it" (2018, preface). Instead of pinning down authenticity, Rickly and Vidon suggest attending to "questions of how authenticity is used, who wants or needs authenticity and why, who authenticates, and what authenticity does" (2). In volunteer English-teaching tourism in Chiang Mai, the volunteer tourists and their expectations, the novice and teacher monks, and the temple space around them all work together to create a sense of "Buddhist authenticity."

Volunteer tourists, being mostly from Europe, North America, and Australia, have a particular kind of Western tourist gaze when considering ideas of Buddhist authenticity. The tourist gaze "refers to 'discursive determinations' of socially constructed seeing," and just "like language, one's eyes are socio-culturally framed and there are various 'ways of seeing'" (Urry and Larsen 2011, 2). A typical, although not universal, Western tourist gaze would find Buddhist authenticity in the calm and simple life of a monk in a tranquil and peaceful temple environment (Bruntz and Schedneck 2020; Geary 2020). This particular gaze would fall under the romantic gaze, where "solitude, privacy and a personal, semi-spiritual relationship with the object of the gaze are emphasized" (Urry and Larsen 2011, 19). However, authenticity exists on a spectrum, revealing differing gazes and expectations based on social patterns and learned ways of seeing (2).

These varying ideas of Buddhist authenticity illuminate the particular positionality of the person vis-à-vis Buddhism. Buddhist authenticity from the Buddhist practitioner gaze would focus on evaluating the most sacred, ancient, and powerful monks and objects as authentic. Of course, there is not a monolithic Buddhist authenticity for the volunteer tourist or the Thai Buddhist practitioner, as any site "can be visually consumed in different ways despite that most are designed and regulated according to specific historic discourse or logic" (Urry and Larsen 2011, 206). For some Thai Buddhists, size matters, with large Buddha statues being perceived as worthy of merit. But for others, historical significance might matter more, regardless of size or the material from which the statue was made. Expectations and previous experiences affect the way one perceives Buddhist authenticity. Imaginaries regarding what Buddhism entails—that is, robed monks, meditation, peace—have come to be perceived as the dominant aspects of the religion from a Western tourist gaze (Geary 2020; Moran 2004, 108). Imaginary, like the tourist gaze, is a key idea in the analysis of anthropology of tourism studies. Both concepts reflect the particular filters—gender, social class, nationality, age, education, religion—through which people approach new environments. As discussed by anthropologists of tourism Noel B. Salazar and Nelson Graburn, imaginaries are defined as "socially transmitted representational assemblages that interact with people's personal imaginings and that are used as meaning-making and world-shaping devices" (2014, 1). Imaginaries connect images and texts to the material world, as they link the individual's thoughts to social locations and specific people (Bruntz and Schedneck 2020). Volunteer tourists' imaginaries of Buddhist authenticity change and adapt as they reflect on their time teaching in the Thai Buddhist temple classroom.

For volunteer tourists' gaze on Thai Buddhism, a Buddhist kind of authenticity is predicated on difference, and difference is contained primarily within one figure: the monk. The Thai Buddhist monk is a symbol of the Thai state and nation (Jerryson 2011, 50). With its majority Buddhist population, the conflation of Buddhism and Thailand becomes a large part of tourist imaginaries of Thailand (Schedneck 2015). As well, the "Oriental Monk" figure within American popular culture, through his nonsexual solitary spirituality, is made acceptable and appealing for mainstream consumption (Iwamura 2011, 22). Monks become representative symbols of Buddhism and values ascribed to it, including peace, kindness, and calmness. Teaching English to monks allows volunteers to interact directly with the people who are perceived to represent the essence of Thai culture.

Volunteer tourists in Thailand choose this alternative mode of travel because of the authenticity it affords, where they are able to directly interact with Thai people.[15] When tourists perceive that they have had intimate encounters with one of the members of the host community, they are likely to interpret their volunteer experience as authentic (Conran 2006, 275). Encountering the other and confronting difference depends of course on one's own lifestyle and worldview, and volunteer organizations employ the perspectives of volunteers from the global North in their promotional materials. The website of Friends for Asia utilizes the ideas of Thailand as a "traditional" society:

> Saffron robes, morning alms and novice monks—and not a tourist in sight. It's hard to believe that such a staunch traditional life still thrives in the 21st century, but Chiang Mai's temple schools are a world away from "everyday." As a volunteer English teacher, you'll experience the difference first-hand. Morning comes early in Chiang Mai's temple schools. As you arrive, novices line up to receive morning announcements from the faculty. Prayer and meditation follow, leading up to the start of class at 8:30 am. Another round of prayer and meditation follows lunch. Education in these temple schools is holistic—a marriage of mind and body rarely seen in the West.[16]

Daily morning activities at a Thai Buddhist temple school here are contrasted with one's life at home. Besides the simplification of daily life in "the West" and the romantic ideas of Buddhist education in Thailand, this statement assumes difference is a sought-after commodity. Why would someone volunteer in a familiar place just like home? The otherness of foreign peoples might aid in "rejuvenating a humdrum domestic culture" (Holland and Huggan 1998, 48). These volunteer organizations have developed specific ways of advertising that display their target audiences' ideas of difference and the other, to create a desire for authentic Buddhist encounters.

Monk teachers understand the appeal of this difference. When I asked why they thought volunteer tourists chose the option of volunteering in a temple school, one monk teacher remarked that the volunteers wanted to exchange (*laek plian*) and experience difference (*prasopkan khwam taek tang*). The volunteer tourists echoed this in interviews, citing the access they, in comparison to regular tourists, had to Thai culture. Felix, a recent college graduate from Germany, reflected: "Monks are interesting students. They pay attention more in the novice school [than in Thai public schools]. You can get some culture in the [Thai] public schools too, but monks can tell you more about Buddhism and Thai culture. . . . The monks, I think, are enjoying how I teach them with the games and entertainment. They really learn something even though the language barrier is big. They come from poor backgrounds, and you can see that this is their only opportunity [to learn and prepare themselves for a job]." The volunteer tourism gaze here sees Buddhist authenticity in the student monks, who embody Buddhist values of discipline and knowledge of the teachings, but who are also part of a student population, which would benefit from volunteers' time in the classroom.

Participating in rituals with Buddhist monks is another experience of difference emphasized by volunteers, which matches their imaginary of authenticity within a Buddhist setting. Hunaid is a middle-aged American who volunteered for two months at Wat Doi Saket. The abbot allowed Hunaid to carry alms for him during the morning alms-round. Hunaid writes: "He also gave me a Thai name, 'Kaa ja-om' which has brought many smiles on Thai faces. It refers to the person who helps the monks on their daily almsrounds. It was a delightful experience as I met many welcoming villagers." He calls volunteering and living in Wat Doi Saket an incredible learning experience: "Without having lived at the wat, I would not have had such a rich experience. Most of all, I would have probably never learned what it takes to go from a novice monk to an ordained monk and what it is like to live as a monk. I did not need an alarm clock as I was woken up each morning at 5am from the sounds of the monks praying and chanting in Pali. Most often, I would go to the mondop [chanting hall] so I could feel the energy of the prayers."[17] For Hunaid, difference relates to the ways he was able to engage with the Buddhist monks and the Thai villagers while following the schedule of daily life in the temple. The idyllic setting of the monks chanting in the temple and collecting alms in the village is part of a Buddhist authenticity that allows volunteer tourists to experience difference along with an intimate encounter with the other.

Volunteers living at the temples in which they taught through the Wat Doi Saket Project were often able to develop relationships with monks, especially those volunteers who were interested in learning more about Buddhism. Brady, an American on a gap year, lived in Wat Sri Soda in Chiang Mai for two months. He wrote of the monks he taught: "The monk friends . . . what can I say? They are awesome. The best people. Most of them are around my age, 18 or 19, and they call me their brother. I hang out with them almost every weeknight, since we all live in the same monastery, and we just seem to connect really well."[18] Similarly, Jonathan, another middle-aged American, wrote to me about his friendships with monks: "I befriended a couple of monks and got to know about their backgrounds and how they happened to become monks. I tutored two novice monks and learned about their life and how they left home and chose to become monks. It was these relationships that engaged me with Buddhism above and beyond just reading about them in some book."[19]

Making friends with these novice students constitutes the authentic interactions that volunteers stress in their communications and memories about their experiences. Felix from Germany also became close with some of the novice monks. He identifies as a Buddhist and discussed this with some of his students one day: "The novice monks always have a good mood. I am impressed the way that everything is connected from their religion and culture. It is surprising to the novices that I am a Buddhist. During lunch one day during the first week, I spoke with the novice monks about this. They had many questions for me, such as, 'How long can you meditate?' When I said I usually meditate about one-half hour to one hour, they got very excited, saying they can only meditate for twenty minutes. They never expected to meet a Westerner who is a Buddhist." Buddhist authenticity involves making friends with the hospitable and kind monks these volunteers encountered.

In the Friends for Asia Teaching English to Monks orientation handbook, one former volunteer advised: "The only thing that's important to remember, especially if you're a woman, is to not touch them. But the distance that comes with that is totally taken away by their friendliness." The genuineness of the novice monks is appreciated and, despite their rules, they make the experience authentic. The difference is also confirmed in the classroom setting. As Chanel, a recent college graduate from the United States, found: "Because of Buddhism, the novice monks respect their elders so much and there is always formality when I start class and when it ends. They [the novice monks] all stand and greet me and thank me at the end. I have never seen such respect, and I think this is the primary thing in their culture." Another aspect of Buddhist authenticity from the volunteer tourist gaze, and reinforced through their experiences, is the calmness and low-stress environment they find in the schools. Felix recalled about the teachers and novice monks: "These are people who do not stress about anything. They are always in a good mood. It is very different in Germany." Not just calmness, but a concern for others is also impressive. Felix continued: "In one class, I have two blind students. The amount of care and attention they receive, you would never see in Germany—it's unfortunate. But they don't have to ask, if they need anything, the other students get up to help them and take them to the bathroom or whatever." While the students were working in groups on a worksheet that he had handed to them, Felix sighed and said to me, "I will really miss this." Specifically, he said he would miss the students. "They all have a smile, laugh, something funny they do. In Germany the students would not act like this. They are more serious, less joyful." Here Buddhist values of friendliness, peacefulness, and a lack of selfishness fulfill the imaginaries of difference and authenticity for these volunteer tourists.

The temple space also serves to create the particular sense of Buddhist authenticity from the volunteer tourist gaze. International volunteers' most memorable moments highlight difference, which engages multiple senses: seeing the sunrise and the orange robes of monks, the novice monks' smiles and laughter, and the glittering golden Buddha statues and hearing the Pali chanting of the monks and bells chiming in the morning and evening. These sensory moments match the experience of visitors hoping for differ-ence. Participating in the daily schedule of the temple can meet sensory expectations of Buddhism. Lauren, a middle-aged American volunteer at Wat Suan Dok, echoes this emphasis on difference: "It was all so different from anything I have ever experienced. The chanting, the rules of respect, taking off shoes. . . . This was all very different for me." Volunteers who live at the temple process difference and authenticity through the aesthetic beauty of the temple and Buddhist material culture. Brady commented on his blog about the beauty of the architecture, murals, golden statues, and pillars and also the sonorous sounds of chanting: "Every morning and evening, close to dawn and dusk, the temple grounds are filled with the wholesome, peaceful sound of the monks chanting in the ancient Buddhist language of Pali." But he also points out other forms of difference that are not as pleasant: "In other places, it is not so beautiful, such as in the perma-nently damp bathrooms (all of them are uber moist!), or in the massive and fragrant open-air garbage dump that sits just outside the . . . cafeteria. Yum."[20] The negative and positive forms of difference are interesting here, as both are still very far from his life in the United States. But since Buddhist forms of authenticity for the volunteer tourist are located within a develop-ing country, the lack of modern amenities and waste systems are an expected part of difference.

Victoria, a recent college graduate from England, wrote that a favorite activity during her volunteer period was meditating in temples—an authentic experience and encounter with difference in the space of the cultural other. She also experienced such moments during the school day: "Before lunch there's always a chanting of thanks, which completely moved me to my very soul the first time I heard it. It was all overwhelmingly beautiful, the temple, the kindness, the peace and serenity of it all, I shall never forget those first feelings."[21] The difference of the ritual and the sounds and participation in the life of the temple community create a feeling of wonder that matches the imaginaries of Buddhist authenticity highlighted by volunteers.

Experiencing the temple space, speaking with monks, and being a part of their classroom routine constitute the ideas of Buddhist authenticity and difference volunteers hoped for. In an interview, Nina told me that she wanted to live in a Buddhist temple to learn about new ways of life and cultures: "I want to know who I really am and test myself by entering into new situations. I don't want to be another *farang* [Westerner] in a resort or tourist market." Instead, she sought the authentic experience of meeting and interacting with Buddhist monks. Mary, a young college graduate from Austria who volunteered for two weeks, said about her experience: "You can't get this kind of experience when you are just a tourist. These people [the students and teachers at the temple school] always stay so calm. Everyone in Austria is stressed about everything, but in Thailand there are many holidays. This contributes to the lack of stress." The volunteers are able to encounter the iconic figure of Thailand, the Buddhist monk, who embodies qualities that fit within the imaginary of Buddhism—friendliness, compassion, and calmness. The temple space and the rituals as well, with their aesthetic beauty and difference, highlight the expected Buddhist authenticity that volunteer tourists sought to encounter. Although this expected form of difference is interesting and exciting for volunteers, challenging perceptions of difference and Buddhist authenticity is another possibility of encounter, which can lead to transforming the self.

Challenging Difference and Authenticity

Anthropologist Peter Moran (2004, 89) has found that Western Buddhists living in Nepal after some time had come to develop what they perceived as a "more realistic view of monks," compared to that of tourists who had just arrived and stayed for perhaps a few weeks or less. The same is true in Thailand; as travelers who have had little prior exposure to monasticism spend time with monks, the more realistic the picture gets. Political economist

Nick Kontogeorgopoulos (2016) has found these English-teaching programs to be a good example of how volunteer tourism can disrupt preconceptions. He writes: "Such volunteers are initially attracted to monks and temples because they are seen as esoteric embodiments of essential Thai culture, but direct interactions with monks ultimately shatter these stereotypes and produce a less ethereal image of monks" (9). Rather than confirming religious stereotypes of the authentic monk, the Buddhist volunteer tourism experience allows for change and growth.

Volunteer tourists must deal with cultural perspectives and worldviews that are challenging and surprising given their initial expectations (Skinner and Theodossopoulos 2011). In some intersections of Buddhism and tourism, if expectations of difference are not met, the Buddhist religion, the temple space, and the lives of monks can be critiqued. The Laos government commodified the culture and religion of the country beginning in the early 1990s, especially Luang Prabang, as a place of "romanticism and royal mystique" (Holt 2009, 187). During this period, novice monks' ritual activity of the morning alms-round became a major tourist attraction (197). Because of their expectations of Buddhism and Buddhist monks as exclusively serene and contemplative, French and other Euro-American tourists sometimes critique Luang Prabang's novices (191). This critique is evident when any form of commercial activity is seen in the temple space (Schedneck 2015, 106). The particular Western imaginaries of a Buddhist authenticity is at odds with the reality of novice monks sitting in Internet cafés, being outside of the temple in the afternoon, and answering cell phones (Holt 2009, 193).

As a consequence of the Western imaginaries of Buddhist monasticism, when novices and monks do not act like perfect mindful embodiments of Buddhist ideals, tourists' expectations in Laos are not realized. In contrast to these tourists' impressions in Laos, the volunteers' experiences in Thai Buddhist temples are more immersive. Because they have extended exposure and possibilities for understanding the temple community, their response to the similarly unexpected behaviors and actions of novice monk students was, for the most part, accepted rather than critiqued, adding to the perceived authenticity of the temple setting and the monks themselves. Chanel remarked, "[I] thought there would be strict rules to follow, but once you're here, it's totally different. I heard about all these rules for what monks can and can't do, but there's actually a lot of freedom. It's not what others tell you. You have to experience it for yourself." Authenticity is found in the encounters with monks and other temple community members, even if they are not fully meeting the imaginary of a regimented monastic life held by the volunteers.

What is authentic Buddhism and who are authentic Buddhist monks to volunteer tourists? Unlike authenticity involving cultural tourism to the Trobriand Islands of Papua New Guinea (MacCarthy 2016) or the indigenous hill tribe groups of northern Thailand (Novelli and Tisch-Rottensteiner 2012; Prasit 2005), where there is a vague sense that authenticity equals living in a premodern state with poverty, traditional outfits, and no electricity, there are specific ideas about Buddhism and Buddhist monks' authenticity for volunteer tourists. It is clear from discussions with many of the participants in Buddhist-related volunteer tourism that there is even a kind of cognitive dissonance that exists between their expectations of Buddhist monks and the reality they experience. During one lesson about hobbies, the volunteer teacher's examples included chanting and meditating. To practice the new sentence patterns, she asked one monk if he liked meditating. When he answered, "No, I don't," the volunteer teacher was very surprised, checking to confirm that he had understood the question. This disparity between authentic Buddhism and the real monk, however, does not detract from the overall experience. It is the intimate, genuine encounter with monks, the surprising nature of their performance as monastics, that makes the experience worthwhile and that promotes self-transformation. Intimate experiences in the classroom with monks, rather than confirming the imagined authenticity of the monastic life, actually change volunteer tourists' perceptions about who a monk is and how Buddhism functions in society. As a consequence, volunteer tourists create a new understanding of Buddhist authenticity.

English-teaching volunteers in Thailand expect difference and authenticity where they will come to know the other and gain cultural capital back home. However, most volunteers, after being asked about their experience, respond that Buddhist monks are "just like regular people." This familiarity is surprising but not criticized by the volunteers who were expecting a space apart from modernity. Bridget, a recent college graduate from the United States, said this to me in an interview after her experience teaching for a month at Wat Phra Singh: "I thought the classroom would have a much more serious feel to it." But she learned through her interactions with the novices that "they can be loud and rowdy." Mary, a nineteen-year-old Austrian volunteer, stated with a laugh, "They can even be a little bit flirty." One of the Friends for Asia staff joked that the novice monks were even louder and more excited on that day, when three young ladies (*saw*) were in the classroom—the volunteer, the staff member, and me. Indeed, once when I was observing a female volunteer tourist bending low to write English words on the board, I noticed many of the novice monks looking very intently at her bottom. When I told her that, she laughed and resolved not to bend down so far again. Beyond the aesthetic differences of the temple space and monastic robes, the monastic life is more similar to familiar attitudes than imagined.

The placement coordinator at Friends for Asia stated that volunteers choose the teaching monks program because they want to experience something "other." However, during the course of the teaching, they soon discover that novices are not holy boys, just boys. She remembers that one volunteer was shocked when some novices took off their outer robes and started fighting. Volunteers expect that monks will not break any of their rules and then wonder why they see some monks eating after noon, playing sports, or smoking, all of which are officially prohibited by senior monks. They see monks with smartphones or chatting on Facebook and wonder how they could afford this luxury. Where do they get the money? Shouldn't they live simply? Volunteers are attracted to difference and the experience of a nontypical tourist with special access to the other. When the other acts unexpectedly, volunteers are challenged to think about difference and reevaluate their perceptions of authenticity. Ann, a Friends for Asia volunteer from the United States who taught at the Pali Satit School at Wat Suan Dok, shared similar sentiments from her own experience: "I find myself judging the monks sometimes. The ways they act, like hitting each other. I wonder if this is part of their rules, because it's such a different lifestyle. I see them using cell phones and sitting at cafés. But I learned that their precepts are not like commandments. They are training so they can keep working toward following their goals. They are normal people but wear robes."

Sally, a thirty-three-year-old American, perhaps because of her age demographic, which was higher than that of the mostly gap year or recent college graduates who participate in volunteer tourism, did not totally accept or feel comfortable with the unexpected ordinariness of monks. Although she considered the temple where she taught to be very welcoming and supportive, with a beautiful atmosphere, she found that she became less naive about Buddhism and Buddhist monks: "I have seen a lot of weird things—monks with cell phones, and behaviors, like with women, and experienced a weird interaction with a monk myself, and you also hear similar things I wouldn't expect. I guess you just have to separate monks from Buddhism. It made me a little disillusioned and disappointed. It just rubs me the wrong way, but I guess that is why Thai people have said to me, 'Just respect the robe.' Overall it [volunteer teaching in the temple school] was awesome, but sometimes, I just wonder about the Buddhist religion." Sally experienced learning and growth, but that did not translate into a totally positive experience. The negative things she experienced and heard about the monastic life left her feeling ambivalent about the "authenticity" she encountered.

Popular media and culture perpetuate impossible stereotypes of monks as silent, stoic, wise, and always in a meditative repose. However, when these expectations of monks' behavior and demeanor are not met, for the most part, volunteer tourists adjust their ideas to match reality. Mike, a young man from Switzerland, wanted to volunteer in order to explore an interest in Buddhism he had had since high school. He hoped that by living at the monastery he would experience the lifestyle of a Buddhist. However, he was surprised at how flexible the schedule was and how comfortable the young novices seemed in their environment. Because there was less distance than he expected, he was able to create more close relationships and form a more realistic understanding of monastic life in Thailand.[22]

Authenticity, as a form of intimacy, is found in the encounters with monks, even if they do not fully meet the ideals volunteers hold. Jim took part of his summer vacation to volunteer through Friends for Asia after taking a college course on Buddhism. He was placed at Wat Phan Tao and assisted with conversation classes for first- and second-year middle school students. He was surprised by the technology monks used, as he thought Buddhism valued silence and contemplation. In an interview, he said: "The monks don't follow the rule about entertainment and are clapping, singing, dancing, especially to K-pop [Korean pop music]." He was surprised by this ordinariness: "I think I wanted to see the monks in Thailand with my own eyes, more so than actually learning about Buddhism here [Thailand] academically." The difference of the experience was attractive, but Jim was more interested in reality, as his main objective was to see how monks really lived by observing and interacting with them.

Rather than being perceived as a failure because the experience does not deliver the expected authenticity, volunteer tourism has the potential to challenge and stimulate, leading to insights about the self. Some volunteers are practitioners of Buddhism who want to learn more about the practice beyond meditation, hoping to integrate new knowledge into their lives at home. Jonathan lived at Wat Doi Saket for two months because of his curiosity about lived Buddhism, calling himself a Buddhist. He was interested in volunteering as a way to add a broader understanding of the religion to his planned meditation retreat:

> I did not have any idea whatsoever as to what a life of a monk is like, except that they live in a monastery and go out for alms to deliver blessings to the local residents. I certainly had no idea that there would be novice monks living in the temple; as a matter of fact, I did not even know of the concept of a novice monk or for that matter how a person comes about being a monk. It was my basic understanding that a person can give up their worldly belongings and move into a monastery and start meditating.

He was surprised to find that monks are not all perfect beings who dedicate their lives to silent contemplation: "Now, when I see a monk, I know what he has gone through to get where he is and I see him more as a person."[23] Despite this perceived lack of difference and unmet expectations, Jonathan described himself as a transformed person, intellectually and emotionally, because of this volunteering experience.

In this way, the Buddhist monk becomes not a representative of the culture but rather a unique individual. Teaching the monks, even for a short while, challenges the perspectives of volunteers and debunks some of the popular cultural myths about the monastic life. During one English lesson, when the novice monks were asked about their future plans, the volunteer tourist was surprised by the two most popular answers: to become a soldier and to own a coffee shop. These interactions personalize the monk who volunteers otherwise would imagine to be an isolated, passive figure fully dedicated to the monastic life with no interest or opportunity to speak with them. The thing Jonathan found most surprising was that all monks are different: some are loud, some do not meditate, and some are quiet. He had put monks on a pedestal before, thinking they were more than human. He wrote: "There were many stores inside the temple for monks to buy things for their daily consumption—this I had not expected. I had just never thought about monks having any money to buy simple things. It had never occurred to me that monks have to swim in the same water as we all do."[24] The first realization for many of these participants is that monks are people too. This opens them up for further exchanges that come to be seen as authentically Buddhist despite their unmet expectations of the other. Ideas about Buddhist authenticity from the volunteer tourist gaze can move the monk figure beyond assumptions of calmness and peace, to becoming real people with flaws who are still training to be proper Buddhist monks.

Processes of self-transformation for volunteers occur when differences and expectations are challenged. As the volunteers learn about the monastic life, they gain insight into themselves, often calling their immersive volunteer experiences transformative or life changing.

Transformations of the Self

Stories one tells about oneself serve to construct an identity—one's self, one's narrative. The stories people narrate about travel create a new kind of self, one set apart from their everyday life, and one in which a new identity can form. New information about the self is integrated into one's personal narrative, especially after a challenging experience. Travel reveals a shifting and continually reformulating notion of the self in contemporary life. "Self-transformation" and "self-discovery" are terms used often in tourism literature as well as religious discourses. In this area, travel and religion overlap as ways to understand the self. Anthropologist Erica Bornstein (2012) writes that "the attraction of volunteering lies in its promise of a transformative experience—one that may seem structurally similar to a religious experience; yet it differs from spiritual transformation in its categorization as a secular practice" (119). The real value in the exchange then becomes "the gift of experience from the recipient to the donor" (139). Examined from a history of religions perspective, the idea of the self as lacking and in need of transformation has been found to be regularly patterned across religious traditions but at the same time culturally determined (Shulman and Stroumsa 2002, 4). Buddhist ideas of positive self-transformation bring the person, paradoxically, away from the idea of a permanent self that can be changed, and toward the idea of enlightenment, or *nibbana*, where, from the Buddhist point of view, myths of an independent, inherently existing self are debunked. Religions often put forth these challenging paths toward transformation; however, travel posits, perhaps, a more manageable kind of self-change.

Along with self-transformation, the rhetoric of discovering and searching for the self has been a motif in travel writing and tourist literature.[25] Academic analysis, by contrast, has focused more on the constructed nature of the self, rather than an essential self that one might locate during travel. Nevertheless, whether the self is transformed or discovered, essential or constructed, travel instigates reflection on the self. Unlike pilgrimage tourism, such as walking the Camino de Santiago in Europe (Norman 2011) or attending a meditation retreat in Thailand (Schedneck 2015), where pilgrims and meditators are purposely undertaking a solitary journey, in many cases to work through a problem at home, volunteer tourism is less intentionally reflective. However, research on volunteer tourism has argued that the experience can lead to a greater awareness of oneself and others and contribute to self-development (Wearing 2001). Volunteer tourists, because of the nature of their activities, which often involve challenging one's values and ideals, along with exposure to different ways of life, can lose the sense of self and identity they usually have within their home environments (Kontogeorgopoulos 2017, 4). The nature of difference involved in volunteer tourism, as well as the liminal space and time, serves to create opportunities for self-exploration and self-making (6).

Self-discovery is evident in foreign tourist interactions with hill tribe groups and sex workers in Thailand, where tourists feel a sense of humanity that they discern as real (Johnson 2007). This ability to discern authenticity becomes a part of their new identities. In this way, encounters with Thai people that feel "real," as in sincere and genuine human interactions, become more important than "authentic" settings. I could see this with my university students whenever I took them to have a conversation with Buddhist monks. Even though their conversations were in a small room without many markers of Buddhism, when they talked about each other's daily lives, there was a sense of awe among the students that two people from such disparate backgrounds could communicate and understand each other in such a simple and direct way. When difference becomes familiar, when the idea of authenticity shifts, so can the self in small ways. Because the monks have similar concerns and ideas about the world, their lifestyle is seen not as something totally foreign, but instead as a possibility for reflecting on the tourist's lifestyle at home.

Unlike self-transformation, there were very few narratives of self-discovery and searching for the self among the volunteers I spoke with. Although not encountering and reflecting upon the nature of poverty, like many volunteer tourists, they interact with a classroom filled with young boys and men whose lifestyle is alternative to the ones they are used to. For many of the volunteer tourists, an unexpected shift occurred when asked about their experiences with Buddhism and their takeaways at the end of their volunteer experience. They compared their homes, communities, and countries with aspects of Buddhist monasticism, and sometimes this led to an aspiration to change their lifestyles and values. When volunteers consider the lives of the monks they have taught, they have a different perspective from which to evaluate and judge their own lives.

A number of studies have analyzed narratives of self-transformation within volunteer tourism (Allon and Koleth 2014; Lepp 2008; Wearing, Deville, and Lyons 2008; Wickens 2011; Zahra 2011). This literature highlights newfound perseverance, mental creativity, broadened perspectives, and the ability to challenge oneself, expand one's possibilities, and create a cosmopolitan identity through international friendships (Mostafanezhad 2014, 111; Neumann 1992). Volunteer tourists in India describe a transformative experience that includes "apprehension, anxiety before the adventure, a loss of self and transformation in the rural environment, and a return to their former life with a new perspective and appreciation for their structural position in the world" (Bornstein 2012, 132). Part of this transformation occurs through the realization that although the space the volunteer entered into was entirely alien, it became familiar and intimate over time.

Volunteers in Thai Buddhist temples do not often comment on comparisons between West and East, development and nondevelopment, or materialism and the simple life, but instead remark on particular ways of being that they noticed and valued within a Buddhist culture. Although volunteers' motivations often include "giving back" and "making a difference," the experience serves to mobilize self-reflection and insight into oneself because of the sustained periods spent within foreign communities. Volunteers come to learn about and appreciate Thai Buddhism as they are immersed in a Buddhist environment. However, because of the limited time frame and the lack of thorough study, their knowledge of Buddhist doctrines remains superficial. The volunteers narrated changes in themselves, which were more directly related to the new experiences, the new environment, and the unexpected familiarity of monks' lifestyles than to any particular Buddhist insight into the nature of the self.

In exit interviews with volunteers in the Teaching English to Monks program, the director of Friends for Asia, Todd Cikraji, found that the volunteers often respond that they learned to relax and take a different outlook on life that is less focused on details. In their writings and in my interviews with them, volunteers focus on the experiences that indicate their transformations. Felix, on returning to Germany after four weeks at the Thammaraj School, described how observing the novice monks changed him: "I'm now more calm in many situations than I was before. They [the novice monks] really taught me that even though something goes wrong, this is not a reason to feel bad for the whole day. I guess that's the biggest change that happened to me after I came back to Germany. I'm now just smiling throughout the whole day."[26] Because of the calm and resilience he observed, he has decided to try out different meditation techniques in order to cultivate that demeanor. Buddhist volunteer tourism thus allows one to learn about another way of life and to see which aspects can fit into life at home.

In addition to realigning values and taking on Buddhist practices, volunteers transform themselves by using the body in different ways. Amanda, a young American teacher, commented on how she had to adopt behaviors she was unaccustomed to when teaching the novice monks: "When you pass a monk, get out of the way so he can go first, stay a few steps behind him, lower your head if you are walking by a monk, when you see a monk, wai [a hand gesture to pay respect] deeply to him." This reverence is especially so for women, as she described: "[I learn to] hold an object with both hands and set it down for the monk to pick up, and when he wants to hand something to me, I cup my hands so he can drop the object and we do not touch." She also tries not to sit next to a monk or touch an object at the same time he does. She feels awkward when she looks at a monk for too long or converses with locked eyes. All of this brings an attention to the body that Amanda has not felt before. She also discussed her relationship to her body outside of interactions with monks: "I'm walking slower, breathing slower, I move around things and reposition things with much more precision as I try not to make noises. None of that is necessary, they're just byproducts of being constantly cautious and trying not to offend." She also admits that, surprisingly, she, in turn, is not offended by the ways the monks treat her, calling her fat and commenting when her hair is wet. Uncharacteristically, she is not insulted but instead has learned to "let it go" and not be concerned with how she looks.[27] The distinct social norms and behaviors she encountered in this environment can motivate these personal transformations.

Brady valued the exchange he was able to have with "his" monks, as detailed in his blog post titled "The Size of My Shoes and the Eiffel Tower: A Thank You to ATMA SEVA and My Monks." He describes the shock the monks feel when comparing their foot sizes to this presumably tall foreign man. A similar difficulty is found when Brady attempts to illustrate how tall the Eiffel Tower is. In both instances, Brady finds the monks' lack of worldly experience refreshing and extraordinary. From this experience, he writes: "I hope that I will be able to channel some of the shock I saw in my monk friends, and allow myself to better appreciate just how extraordinary and incredible things in this world really are. Learning to see the world in new ways is one huge benefit I've gained from living in Thailand."[28]

Many volunteers who lived in the Buddhist temple reflect on comparisons between the monastic life and their own. Volunteers noted the ways they think differently as a result of their observations and the lifestyles they experienced at the temple. This is especially evident when they return home. Mike, from Switzerland, reflected on changes in his perspectives of his home country: "I definitely learned a lot and changed quite a bit in different views and opinions. I think one of the most beautiful things I learned is *metta*, the lovingkindness.... And now when I talk to people from home (Switzerland), I realise how different they see certain things. One of my friends for example couldn't believe that people were actually giving food on alms round without expecting anything back. That really shocked me, but also showed me how much I have learned regarding generosity."[29] Mike saw *metta*, or lovingkindness, the attitude of friendliness and generosity, embodied each morning as lay Buddhists offered food to monks. He had internalized this value without noticing it. Only when his Swiss friends at home challenged this value did he realize how the volunteer experience had changed him.

Another aspect of Buddhism that volunteers mark as transformative is its meditation practice. Although these volunteer experiences are not meditation retreats, some volunteers are exposed to meditation for the first time. Sam, a young British volunteer, when asked if his life in England was different after his experience teaching and living at the temple, responded: "The truth is, my time at the temple in Thailand was really my first exposure to a meditation practice and was one of the first steps I took in exploring a contemplative lifestyle. Now I am deeply involved in several types of spiritual practices, including meditating as often as possible, and I have started to make a 'career' out of creating spaces for people to have transformative experiences. I can trace my experience at the temple as being one of the first major events that set my current path in motion."[30]

After Sam took the opportunity to practice meditation while teaching the novice monks, this initial exploration led to a deep involvement in meditation and spiritual practice. Joanie, a British volunteer in her thirties at Wat Saraphi, has also taken Buddhist meditation seriously as a result of her encounter with the temple and monks: "I've always wanted a peaceful and happy life, so Buddhism and I go wonderfully together, but meditation has definitely helped me to be wiser and even more patient and I'm already very laid back! Buddhism has helped me to find faith in humanity again."

She credits the older novices and monks with teaching her how to meditate and breathe, which she finds not only deepens her values but also helps her to be a better person.

Along with the expected difference of being exposed to Buddhist teachings and meditation, volunteers also highlighted their interactions with monks as creating changes in themselves. Jonathan describes his volunteering at Wat Doi Saket as transformative: "It was the monastic life and its connection to the people that have stood out the most and which I feel has given me a day to day perspective where things that seemed so frustrating in the past are just not as important. . . . For me, even at this late age, spending 2 months in Chiang Mai was a life affecting experience . . . the 2 months at Doi Saket has given me a new point of reference."[31]

Encountering new lifestyles allows volunteers to reflect on their own worldviews, while the difference of the environment reminds them of the newness and unfamiliarity of the experience. Their volunteer work is centered not on improved material development but on interpersonal interactions with their hosts. This becomes one of the most salient and transformative aspects of Buddhist volunteer tourism.

Joanie also discussed the ways the unexpected familiarity with the monks changed her focus from not just learning about Buddhism to also teaching the monks English. She said: "I was surprised, nicely surprised, with the way the novices took to me and made me feel a part of the school, wanting to talk to me outside lessons, and the patience and compassion that goes with the teaching at the temple school is just bliss. The novices made me want to stay and try to be a good teacher for them—they made me change my mind about being a teacher."

From these narratives it is clear that volunteers learned not only about Buddhism and how to teach English, but also about themselves. For many, the trip to Thailand is taken as a wish for personal change, using tourism as transformation. The experience offers a model of an alternative way of life that is informed by both the expected differences and the unexpected familiarity of the temple environment and the lives of the novice monks.

Along with experiencing and questioning difference, the appeal and goal of volunteer tourism for international visitors is the possibility of sampling and experimenting with not just Buddhist ideas but a distinctive way of life, leading to transformations of the self. Although some of the similarity is unexpected, as the monks' lives are more modern than imagined, this makes the volunteers' interactions more memorable. It is the mixture of experiencing difference as well as challenging ideas of Buddhist authenticity that aids in transforming the self for volunteers in Buddhist temple schools. Learning about oneself, gaining experience, and experiencing a new region of the world are some of the benefits that have taken on increased significance in the business of volunteer tourism. Instead of making a developing region more developed, volunteer tourists seek to take away new models and lifestyle aspirations from their experiences in the Buddhist temple schools' classrooms.

These encounters illustrate one of the ways that Buddhism reaches out to new communities, leading to new formations of the self for foreign volunteer tourists. Travelers do not often commit fully to the religion but are, nonetheless, transformed in significant ways, pointing to Buddhist values of loving-kindness, calmness, and mindfulness. Instead of an interest in philosophical and complex Buddhist teachings, travelers who engage with Buddhism in long-term contexts report subtle changes such as an increased attention to the body and enhanced value placed on generosity. The literature on self-transformation through travel demonstrates how the experience often serves to mobilize self-reflection and insight into oneself because of the sustained periods spent within foreign communities (Bruner 1991; Wickens 2011; Zahra 2011).

Cultural difference can often be detected and expressed at the level of the body (Jobs and Mackenthun 2011, 9). It is first noted within physical difference—dress, behavior, and movement. Because communication is often difficult within cultural and religious encounters, bodily appearances take on heightened importance. Volunteer tourists noticed the different dress of the monks they were teaching but were also focused on the ways they had to present themselves—moving carefully, behaving calmly, and not getting too close to their students, especially for women. As a result, changes in the body are one of the ways tourists understand their own self-transformation after encountering Buddhism. Noticing small movements while walking, eating, and teaching, volunteer tourists narrate a heightened awareness of the self in relation to others. In noticing these changes during religious encounters, a new knowledge of the self is formed, so that volunteer tourists begin to describe their values in new ways. Volunteer tourists express increased commitment and openness to alternative lifestyles and, for some, Buddhist practice and a Buddhist religious identity.

English-teaching volunteers in Thai temple schools seek what they understand to be a Buddhist authenticity and difference. Buddhist temple spaces, from the volunteer tourist gaze, are imagined as pristine, beautiful, and quiet enough to meditate in. In some cases, this is found through sensory modes, as volunteers, in interviews and blog posts, often mentioned listening to chanting every morning and evening, seeing the gold statues in the temple buildings, and smelling the incense, candles, and flowers during rituals. The imaginary of the Buddhist monk fulfills initial ideas of Buddhist authenticity through embodying values of peace and calmness. However, beyond this superficial difference, the temple has many surprisingly normal and modern elements, including coffee shops and commercial items available in the temple, along with cheeky, undisciplined novice monks who have a surprising knowledge of global popular culture. These similarities between the volunteers and the monks are accepted rather than critiqued, creating a new, more realistic idea of Buddhist authenticity and indicating that volunteer tourism functions differently than other forms of tourism. This occurs because of the nature of the exposure to local life and the length of time many of the volunteers spend in Thailand. Volunteers come to understand monastics as regular people but are also able to imagine an alternative worldview and take some of these ideas and practices into their own lives.

Both the expected difference and the unexpected familiar offer an opportunity to reflect on the self and how one has changed. The volunteers are proud of their new knowledge, their understanding of new social norms, and their ability to debunk the popular myths of Buddhism and the monk's life. These discourses of self-transformation do not include broad reflections on materialism or capitalism but tend to be grounded in interactions with people and the temple space. Volunteers' encounters with monks, the temple community, and the aesthetic environment of the temple demonstrate that difference as well as familiarity can be significant for narratives of self-transformation.

The dynamic encounter process, as has been observed in India, "produces and transforms notions of cultural boundaries" (Viehbeck 2017, 10). A focus on relational encounters helps to highlight how volunteer tourists in Buddhist temple schools understand and process their own experiences. Having what they describe as an authentic experience with a Buddhist monk is a highlight for many tourists and students who visit Chiang Mai. In a number of instances, an ongoing relationship is formed where the monks and travelers keep in contact via email and Facebook. These friendships signal a cosmopolitanism for both parties—where difference indicates a cultured person who has relationships with many kinds of people. These visible friendships, especially with photos on Facebook and Instagram, allow both monks and foreign travelers to declare to others their status and the type of person they are. In this way, both groups desire to learn about and have an authentic, intimate (if also reproduced on social media) experience with the other.

Personal growth and transformation is one of the results of Buddhist encounters in Chiang Mai. The global connections between volunteer tourists and Buddhist monks are not always smooth, but for those volunteer tourists who engage with the religion for a sustained period, the connections demonstrate the possibilities of encountering Buddhism and returning home with increased reflexivity and new, enhanced values. The friction of volunteer tourism creates pathways for global motion and encounters, and its effects can be inspiring and empowering.

CONCLUSION

SPACES OF ENCOUNTER OFFER A WINDOW INTO THE WAYS BUDDHISM is constructed in global contexts. Buddhist encounters do not simply occur naturally because of education, tourism, and urbanization. Instead, Buddhists utilize these conjunctures when creating programs, opportunities, innovations, and resources in order to engage with the friction of global connections in ways that benefit their communities, temple spaces, and religion. Thai Buddhism is continually reproduced and coproduced in its interconnection across difference. Despite what might seem to be awkward, unequal, and unstable qualities of these encounters, student monks in Chiang Mai have focused on the creativity possible through exchange. Although commodification and city life may appear to overwhelm sacred spaces and infringe on their authenticity, urban lifestyles do not signal only shopping malls and noisy tourists with cameras. Urbanization also has generated spaces for religious and cultural exchange.

The city of Chiang Mai is a magnet for different people for different reasons. For young Buddhist men from Thailand or other Theravada Buddhist regions of Asia, Chiang Mai is a center of Buddhist education where they can also learn and practice English. For Chinese tourists, Chiang Mai is a trendy spot to spend a few days after seeing the natural landscapes, Buddhist temples, and amenities featured in the Chinese movie *Lost in Thailand*. For English-speaking tourists, the city is part of the national brand and image of Thailand as a Buddhist country filled with ancient culture. Along with the city of Chiang Mai, the Buddhist temple has different meanings and resonances. Student monks notice Western tourists who are eager to converse with them in Monk Chat and join their classrooms as volunteer tourists. Many Westerners use the space as a site of learning and

158

engagement with the religion and culture, and student monks praise this. The student monks also see Chinese tourists who are interested less in engagement than in taking pictures and hurrying through the space. Such tourists have some devotional practices that are different from Thai prostration, and the monks respect that they are worshipping the Buddha in their own way. Thai Buddhists, the student monks told me, know how to act in this space and support Buddhism, although local Thai Buddhists may not be interested in learning from student monks. For student monks, the temple is a place to live, get an education, and meet with friends and teachers, and it is the space where they enact their roles as monks by conducting ritual activity, preparing for ceremonies, and spreading the Buddhist teachings. That the temple space contains different meanings for different groups signals the unstable aspects of global interaction. However, Thai Buddhist monks attempt to assert and maintain their view of the space with signs, fees, and regulations for non-Buddhists entering the temple.

Some senior monks, who are focused on administration and temple management, view the different tourist groups through a distinct lens. Chinese tourists can be disruptive to the site through their behavior, as they are known to be less concerned about the sacred nature of the temple. Western tourists can also be problematic when they use the space in their own ways, such as practicing yoga on temple grounds or wearing inappropriate beach clothing to the temple (Schedneck 2020). For senior monks, the most important temple visitors are the Thai Buddhists, whether they are domestic tourists or locals. These visitors know how to make merit, an important part of the temple experience, which generates donations. Although senior monks are often more wary of non-Buddhists than the student monks are, it is clear that the friction of such encounters is not a "synonym for resistance" (Tsing 2005, 6). There is compromise in this friction and contestation over the nature of the temple, but there is no opposition to tourist entry.

The heightened levels of tourism and urbanization in the city of Chiang Mai have created debates about the nature of the temple's place within an urban environment. Some temples have taken advantage of new populations by creating fee structures and shops to generate income, not without criticism. The various audiences that participate in Buddhist cultural exchange programs have generated varying attitudes toward religious others for monastic participants. Members of one particular group, Western tourists, are seen to be the most likely candidates for spreading Buddhism. Because of tourists' interest in Buddhism, cultural exchange programs become a way for monks to practice English and also to think about both informal and formal practices of Buddhist missionizing. The economics of sacred spaces, attitudes toward religious others, and the meaning of the missionary category are significant results of the conjunctures of education, tourism, and urbanization in Chiang Mai. As well, when communities of Buddhist monks encounter religious and cultural others, self-transformation can often result. For volunteer tourists, this is a new sense of authenticity, and for student monks, personal development and renewed commitment to Buddhism.

Effects of Buddhist Encounters for Student Monks

Buddhist monks mention their expanded view of the world and broader aspirations for travel, study, and missionizing as a result of encountering foreigners. In response to the question "How have you changed as a result of participating in Buddhist cultural exchange programs?" student monks narrated their new ideas, personal developments, and increased study, faith, and dedication to their religion. Some student monks compared tourists and monks, or Westerners and Asian people. Phra Maha Mitra said of the volunteer tourists he has worked with: "It's a big thing for them, the volunteers, I think, because they come so far and are in a new place with new people and culture. They have big idea to teach, to help, they have volunteer mind to teach English to us. Maybe it [the experience] is bigger for them than for novice monk. When volunteer comes, they [the novices] just laugh, it's [learning/speaking English] very funny for them."

Although the experience is perhaps more novel and stimulating for volunteer tourists, Monk Chat monks often articulate the new ideas that arise from speaking with foreigners. Phra Maha Mitra has experience as both a student of volunteer tourists and a Monk Chat monk: "[The tourists] give me new ideas I would never think about. One man came and he showed us how to make a logo on Photoshop. I would have never thought to do this. The foreigners always think big, have ideas to change things and see problems, but we don't think this way."

Other monks also found the experience of speaking with international travelers every day opened them up to new perspectives and ways of thinking. Phra Bunmi, from the Shan State in Myanmar, felt that he had changed much during his three years at Monk Chat: "I learned a lot, not just about Buddhism but the way other people behave, and their lifestyle. I improved how to communicate with strangers. The foreigners ask questions and it trains us to improve critical thinking, challenges us to answer, because foreigners ask different kinds of questions we are not used to from our study." Naen Maha Tri found that after talking to many people over two years, he has more of an open mind to exchange and experience culture: "I see that no one is perfect, we are all so different and should just develop ourselves better. This is better than criticizing other people." He explained that he used to criticize: "One American got mad at us when I said we Buddhists don't believe in God. I thought maybe Americans are like this. The Chinese are always sitting here at these benches, speaking loudly, smoking. But now I know people are all unique. What is the point of judging? I know that is the culture of Chinese now. I learned this from some Chinese who came here, and now I am used to it." The ability to continually be in contact with people from different backgrounds allowed this student monk to accept differences, rather than judge people negatively for not being like him.

Phra Atid spoke of his own development after four years of attempting to explain Buddhism to tourists: "At first I felt stressed if I can't answer the question, because foreigners have a lot of expectations to talk and learn something from the monk. So, I felt sad with myself. Now I know the way to explain to foreigner. I can give good answers, and many appreciate this. Sometimes it makes them cry when I explain about the truth of life, the three characteristics [non-self, suffering, and impermanence, called the Three Marks of Existence in Buddhism]. I teach it in a simple way just a little bit but not too deep."

Phra Atid is proud of his transformation, which he marks by comparing his first conversations with foreigners with those during his fourth year of university. Naen Samrin highlighted how, through his interactions with foreigners, he became more committed to Buddhism: "Before I didn't know why I am a monk. With the foreigner questions, I could think more deeply, what is the real use of what I am and what is Buddhism? They have questions like 'Why do you wear the robe?' and now I think about the robe and why my head is shaved. I never thought about this before. I just accepted. Now I see more the wisdom of Buddhism." His understanding of Buddhism deepened as he considered the reasons for the markings of monasticism and how they relate to the Buddhist teachings and their goals.

Monk Chat monks were able to reflect on their own development, what they have learned about themselves, Buddhism, and the world, through their encounters and conversations with international travelers over a sustained period of four years. In contrast to volunteer teachers, student monks are not concerned with the authenticity of their interlocutors. Instead, the student monks find the difference of the tourists leads to new understandings about themselves, their abilities, and Buddhism. They are able to consider different questions and new ideas, which can result in the transformation of their perceptions of the world and goals for the future.

Buddhist Encounters in Southeast Asia

Chiang Mai is not the only place where Buddhist temples and monks are encountering international communities and urbanization. Cities that are hubs for education and tourism are equipped for such exchange opportunities within mainland Southeast Asia. Conjunctures of urbanization, monastic education, and volunteer tourism have created opportunities for Buddhist cultural exchange programs in the cities of Mandalay, Myanmar, and Phnom Penh, Cambodia. Both of these locations have monastic schools where volunteer tourists are welcome to stay and teach English. In Mandalay, the Phaung Daw Oo (PDO) Integrated Monastic Education School has been in operation since 1993, and the school has received foreign volunteers since 2000. PDO affiliates with Volunteers in Asia, the Oxford Burma Alliance, and various universities in the United States. Some of the volunteers learn about Buddhism during conversations with Venerable U Nayaka, the founder and director of PDO, and through taking advantage of facilities for meditation.[1] The mission of PDO is to help students get accepted into good colleges or universities and receive scholarships to study abroad.[2] Because the school's aim is focused exclusively on secular rather than Buddhist education, U Nayaka stated that most of the volunteers are not interested in Buddhism, as many of them are Christians who hope to share their knowledge with less privileged children. In Phnom Penh, Wat Nighrodhawann has affiliated with the volunteer tourism company World Service Group since 2013. Wat Nighrodhawann, located ten kilometers outside of Phnom Penh City, houses around two hundred monks and nuns and has a reputation of strict meditation practice and Buddhist study. World Service Group began the connection with Wat Nighrodhawann by speaking with the monks there. After considering the mutual benefits, both parties involved decided the volunteer program was a good fit with the monastery because of the school and homestay nearby.[3] One monk at Wat Nighrodhawann, Venerable Sopheara, stated in an interview that the abbot agreed to World Service Group's proposal because he wanted to spread the dhamma. Because this abbot has studied in Sri Lanka and traveled to the United States and Europe, he is open to foreign communities and wants Buddhism to be available outside of Cambodia. The twenty volunteers who come each year are part of a "Buddhist immersion program," where they participate in volunteering activities such as teaching English to the nearby schoolchildren and taking part in meditation sessions. Buddhist cultural exchange programs are slowly proliferating in mainland Southeast Asia for those temples and monastic schools that either are interested in spreading Buddhism or have educational needs, or both.

In East Asia, however, there is less need for educational aid or any kind of volunteer tourism, due to the higher socioeconomic status of countries in the region. Despite that, creative and innovative programs have engaged new audiences there.

Buddhist Cultural Exchange Programs and Innovations in East Asia

Although Chiang Mai's Buddhist cultural exchange programs were created as a way to respond to increasing curiosity and numbers of tourists in Thai Buddhist temples, Korean Templestay had a more specific reason. In 2002, as Korea cohosted the Fédération Internationale de Football Association (FIFA) World Cup with Japan, the Ministry of Culture and Tourism was concerned the country might not have enough accommodation for all the foreign visitors, and so the idea of housing them at Buddhist temples of the dominant Chogye Order was proposed. And instead of just offering football fans a place to sleep, it created an entire spiritual and cultural experience (Kaplan 2010, 131–32). Since that time, the Korean Templestay program has grown in the number of temples and visitors it accommodates each year. This growth has also resulted in the Templestay program receiving attention from researchers who focus on the branding of the experience for domestic and foreign participants (Kaplan 2010; S. Kim 2017). They argue that the program changes the nature of the temple space from a living temple to a kind of heritage museum of Korean culture. The branding of the temple as a cultural space opens it up for non-Buddhists while simultaneously allowing for the propagation of Buddhism.[4]

This Korean Buddhist cultural exchange program is more formalized than the institutional structures within Thai Buddhism. The administration of Thai Buddhism is diffuse, with abbots having a degree of autonomy to innovate within their own temples. Since individual Thai Buddhist temples maintain independence, for the most part, systematic, nationwide programs are unlikely to emerge. In contrast, the coordinated maintenance of the Templestay program in Korea is possible because of the Korean Ministry of Culture and Tourism's involvement and connection to one sect of

Korean Buddhism, the Chogye Order. The Templestay booklet from 2016 highlights the sixteen temples with English-speaking programs available and states that over ninety thousand foreigners have participated in these programs since its inception. The Korean Templestay program is a service provided with numerous volunteers and English-speaking staff to help coordinate activities, such as chanting in the morning and evening, performing the 108 prostrations, copying sutras, meditating, drinking tea with monks, and hiking. For these services, a typical two-night visit costs about seventy thousand Korean won (US$70). With a functioning website, newsletters and other publications, and a headquarters situated in downtown Seoul, this Buddhist cultural exchange program is accessible and easy to navigate.[5]

Visitors to the Korean Templestay program not only see what it is like to live in a Buddhist temple, with rituals and the monastic life, but also become immersed in Korean cultural activities, such as paper folding and tea ceremonies (Kaplan 2010, 128). These activities become a symbol of Korean culture, packaged for tourists, as represented by the Templestay program.[6] Through these hybrid activities, Templestay displays its twin goals of "Buddhist universalistic intention" and "touristic nationalistic intention" (Kaplan 2010, 133). While the Templestay program is interested in showcasing aspects of Korean culture, it is also an opportunity to spread Buddhism, however informally, among a curious population of international visitors. Scholar of Korean Buddhism Uri Kaplan (2010, 140) confirms that propagating Buddhism is one of the main objectives of this program based on interviews with those involved at the temple level and on a review of Templestay publications. Kaplan remains unsure whether Templestay counts as missionary work because the program does not actively attempt to convince participants to consider further joining the Buddhist path. However, inspiring tourists to become Buddhists is not the goal of many Buddhist missionaries. Creating a program where an experience of living in a Buddhist temple is possible spreads Buddhism by piquing the curiosity of those interested and planting seeds for further engagement with the religion in this lifetime or future ones.

In China and Japan, Buddhist monks who aim to increase traffic in their temples have received considerable media attention. Worried that modern and global trends within youth and consumer culture are taking over the relevance of Buddhist traditions, some monks are creating distinctive ways to attract new audiences. In one unique case in China, the robot monk Xian'er in Longquan Temple has captivated Chinese tourists as well as international journalists. The *New York Times* cites a monk at Longquan explaining that the point of the robot is to use modern ways of spreading Buddhist teachings.[7] The *Guardian* quotes the robot's creator, Master Xianfan, stating that this robot embodies the innovative spirit of Buddhism, which will help the religion reach a wider public.[8] In an article published by CNN, Master Xianfan describes Xian'er as sparking interest in Buddhism among both Buddhists and non-Buddhists.[9] Longquan Temple offers both technological developments, such as the abbot's blog and animated cartoons illustrating Buddhist ways to cultivate the mind, and physical programs, such as temple stay and meditation retreats for members of the community and tourists (Bruntz 2020). Although this case is not representative of trends in contemporary Chinese Buddhism more broadly, this particular temple hopes to spread the Buddha's teachings so that participants can engage with Buddhism as a source of wisdom to implement into their daily life.

For Japan, one innovative way for spreading Buddhism is a bar in Tokyo called Vowz, run by Japanese Buddhist monks. The monks hope to insert themselves into modernity, not through technology, but through young professional culture. With busy lifestyles and long working hours, the center of the community in Japanese cities is no longer the Buddhist temple. However, a Buddhist temple-like atmosphere in a bar setting, as monks at Vowz attest, allows customers to loosen up and talk about their problems with Buddhist guidance. The bar, and the monastic rock band it features, fans argue, can reach a broad audience, exposing them to the Buddhist way of life.[10] Buddhists in Japan seek "to domesticate an understanding of Buddhism so that it responds to and privileges the patterns, preferences, and concerns of a person's life" (Nelson 2013, 27). As Buddhism is slowly losing popular support, its sites shift toward focusing on casual tourism and cultural heritage (19). In order to maintain the relevance of temples, new resources are necessary. Social activism, creative initiatives, and programs of progressive monks serve to reinvigorate Buddhism within modern Japanese societies (xvi). Examples such as concerts in temples, chanting monk performances in jazz clubs, and fashion shows featuring Japanese monks demonstrate the extent to which Japanese Buddhists are aiming to stave off the decline in interest and value placed on their religion today. In this way, these creative innovations are following the trend toward informal missionizing activities. These new spaces for Buddhism, entering bars and the technological world, from a Buddhist point of view, are a way to show Buddhism to a wider audience than would likely frequent a traditional temple.

One of the major reasons for these creative developments, inside and outside Buddhist temples, is the perception that Buddhism is in decline.

Buddhism in Decline?

Cultural exchange programs and other innovations in informal missionizing often come in pairs. Along with the Buddhist monk's duty to spread Buddhism, the idea that Buddhism is in decline is another part of the context for these programs. When Buddhist teachings are being spread across the world, people are practicing Buddhist meditation and participating in temple activities, and Buddhist monks are meticulously living their monastic lifestyle, then Buddhism can be said to be thriving. However, Buddhism seems to be in decline if the global, national, or local opinion of Buddhism is low, not many people are engaging in Buddhist practice or coming to the temple, and Buddhist monks are not following their rules. All of these factors figure into the ways both Thai Buddhist society and student monks consider the status of Buddhist presence in the world today. From a Buddhist perspective, Buddhist cultural exchange programs help to protect and propagate the teachings and practices of the religion.

Religious institutions in crisis and the unstoppable forces of modernity that have taken their place is a compelling story throughout much of Asia. In Japan, a "temple Buddhism crisis" is voiced by many Japanese Buddhist monks of all sects (Reader 2011). Lack of support from Japanese Buddhists, a decreased population of monastics, and temple closures solidify this crisis for Buddhists in modern Japan (233). Demographic shifts from rural to urban areas mean that long-standing familial relationships with temples are severed. As well, the freedom to choose temple affiliation in urban environments is a new and complex issue for Japanese Buddhism (Nelson 2013, xv).[11] In part, the examples of cultural exchange programs and innovations above point to Buddhists' interest in maintaining relevance in their urban environments, so that these issues can be ameliorated, avoided, or prevented.

But in contemporary Thailand, this narrative of Buddhism's decline in modern societies is not as clear, as not all Thai monks are in agreement about their state of affairs. Instead, the issues of declining Buddhism are espoused mostly in the Thai media. And it is not a decreasing population of Buddhists attending temple services or donating to maintain temple structures that constitute the arguments of decline. Unlike in Japan, in Thailand monastic behavior is the main culprit among the reasons for Buddhism's decreasing impact on Thai society. An article in the *Bangkok Post* in 2015 titled "Chequebook Buddhism: Threat to Buddhism in Thailand?" exemplifies the ways the media, both foreign and Thai, frequently constructs Buddhism in Thailand as existing in a state of collapse: "In deeply religious Thailand, monks have long been revered. But badly behaved clergy, corruption scandals, and the vast wealth amassed by some temples has many asking if something is rotten at the heart of Thai Buddhism. From selfies on private jets to multimillion-dollar donations from allegedly crooked businessmen, Thailand's monks are coming under increasing fire for their embrace of commercialism."[12]

In many opinion pieces in English and Thai media outlets in Thailand, Asia, North America, and Europe, Buddhism in Thailand is portrayed as a religion in dire need of transformation, reform, or even an entire overhaul. The highest-ranking monks, called the Sangha Supreme Council, are criticized for lack of control over the scams and scandals of Thai Buddhist monks involving money, sex, alcohol, and drugs, as well as council members' own luxurious lifestyles.[13] Thai Buddhists are constantly being reminded of the state of their religion through the media.[14]

Such assertions concerning Thai Buddhism, forces of modernization, urbanization, secularization, and consumerism butt up against an idealized picture of peace-loving Buddhists. Media articles often write nostalgically about an idyllic past when the temple was the center of the community, Thai society followed Buddhist morality, and there was no consumer culture to be a part of. The narrative contends that modernity has confused Thai Buddhist monks, causing one of the major national institutions to become unstable, if not completely broken.[15] A note of loss characterizes these pieces, along with the accusation that a once devoutly Buddhist nation has strayed far off its path. These media narratives are backed up by well-known, high-profile Buddhist monks. Phra Paisal Visalo and Phra Phayom Kalyano decry the rise of consumerism and materialism, among both the monastic institutions and the societal values at large.[16] Phra Paisal is especially critical of commercialized Buddhism, in which he finds that the temple has become like a marketplace specializing in objects that can increase wealth instead of a place of long-term practice (Scott 2009, 176). One of the solutions for Thai Buddhism's crisis, as Phra Paisal sees it, is to separate consumerism from Buddhism. However, as he observes in Thai society currently, Buddhism and consumerism are indistinguishable. He even names this phenomenon "the Religion of Consumerism."[17]

Phra Phayom Kalyano also seeks to draw Thai Buddhists' attention back to the "core" of Buddhism through highlighting the ridiculousness of the popularity of material objects thought to bring wealth, especially Chatukham-Rammathep amulets, which were immensely popular in 2006 and 2007. His critique took the form of Chatu Kham cookies (a play on Chatukham, in this case meaning "four bites"). His cookies were a parody of the shape and design of the Chatukham amulet, but contained Buddhist teachings about wealth. His intention was to direct Thai people away from attachment to material wealth (Scott 2009, 182). Other monks, lay Buddhists, journalists, and bloggers, too, create a stark binary between materialism and pure Buddhist teachings, modernity and traditional Thai lifestyles, misbehaving monks and pure monks, corruption in the sangha hierarchy and enlightened leadership. But this kind of rhetoric is seen especially in connection with ideas of a crisis and decline of Buddhism in Thailand.

Student monks at the Buddhist universities in Chiang Mai, unsurprisingly, express alternative ways to understand this presumed threat of Buddhist decline in Thailand. Monks agree that there are problems within Thai Buddhism, but they do not bring up the power of modernity or materialism as a factor. Student monks in Chiang Mai are cautiously hopeful about the state of Buddhism in Thailand. The situation is not quite so urgent for them, as they do not mourn for a time when Buddhism and society were more closely aligned, nor do they perceive modernity to be at odds with Buddhist teachings. They are not attached to past memories of Buddhism, allowing for a creative interplay between Buddhism and modernity, Buddhism and consumerism. Phra Sek, from Cambodia, who attended high school and university in Chiang Mai, in generalizing the issues Thai Buddhism faces, reflected: "This is not the end of Buddhism, just basic problems. Buddhism is still here, no one can just take it away as if a bomb had gone off." Through comments like this, student monks distinguish between Buddhism and Buddhists. They emphasize that Buddhism is not in decline but that the monks and laity who practice Buddhism can lose sight of the teachings. They believe it is wrong to criticize a few monks' actions as if they reflect all of Thai Buddhism.

The young monks understand the role of media in influencing Thai society. Phra Sek explained: "This [monks, in general, behaving inappropriately] is spreading now because of all the media about monks. In the past, maybe there were also monks like this, but now everybody knows about it." They could understand the situation of monks accused of behaving badly. "Many of these monks in the news are novice monks. They do not yet know the rules," said Phra Chaiya, from Thailand. "This is the main problem in Thai Buddhism that can be easily fixed. But some monks are naughty and do not know how to practice or follow the Vinaya [rules of the monks]. Just like in the outside world, some people are bad. It is unavoidable in monks too." Their reasoning for scandals is more grounded in the everyday structures of temple life, rather than in secular socioeconomic forces. Student monks do not compare modern Thai Buddhism with a past when all monks were pure, and all laypeople could look up to them.

Another problem that the student monks at Chiang Mai's Buddhist universities discussed involves senior monks who attain high-level positions within the Buddhist hierarchy. Instead of framing the issue as monks being attracted to modernity, as the media often does, they reference instead the Buddhist teachings. High-ranking monks who are interested in power could, one monk, Phra Chet, asserted, "forget about the dhamma and Vinaya. They intimidate their disciples and laypeople and just do what they want without thinking about the people." Many of the student monks emphasized how laypeople believe that high-ranking monks are purer, but this is not always true. Instead, some high-ranking monks, as Phra Chet described them, "care about building big buildings but not building people." These student monks are concerned with teaching other monks and laypeople how to become better Buddhists, not pushing away modernity. They direct their criticism toward particular Buddhists, such as high-ranking monks not focused on education, or toward Thai people who are surrounded by Buddhism but do not take advantage of these teachings and opportunities to practice. However, their negative opinions of these people, for student monks in general, do not constitute a crisis at the level portrayed by the Thai media. As student monks explain, these are simple problems and not an indication that all of Buddhism is declining.

Buddhist cultural exchange programs provide a venue where these monks can express and explain these teachings. The situation is not quite so urgent for them, as they do not mourn for a time when Buddhism and society were more closely aligned. They do not perceive modernity to be at odds with Buddhist teachings. They see problems with Buddhist monasticism, but emphasize that there is no problem with Buddhism itself. They can see this when international travelers come to their temples to volunteer or simply to have conversations with monks. In the curiosity of many tourists, student monks see opportunities to spread Buddhism. Through answering foreign tourists' and volunteers' questions, these student monks gain a deeper appreciation of Buddhist teachings, their depth and profundity. Instead of considering Buddhist cultural exchange programs as a way to prevent decline, student monks find in these programs proof that Buddhism is not in decline after all.

Through global connections, Buddhists encounter the friction of new opportunities and challenges. These encounters often result in creative ideas and programs to engage new audiences and the ability to take in new resources for the survival of the religion. Buddhism needs both people and monetary resources to survive. These two in combination have been the impetus for Buddhist monks to engage with modern, global, urban trends in cities. They search for both new revenue streams and people to spread Buddhism to. This does not mean that all Buddhists and non-Buddhists are equal. As we have seen, there is a variety of attitudes toward different audiences who visit Buddhist temples in Chiang Mai.

Both Buddhist monks and tourists can be altered by their exchange. Volunteer tourists, who spend significant time in temples teaching monks, have a chance to encounter difference and an unexpected authenticity from this backstage view of the monastic life. The student monks who participate in Monk Chat reflect on how the difference of the religious and cultural others whom they meet allow them to change and grow. Although authenticity is less of an issue for them, monks feel that explaining Buddhism helps them understand their religion's wisdom. Other countries and cities recognize the fruitful nature of cultural exchange programs, as volunteer tourism has entered into Mandalay and Phnom Penh. The student monks in Mandalay and Luang Prabang, Laos, often strike up conversations with foreigners, hanging out where tourists are likely to be. These monks recognize the need to practice English and engage with the international community. Without support from their temples or the official monastic structure, informal conversations are the next best option. While wearing their robes, Buddhist monks can never escape their role as representatives of Buddhism. Because of that, they are unlikely to be only practicing English; if only in small ways, they also make Buddhism more present in the world through their conversations.

Besides transformation, encounters between Buddhist temples, tourism, and the urban environment necessarily concern the economic, social, and religious spheres. Buddhist monks have varying opinions on the nature of the temple space as wholly sacred or as a place where some profane commerce can exist. As tourism increases and changes, temple leadership must consider the nature of their space and how fee structures and commodities can or should relate to it. Specifically, Buddhist cultural exchange programs in Chiang Mai inform Buddhist attitudes to religious others. Because monks interact with different groups of people, tourist urban encounters facilitate their understanding and comparison of how these groups associate with Buddhism. Finally, cultural exchange programs allow for an analysis of Buddhist missionizing. Although Monk Chat, temple stay programs, and volunteer tourism opportunities are informal ways of spreading Buddhism, they reveal the strategies of Buddhist missionaries. They are interested in showing Buddhism to those who are already curious, as they believe Buddhist teachings will help to reduce the suffering of all people.

In East Asia, there are interesting comparisons to be made with the cultural exchange programs of Chiang Mai. In cities of Japan and China, there are attempts to engage local and international communities in Buddhist temple and monastic activities. In Japan, moving Buddhism out of the temple seems to be a trend, with Buddhist monks setting up bars, performing chanting in jazz clubs, and modeling monastic wear on fashion runways. In China, technology is used to engage youth and others who might be attracted to innovative ways of learning about Buddhism. Korea uses its national heritage of Buddhism and the global appeal of Buddhist teachings to create an atmosphere where Korean and international guests will want to visit and participate in its Templestay programs. All of these programs and innovations have taken place, at least partly, in order to stave off a perceived threat to Buddhism. Especially in Japan, temple closure is a real issue that forces monks to consider creative ways to fundraise and raise the profile of Buddhism in their communities.

In Thailand, temple closures and demographic shifts of the lay and monastic Buddhist population are not the cause of perception that there is a crisis. Instead, it is the actions and behaviors of individual monks: alcohol and drug use, sexual activity, possession of luxury items, and involvement in financial scandals appear in Thai media reporting on Buddhism. Corruption among the seniors of the monastic hierarchy and their lack of effectiveness in curtailing the inappropriateness of their junior monks is often criticized. Reform-minded monks such as Phra Phayom Kalyano and Phra Paisal Visalo agree that there need to be some changes for the monastic institution to survive. However, the student monks of Chiang Mai, the main voices of this book, express different perspectives. They are not concerned with a decline of Buddhism because they do not see a crisis. They see opportunities to engage the international community and Thai Buddhists with the teachings of Buddhism. They would like to increase these opportunities for teaching in the temple so that it is a relaxing and learning space for all who enter. These monks do not criticize or blame younger monks for small infractions but do think the monastic leadership could focus more on education. Education would allow more monks to be able to spread the Buddhist teachings to all who are curious.

Within contemporary Buddhism, these encounters will continue to result in unique programs and innovations, but they will also be debated and grounded within Buddhist teachings and traditions. This is part of the friction of global connections and negotiation of difference within encounter (Tsing 2005, 6). The student monks of Chiang Mai must compromise some of their ideals about the welcoming nature of Buddhism by living in temples that have instituted fees for foreigners. They also are concerned about the genuine interest of some Thai Buddhists and Chinese tourists. But ultimately, they appear to be empowered by global connections. They debate about the best ways to use the temple space and spread Buddhism, but the fact that student monks have these conversations is exciting to them. The possibility of hosting curious foreign non-Buddhists and being able to show and teach them about Buddhism is a major part of the creative, productive friction of the student monks of Chiang Mai with education, tourism, and urbanization.

NOTES

1 Buddhist cosmology covers heaven, hell, and earthly realms, incorporating humans, animals, hell beings, and gods. At the center of this universe is Mount Meru, below the heaven realms but towering above the southern continent of Jambudvipa, where human beings live. Below this are the various hell realms. A developed version of this cosmology is located in the Buddhist texts of the Abhidharma (Gethin 1998, 118). But Thai people would know this cosmology from the fourteenth-century work *The Three Worlds according to King Ruang* (Traiphum Phra Ruang).

2 Sacred space becomes especially important for Chiang Mai during times of political upheaval, such as the late eighteenth century, when Chiang Mai began to break from its Burmese overlords, who had occupied the area since 1558, and align with Siam (Easum 2013, 214).

3 This figure is an estimate by the Thailand National Committee for World Heritage in its application to the United Nations Educational, Scientific, and Cultural Organization's (UNESCO) World Heritage List, http://whc.unesco.org/en/tenta tivelists/6003, accessed July 2, 2018.

4 Anthropologist Nancy Eberhardt (2009) has researched two well-known Shan temples in Chiang Mai, Wat Ku Tao and Wat Pa Pao, which host a famous ordination ceremony every year called Paui Sang Long. Other temples, such as Wat Dao-wadung in the old city of Chiang Mai, have large populations of Karen people.

5 Most notably, anthropologist Andrew Alan Johnson (2014) and sociologist Kazuo Fukuura (2011) have studied spirit mediums and their practices of mediumship in Chiang Mai. Fukuura notes the ways spirit mediums must negotiate with Buddhist values, paradoxically, in order to maintain their independence and expertise during city rituals such as the annual Inthakin Festival, or worship of the city pillar (*lak mueang*) located at Wat Chedi Luang (Fukuura 2011, 109).

6 Historian Nidhi Eoseewong ([1991] 2003) writes that, more than other religions, Buddhism has a special status within Thailand, making it the de facto Thai

national religion. Although Buddhism is not listed in any of the Thai constitutions as the state religion, Thailand has a large majority of citizens (93 percent) who identify as Buddhist, and the king of Thailand, who officiates at important Buddhist ceremonies, must be a Buddhist. Within Theravada Buddhism, the king is the traditional protector of Buddhism, and more recently this idea of protection has merged with nationalism. "To be Thai is to be Buddhist" is a common saying, linking being a proper and patriotic Thai to identifying as a Buddhist. This link was used by the monarch and, later, the state to distinguish Thailand from the West, but at the same time to claim a religious culture as rich as Christianity. Although the discourse of Thai identity, or Thainess (*khwam pen thai*), often includes Central Thai (Bangkok) language and values, as can be seen in the Cultural Mandates of 1939 (Reynolds 2006), recently local and regional Thai cultures have experienced a renaissance, especially the Lanna culture of northern Thailand, due to international but especially domestic tourism (Schedneck 2017b).

7 Pairat Temphairojana, "Thailand Expects Record Tourist Arrivals in 2016," Reuters, January 6, 2016, www.reuters.com/article/us-thailand-tourism-idUSKB NoUKoIU20160106.

8 The *Jakarta Post* reported this statistic in "Increasingly Popular Chiang Mai Gears Up for Changing Tourism Trends," December 25, 2018, www.thejakartapost.com /travel/2018/12/24/increasingly-popular-Chiang-mai-gears-up-for-changing -tourism-trends.html.

9 Through investigating the Primary Information of Buddhism document from 2017 by the Office of National Buddhism, my research assistant, Phra Maha Milan Shrestha, found that, at that time, there were 2,866 monks and novice monks in Chiang Mai City and 11,682 monks and novice monks in Chiang Mai Province.

10 It is common within Southeast Asian nations to have a large capital, which dwarfs the next largest cities in the country in size and influence (Rimmer and Dick 2009, 83).

11 Movies such as 2004's *Jod mai rak* (The letter) and 2010's *Laddaland* (Golden land) depict Chiang Mai as a space that retains Thai culture and identity, in contrast to Bangkok. For scholarship on this trope of urban versus natural lifestyles in Thailand, see Johnson (2014, chap. 1) and Knee (2015).

12 Tourism Authority of Thailand, "Religion," www.tourismthailand.org/About -Thailand/Religion, accessed November 21, 2016.

13 Chiang Mai International Airport is expected to service about twelve million passengers by 2020. "Chiang Mai Being Developed as a Creative City," UNESCO Bangkok, February 24, 2011, www.thaiembassy.sg/press_media/news-highlights /Chiang-mai-being-developed-as-a-creative-city.

14 According to *Bloomberg*, 8.8 million Chinese tourists arrived in 2016, tripling their numbers from the previous five years and accounting for a quarter of all foreign tourists to Thailand. "Chinese Tourists Could Cause Years of Misery for Thai Airports," *Bloomberg*, December 20, 2017, www.bloomberg.com/news

/articles/2017-12-20/thai-airport-misery-may-last-years-as-chinese-overwhelm
-upgrades.

15 Searching "Chinese tourists behaving badly in Thailand" on Google reveals more
than 366,000 videos and articles. For an example article on the temporary Chinese boycott of Chiang Mai, see "TAT [Tourism Authority of Thailand] Desperate to Bring Chinese Tourists Back after They Boycott Thailand," *Coconuts Bangkok*, July 27, 2016, https://coconuts.co/bangkok/news/tat-desperate-bring
-chinese-tourists-back-after-they-boycott-thailand.

16 "Desperate Times: Chiang Mai Trying to Win Back Chinese Tourists," *Coconuts Bangkok*, August 1, 2016, https://coconuts.co/bangkok/news/desperate-times
-Chiang-mai-trying-win-back-chinese-tourists.

17 In a 2013 survey of Chinese tourists in Chiang Mai, tourism researcher Korawan
Sangkakorn (2013) has found that four out of their ten top destinations were
Buddhist temples.

18 I did not interview Chinese tourists mostly because I do not speak Chinese.
The Thai tourists are so numerous that it would be difficult to get any kind of
representative sample. Instead, as I explain in chapter 5, I focused on volunteer
tourists, who reside in Chiang Mai for a longer period than typical tourists.

19 The two sects in Thai Buddhism are Mahanikai and Thammayutnikai. Mahamakut Buddhist University (MBU), located at Wat Chedi Luang, is part of the
Thammayutnikai. Mahachulalongkorn Rajavidyalaya Buddhist University
(MCU), located at Wat Suan Dok, is part of the Mahanikai.

20 The estimated population of precept nuns is twenty thousand. In Thailand, these
precept nuns are called *mae chi*. Even though *mae chi* are accepted within the
Thai Buddhist sangha, they do not reach high levels of authority because they
are limited to 8 precepts, instead of the 227 rules of male monks. For information on *mae chi* educational institutions, see anthropologist Monica Lindberg
Falk's (2007) ethnographic study. Female monks, or *bhikkhunis*, keep 311 precepts; however, they are not accepted in the Thai Buddhist sangha. Since 1928,
female monk ordination has been banned in Thailand. Today Thai female monks
are ordaining in Sri Lanka and have set up several *bhikkhuni* communities in
Thailand. In Thailand, there are roughly about three hundred thousand male
monks, while female monks number just over two hundred.

21 Group interview with monks at Wat Chedi Luang, June 20, 2018. Except for two
instances of group interviews, all individual interviews are cited in the reference list.

22 My discussion of typical mobility situations of student monks in Chiang Mai
is based on my research into monastic school populations. I have discussed
with student monks their living situations and how they navigate the city with
limited funding.

23 Important works that focus on historical encounters between religions and
cultures include Audrey Truschke's (2016) investigation of the Mughal Empire's
(1560–1660) ongoing cultural encounters with the Sanskrit tradition through Jain
and Brahman intellectuals; Ahn Q. Tran's (2018) study of Christian encounters

with Vietnamese religion in the eighteenth century; and Webb Keane's (2007) work on the Christian missionary encounter with the Sumbanese in Indonesia.

24 Theorists of urbanization and global cities have neglected the importance of religiosity in urban environments, assuming that the rural is religious and the urban is necessarily secular (Cornelio 2015, 72).

25 One of the first ethnographic examples of Buddhist communities encountering Western societies, by Penny Van Esterik (1992), concerns Lao Buddhists in the diaspora of North America. Monographs that focus on race as part of the Buddhist experience abroad include Joseph Cheah's (2011) ethnography of a Burmese temple in California. Outside of the United States, Cristina Rocha's *Zen in Brazil* (2006) explores Buddhism as a part of cosmopolitan aspiration in Brazil.

26 Occasionally, some foreign monks become fluent in Thai. In these cases, we would sometimes speak in Thai together.

CHAPTER 1: A MODERN HISTORY OF BUDDHIST ENCOUNTERS IN CHIANG MAI

1   The Doi Kham chronicle is a translation of a published account by Phra Khru Paladphin, the abbot of Wat Phra That Doi Kham (Swearer, Premchit, and Dokbuakaew 2004, 70). The *Tamnan Phra That Doi Suthep* is taken from a palm-leaf manuscript from Chiang Mai dated to 1824 (Swearer, Premchit, and Dokbuakaew 2004, 70). The *Camadevivamsa* is a northern Thai chronicle (*tamnan*), which was composed in Pali by Mahathera Bodhiransi in the 1400s (Johnson 2014, 42).

2   The drama of the giants is reenacted annually with spirit mediums of Grandmother and Grandfather Sae eating raw buffalo flesh at the base of Doi Kham (Johnson 2014, 45).

3   Tourism researchers Jaeyeon Choe and Michael O'Regan (2015, 194) use the Association of Southeast Asian Nations' (ASEAN) international visitor arrivals statistics for 2013, which list Thailand as having the second-largest number of visitor arrivals (after Malaysia) in the region, with 145.5 million visitors, accounting for about 6–7 percent of the nation's gross domestic product (UNWTO 2011, 275).

4   Chiang Mai has won a number of awards from travel magazines, including *Travel + Leisure* and *Condé Nast Traveller*. In *Travel + Leisure*'s 2020 list of the world's top fifteen cities, Chiang Mai came in fourth. Sara Clemence, "The Topic 25 Cities in the World," *Travel + Leisure*, July 8, 2020, www.travelandleisure.com /worlds-best/cities. In 2014, the city was voted among the top twenty-five cities in the world by *Condé Nast Traveller*'s Readers' Choice Awards. "Bangkok and Chiang Mai Named World's Top 25 Cities," *TAT News*, October 31, 2014, www .tatnews.org/bangkok-and-Chiang-mai-named-worlds-top-25-cities. According to the Tourism Authority of Thailand, in 2015, Chiang Mai received 2.8 million international visitors and its hotels had more than forty thousand rooms. "Chiang Mai Tourism Stakeholders Reiterate Readiness in Welcoming Chinese Tourists and All," *TAT News*, July 30, 2016, www.tatnews.org/Chiang-mai

-tourism-stakeholders-reiterate-readiness-in-welcoming-chinese-tourists-and-all.

5 UNESCO, "Monuments, Sites, and Cultural Landscapes of Chiang Mai, Capital of Lanna," September 2, 2015, http://whc.unesco.org/en/tentativelists/6003.

6 Tourism Authority of Thailand, "Chiang Mai," www.tourismthailand-middleeast.org/en/all-destinations/northern/1/Chiang+Mai, accessed October 12, 2018.

7 Lonely Planet, "Welcome to Chiang Mai," www.lonelyplanet.com/thailand/Chiang-mai-province/Chiang-mai, accessed October 12, 2018.

8 Rough Guides, "Chiang Mai," www.roughguides.com/destinations/asia/thailand/north/Chiang-mai, accessed October 12, 2018.

9 Frommer's, "Things to Do in Chiang Mai," www.frommers.com/destinations/Chiang-mai, accessed October 12, 2018.

10 Urbanization is here defined as a concentration of people at a location, which can be called a city, and which is connected to suburban and rural areas (Toh 2012, 116).

11 These statistics are from the graph and description in Statistica, "Thailand: Urbanization from 2009 to 2019," www.statista.com/statistics/455942/urbanization-in-thailand, accessed March 4, 2019.

12 The Thai census last occurred in 2010, so it is difficult to find up-to-date information from the Thai National Statistics Office. These statistics are from Thai Wikipedia, s.v. "Chiang Mai Province," https://th.wikipedia.org/wiki/จังหวัดเชียงใหม่, and "Chiang Mai City," https://th.wikipedia.org/wiki/อำเภอเมืองเชียงใหม่, updated in 2018.

13 Religious relationships within northern urban centers are part of a Buddhist pilgrimage network, which consists of twelve stupas marking the twelve animal years of the northern Thai calendar. This system contains stupas in Lanna, Laos, Burma, northern India, and heaven, creating a center and peripheries tied together as moral communities and sacred lands (Keyes 1975b).

14 A world city would be classified by its global service functions such as financial centers, transportation centers, and international institutions. A megacity would have a population of over ten million people (Toh 2012, 123).

15 This section provides an overview of the types of encounters with Buddhism historically possible in Siam and the Lanna Kingdom, and today in Thailand, Chiang Mai in particular.

16 Philachan Kornkrai Benedetto (1999, 67) writes that some early missionaries attacked and insulted Buddhism without having much knowledge of the religion, and this not only caused a negative reaction among the Siamese but hurt the missionaries' chances at making headway toward conversion. The example Philachan Kornkrai gives is of Monsignor Pallegoix, whose missionary work took place from 1841 to 1862. In an 1846 book by Pallegoix, consisting of questions and answers about Buddhism, he declares that Buddhism is not a religion of truth (Philachan Kornkrai 1999, 48). The book's distribution was halted by King Rama III and caused distrust among Buddhists toward Catholics.

17 "Woman Sitting in Lap of Buddhist Statue Draws Ire Online," *Bangkok Post*, March 9, 2018, www.bangkokpost.com/thailand/general/1425330.

18 Soonthorn Pongpao, "Tourists Charged with Climbing Ruins at Historic Site," *Bangkok Post*, February 26, 2018, www.bangkokpost.com/news/general/1418795.

19 "Villagers Feel Disheartened as Tourists Crowd to Stick Stickers throughout Temples in Pattaya" [in Thai], *Sanook News*, June 21, 2018, www.sanook.com/news/6892326.

20 Nujaree Raekrun, "Malaysian Buddhists Attend Annual Ordination in South," *Bangkok Post*, April 22, 2017, www.bangkokpost.com/news/general/1236546.

21 Melissa Locker, "*The Bachelorette* Recap: Before Fantasy Suites, Becca Gets Ready to Thai the Knot," *Time*, July 24, 2018.

22 The Monk Chat program began in Wat Suan Dok in 2000. Wat Chedi Luang followed this trend next, with its Monk Chat program beginning in 2005. Wat Srisuphan started its program in 2008.

23 Phra Saneh Dhammavaro, one of the founders of Monk Chat, relates its purpose in a booklet from 2009. He explains that its aim, reproduced below as written, is to

> fulfill the aspiration of the foreigners whom approached monk at Wat Suandok with a lot of doubts and questions regarding Buddhism, Buddhist way of life, life of monk and meditation etc. So the main purpose of the Monk Chat Programe are 1) to provide and opportunity for the foreigners to chat with monks informally on general topics, 2) to provide and opportunity for the foreigners, monks and novices to learn, exchange and discuss the general ideas on Buddhism, Buddhist way of life and Thai culture, 3) to provide and forum for monks and novices to exchange ideas with people from different cultures, faiths and ways of life. (Dhammavaro 2009, foreword)

24 Wat Suan Dok's Monk Chat program has a website: www.monkchat.net. The other two programs rely on Facebook groups, which the leaders continually update with photos and videos.

25 During the beginning of my research, the foundation's program was called the Wat Doi Saket Project. The project was founded in 2009 when the temple's abbot asked ATMA SEVA, the nongovernmental organization (NGO) that Wat Doi Saket has worked with since 1990, for increased English learning opportunities for the resident monks. Starting in January 2014, the Wat Doi Saket Project became part of a larger organization called the FutureSense Foundation and changed its name. In 2017, the FutureSense Foundation moved to another area of northern Thailand. I discuss the implications of this move in chapter 5.

26 The program maintained an affiliation with Phra Maha Insorn Khunawuttho, principal of the school at Wat Nong Bua, Doi Saket, Chiang Mai.

27 On the costs for these programs, which vary depending on how long one stays, see chapter 5.

28 As part of my position at the Institute of Southeast Asian Affairs, Chiang Mai University, I took groups of American students to Plik Wiwek in 2013 and 2014.

29 The program hopes to offer its participants five main objectives: the opportunity to (1) live in a temple, (2) learn the basics of Buddhist beliefs and practices, (3) participate in a meditation retreat near the temple, (4) interact with the novice monks and help them become comfortable with the basics of English, and (5) ordain as a novice monk.

30 Phra Ajahn Dr. Abhisit grew up in this community of downtown Fang and returned to take the position of abbot upon the death of his teacher, the former abbot.

31 Phra Ajahn Dr. Abhisit's Best Together Foundation (www.bcdcfang.org) has a number of projects designed to aid the people of Fang, including a health center, a park, and scholarships for local children. This program is funded by donations, which support the maintenance of the facilities as well as Phra Ajahn Dr. Abhisit's development projects for Fang.

32 *Vipassana*, as part of the Theravada Buddhist tradition, is usually translated as "insight" and is a technique of meditation that aims to "see things as they are" through close self-observation of the mind and body and gaining insight into the unsatisfactory, impermanent, non-self or non-substantial nature of all phenomenon. An example of a strict *vipassana* meditation center is Wat Rampoeng in Chiang Mai City (www.palikanon.com/vipassana/tapotaram/tapotaram.htm). Over twenty-six days, one starts meditating seven to eight hours per day and reaches a determination period of nonstop meditation. The increased emphasis on *vipassana* meditation at Wat Sri Boen Ruang is marked by a new name. Instead of Temple Stay and Retreat program, the name is now Vipassana Meditation Center–Wat Sriboonruang (http://vipassanameditation.asia). I continue to use the name Temple Stay and Retreat because all of my research took place before the program's name change.

33 A shorter version of this summary of the Buddhist cultural programs can be found in Schedneck (2020).

34 Both Prince Wachirayan and Prince Damrong were sons of Rama IV, King Mongkut (1804–1868), and half brothers of Rama V, King Chulalongkorn (1853–1910). They also were closely involved with the Thai educational system, monastic and secular, during the reign of Rama V. For more information on their influence, see Reynolds (1972) and Wyatt (1969).

35 King Mongkut, while an ordained monk, established the Thammayutnikai, or reform sect of Thailand, in 1833. Thereafter, the Thammayutnikai has been associated with the royal family. The monks who did not ordain into this sect became known as the Mahanikai sect.

36 Thammayut's Mahamakut College became Mahamakut Buddhist University in 1945 and Mahanikai's Mahachulalongkorn College became an officially accredited monastic university in 1947 (Phibul 2015, 436).

37 When a monk has reached the third level of Pali exams, his title changes to include "Maha," as in the case of my research assistant, Phra Maha Milan.

38 This kind of mobility for university students would be considered vertical because they are moving from countries with lower levels of educational institutions compared to those of Thailand (Salazar 2018, 96). They are also motivated by

degree mobility, as they seek to attain a better education than is available in their home country.

39 These changes were met with resistance, as the well-known story of the Buddhist monk Kruba Sriwichai details. Kruba Sriwichai continues to be revered in northern Thailand because of his building and renovation of many temples in the region. See Ratanaporn (2018).

40 For this section, I thank Phra Maha Milan for his research assistance with the MCU curriculum. The in-depth curriculum of the university's system can be found at Mahachulalongkorn University, "Bachelor of Buddhism, Department of English" (Laksut phutthasat banthit sakha wichakan phasa angkrit), http:// mcuaad.mcu.ac.th/ac/curr/_tqf2/file/16de0f22af5e53f2da43eaab74f596ff.pdf, accessed September 23, 2020.

41 In 2020, undergraduate tuition per semester for first-year monks at the MCU Chiang Mai campus was 2,625 Thai baht (US$85) for monks studying in the English and bilingual programs and 3,750 Thai baht (US$120) for lay students.

42 I thank Phra Maha Milan for his research assistance with the MBU curriculum. The in-depth curriculum of the system can be found at Mahamakut Buddhist University, "Department of English Language Teaching" (Sakha wichakan son phasa angkrit), www.mbu.ac.th/index.php/2012-11-14-02-12-21/2013-02-14-07 -25-27/2013-05-20-04-04-58/2013-05-20-04-41-09#.X2uQm5NKhKc, accessed September 23, 2020.

43 In 2018, tuition per semester at the MBU campus in Chiang Mai was 2,475 Thai baht (US$80) for monks and 4,850 Thai baht (US$155) for lay students. I thank Phra Artit, a student monk at MBU for this information.

44 Personal communication with a lecturer in English at MBU, Wat Chedi Luang, March 20, 2018.

45 This information comes from National Office of Buddhism, "The Statistics of Dhamma Study and Pali Examination of North Thailand," http://deb.onab.go .th/images/stories/Pali/PDF/north61.pdf, accessed May 28, 2018.

46 Monk-scholar Khammai Dhammasami's (2018) book *Buddhism, Education and Politics in Burma and Thailand* explores this important debate concerning the nature of Buddhist education.

47 A narrative description of this monastic education summary in Chiang Mai can be found in Schedneck, Khansamrong, and Epstein (2019).

48 My focus on encounter and life narratives is part of a larger conversation among scholars of Buddhism about the importance of studying real-life practices. Recent Buddhist studies textbooks have started to recognize the importance and need for understanding Buddhist life stories. See *Buddhists: Understanding Buddhism through the Lives of Practitioners* (Lewis 2014) and *Figures of Buddhist Modernity in Asia* (Samuels, Rowe, and McDaniel 2016).

49 Email communication with Phra Le, April 12, 2018.

50 Email communication with Jen, June 14, 2016.

51 Email communication with Jim, July 15, 2014.

52 Ileana, blog post on finding spirituality, September 2017.

53 Seema, blog post on Monk Chat, October 2018.

54 The themes of expected and unexpected difference are explored in depth in chapter 5.

55 David, blog post on traveling in Thailand, October 2018.

56 TripAdvisor, "Has Anyone Been to the Monk Chat?," https://en.tripadvisor.com .hk/ShowTopic-g293917-i9325-k2069039-Has_anyone_been_to_the_Monk_Chat -Chiang_Mai.html, accessed October 12, 2018.

57 TripAdvisor, "Has Anyone Been to the Monk Chat?"

58 Nelson, blog post on Monk Chat, October 2018.

59 Fodor's Travel, "Monk Chat," www.fodors.com/world/asia/thailand/Chiang-mai /experiences/monk-chat-88442380, accessed October 12, 2018.

60 Lonely Planet, "Chiang Mai in Detail: Monk Chat," www.lonelyplanet.com /thailand/Chiang-mai/in-location/activities/fbc16840-f31c-4b81-8042-05d909a 1c672/a/nar/fbc16840-f31c-4b81-8042-05d909a1c672/357655, accessed October 12, 2018.

CHAPTER 2: THE AGENCY OF BUDDHIST MONKS IN THE TOURISM LANDSCAPE

1 Tourism can be considered a form of neocolonialism when a space's cultural and religious meaning is redefined and commoditized by the tourism industry. I argue that this is not the case for Chiang Mai City's old city temples. For an example of tourist neocolonialism in Borobudur, Java, see Cywinski (2015).

2 See, for example, the essays collected in Juliane Schober and Steven Collins's (2017) edited volume *Theravāda Buddhist Encounters with Modernity*.

3 Historian of religion Anne Ruth Hansen (2007) has discussed changes in ethical conduct in the context of colonial Cambodia in her book *How to Behave*. In Thailand, King Mongkut began the reform sect, Thammayutnikai, in 1833. In East Asia, by the end of the 1800s, Japanese thinkers were actively trying to create New Buddhism (Shin Bukkyo). In the 1920s, the Chinese monk Taixu started to define humanistic Buddhism (*renjian fojiao*).

4 The topic of Buddhist economics was first written about by economist E. F. Schumacher after a trip to Burma and a meeting with then prime minister U Nu in 1955. His piece "Buddhist Economics" appeared in a group of his essays titled *Small Is Beautiful* (Schumacher 1999). His ideas were extended by P. A. Payutto (1998) in five essays translated and collected in his book *Buddhist Economics*. The term is used by both authors in order to contrast what they perceive as the human-centered approach of Buddhist teachings as applied to economics with the profit- and greed-driven approach of Western capitalism.

5 The alternative, of city monks not handling any money, is hard to imagine. If all city monks were unable to carry money, they would require lay Buddhist assistance for all their daily travel and monetary needs. This practice can be enacted for high-level monks. But creating a system where all monks in Thailand would always have a lay Buddhist nearby to handle funds would be logistically impossible.

6 For forest monks, money is best used when it goes toward the collective benefit of the community, and not when it is for an individual. Buddhist studies scholar

Kamala Tiyavanich (1997, 204) writes that a forest monk named Fan told villagers that they could pay a ritual specialist to remove the spirits from their village, but only if that ritual specialist used their money to "build a *wat* or facility for public use." But if their payment went toward the ritual specialists' own use, then it would not be worth paying him.

7   Durkheim ([1912] 1995, 37) found that sacred things are by definition separate, asserting that they "cannot be fixed once and for all; [their] scope varies endlessly from one religion to another." Each religion, therefore, identifies different objects, times, and practices as sacred; however, for all religions, the sacred is set apart. Durkheim's strict dichotomy of sacred and profane is murkier in urban space. Eliade (1957, 11) created the term "hierophany," which he defined as the manifestation of the sacred. Art historian Angela Chiu has found that hierophany could describe a Buddhaland, or *buddhadesa*, as portrayed by Lanna chronicles, which connect the land of Lanna to the presence of the Buddha. Aligning with Eliade, Chiu (2017, 84) argues that from the Buddhist perspective, the Buddha's agency does not transform the land into something sacred, but, instead, the land is already sacred and the Buddha travels to Lanna because he recognizes it as such.

8   For an overview of how the Thammayutnikai reform movement in Thailand relates to the forest tradition, see Thanissaro (2005).

9   Through personal communication with an abbot in the northeast of Thailand, Kamala Tiyavanich found that in public, Thammayutnikai monks do not touch money, and if they find a temple boy spending money, they will beat him severely. But if a similar situation happens in a Mahanikai temple, the monks will beat him less harshly because they are allowed to handle money (Kamala 1997, 350n46). These examples demonstrate that because they are stricter, Thammayutnikai monks have to be more wary of public perception.

10 Theravada Buddhist Renunciate Communities, *Discipline and Conventions of the Theravada Buddhist Renunciate Communities: A Guide for the Western Sangha*, www.budsas.org/ebud/ebdha116.htm, accessed June 12, 2018.

11 Personal communication about usage of money in the Thai forest tradition during my stay at Wat Pah Nanachat (International Forest Monastery) in Ubon Ratchathani, northeastern Thailand, January 2010.

12 Buddhist studies scholar Anthony Lovenheim Irwin (2017, 90) argues that *barami* is a central concept in understanding Thai Buddhism. *Barami* is the Thai version of the Pali word *parami*, meaning "perfection." The ability to build and renovate temples is associated definitively with *barami*. Therefore, the way for monks to prove *barami* is to enact building projects. If a project does not get enough funding and is not completed, Irwin explains, "people give an overarching explanation: that the *barami* of the leading abbot was simply not sufficient to carry out this type of work" (96), or, in Thai, "Barami mai theung."

13 With more building projects needed to maintain the Kruba title and increased expectations of expensive and lavish constructions, local communities cannot support all of these demands. Wealthy urban patrons have come from

Bangkok to contribute to these financial needs. As a result, some Krubas succumb to donors' influence regarding the direction of future projects (P. Cohen 2017, 21).

14 In *The Religion of India*, Weber (1958, 207) famously posited that Buddhist monks held an otherworldly, ascetic orientation. Weber describes ancient Buddhism as essentially a technology of wandering for intellectual mendicant monks (206). He conceived of a radical separation between Buddhist monks and the laity, whereby Buddhist monks would compromise their charisma in the eyes of the laity if they used money and did not wander. He writes, "A rational economic ethic could hardly develop in this sort of religious order" (216).

15 "Monks Told to Stop Selling Holy Items in Ubosots," *Bangkok Post*, October 3, 2017, www.bangkokpost.com/news/general/1335363.

16 The sign at the entrance to Wat Phra Singh reads: "Don't sell any merchandise inside the temple, except in shops in the temple and school, which are already approved. The temple will follow the law for someone who breaks this rule" (my translation).

17 This idea of the degrees of sacredness exists not only in Thailand but throughout Buddhist Asia. See Bruntz and Schedneck (2020).

18 These discussions of the appropriateness of temple activity and monk behavior are contingently framed. In nineteenth-century northeastern Thai villages, Kamala Tiyavanich (1997, 24) has found, when "monks were not gifted in oratorical, artistic, or healing skills (which brought in donations), the *wat* had to survive any way it could. In many locations, monks had to work to support the monastery by growing vegetables, tending orchards, carving boats, or raising cattle and horses." That monks took on this kind of labor was typical and considered appropriate at this time and place. Today, in Chiang Mai City, this would not be considered appropriate, so other ways of maintaining the temple are sought.

19 Ben Hooper, "Thai Monk Says Winning Lottery Number Came from Examining a Tree's Textures," United Press International, September 2, 2016, www .upi.com/Odd_News/2016/09/02/Thai-monk-says-winning-lottery-number -came-from-examining-a-trees-textures/1161472832843.

20 Dhamma Study and Support Foundation, "Dhamma Discussions," http://dham mahome.com/webboard/topic25111.html, accessed September 15, 2016.

21 Pantip discussion forum, http://pantip.com/topic/33161418, accessed September 15, 2016.

22 Religious studies scholar Rachelle M. Scott (2017, 230) finds that there is no specific reference to gambling in the 227 monastic rules for male monks in the Patimokkha; however, one could interpret the second precept against stealing and the tenth precept against handling gold and silver to function as prohibitions against gambling. Monks who gambled were common in nineteenth-century Thailand, although, as today, these activities did face scrutiny and debate concerning the appropriate behavior of monks (232).

23 Sanitsuda Ekachai, "Dhammakaya Is Only a Symptom," *Bangkok Post*, February 2, 2015, www.bangkokpost.com/opinion/opinion/483196.

24 Many articles were written on this story throughout Asia. See, for example, Auk-karapon Niyomyat and Patpicha Tanakasempipat, "Thai Police End Search of Temple without Finding Monk," Reuters, March 10, 2017, www.reuters.com /article/us-thailand-buddhism-idUSKBN16H18Q.

25 "Buddhist Followers Cling to Their Beliefs in Wake of Temple Fund Embezzle-ment Scandal," *Bangkok Post*, June 10, 2018,www.bangkokpost.com/thailand /general/1482169.

26 Many Thai lay Buddhists have faith in these Buddhist monks and hope that things will go back to normal quickly. Another perspective faults the National Office of Buddhism, blaming it for false accusations, and claims that Thai lay Buddhists do not need it to regulate who and where they should worship. See, for example, "Followers' Faith in Busted Monk Strong as Ever," *Bangkok Post*, June 10, 2018, www.bangkokpost.com/thailand/general/1482189; "Dragnet Likely to Snare More Monks," *Bangkok Post*, June 12, 2018, www.bangkokpost. com/thailand/general/1483081; and "CSD [Crime Suppression Division] Closes in on Former Abbot," *Bangkok Post*, June 14, 2018, www.bangkokpost.com /thailand/general/1484577.

27 Within the walls of the old city of Chiang Mai, Wat Si Koet and Wat Tung Yu have donation boxes set up for their parking services. As well, one Thai monk who had recently graduated from MCU at Wat Suan Dok maintained that his temple makes enough money to meet its monthly budget from the parking lot donations alone.

28 Personal communication with Khun Ou, Wat Buppharam, September 20, 2016.

29 "Wat Chedi Luang Collects Fee to Visit" [in Thai], *Chiangmai News*, June 1, 2016, www.Chiangmainews.co.th/page/archives/490133.

30 It is difficult to determine when exactly this fee was instituted. Monks who have lived at Wat Doi Suthep for many years estimated that it has been in effect for over thirty years.

31 TripAdvisor, "Wat Doi Suthep," www.tripadvisor.com/LocationPhotoDirect Link-g8286767-d456320-i99416136-Wat_Phra_That_Doi_Suthep-Doi_Suthep .html, accessed June 17, 2018.

32 ThaiVisa Forum, "Abbot of Doi Suthep Having a Great Time in the USA," www .thaivisa.com/forum/topic/727505-abbot-of-doi-suthep-having-a-great-time-in -the-usa, accessed June 17, 2018.

33 TripAdvisor, "Review of Wat Chedi Luang," www.tripadvisor.com/ShowUserRe-views-g293917-d447585-r438913257-Wat_Chedi_Luang_Varavihara-Chiang_Mai .html, accessed June 17, 2018.

34 TripAdvisor, "Wat Phra Singh," www.tripadvisor.com/Attraction_Review -g293917-d447648-Reviews-Wat_Phra_Singh-Chiang_Mai.html, accessed June 17, 2018.

35 See, for example, the "Wat Bupharam" review on TripAdvisor, www.tripadvisor .com/Attraction_Review-g293917-d552531-Reviews-Wat_Bupharam-Chiang _Mai.html, accessed June 17, 2018.

36 In Thailand it is common for men to ordain temporarily—either for a few days or for a few months. Many men become fully ordained monks for the rains

retreat (July–October), and many boys ordain as novice monks during their school vacation (March–April).

37 According to Phra Maha HaOrn, the temple started to build the coffee shop in 2013, and within a year, about 2014, it opened.

38 If a foreigner lives in Thailand, can communicate in Thai, and has contact with a temple community and abbot, then he would be able to ordain without the aid of the Temple Stay and Retreat program.

39 For an argument pointing to the nature of lived religion, which draws on the data about volunteer tourism at Wat Nong Bua and Plik Wiwek, see Schedneck (2019).

CHAPTER 3: RELIGIOUS OTHERS IN THE BUDDHIST EYE

1 A series of articles have appeared in Thai media outlets concerning "Chinese behaving badly," that is, not following Thai etiquette. One article elaborating on the situation is Khaosod English, "'Chinese Tourist' Filmed Kicking Chiang Mai Temple Bell," February 22, 2015, www.khaosodenglish.com/life/2015/02/22 /1424603910.

2 This incident was also widely covered. See, for example, "Monk Calls on Govt to Burn Down 1 Mosque for 1 Dead Buddhist Monk," *Coconuts Bangkok*, November 2, 2015, https://coconuts.co/bangkok/news/monk-calls-govt-burn-down-1 -mosque-1-dead-buddhist-monk.

3 Scholar of Buddhism in Thailand Peter A. Jackson (2014, 4) calls the dialogue between ascendant doctrinalism and resurgent magic a paradox, as both of these modes of religiosity are present within modern Southeast Asia.

4 For historical examples of Buddhist attitudes toward religious others, see Burton (2010), Elverskog (2011), Jayatilleke (1975), Makransky (2003), Suwanna (2003), and Thongchai (2015). For theological examples of Buddhist relations with religious others, see Kiblinger (2005), Schmidt-Leukel (2007), and Vélez de Cea (2013).

5 Scholar of Theravada Buddhism John Holt (2009, 191) finds some conflict between tourists and novices in Luang Prabang, asserting that "some of the harshest critics of Luang Phrabang's *samaneras* (novices) are French expatriates with decidedly Western understandings of what it means to be Buddhist." During interviews with Luang Prabang's novice monks, Holt found that most likely more than two-thirds of them regularly converse with tourists. One of their major motivations is to practice English (206).

6 The Monk Chat program at Wat Suan Dok has twenty to thirty regularly participating members. Wat Chedi Luang followed this trend with its Monk Chat program beginning in 2005, with about one hundred members. Wat Srisuphan started its program in 2008 and has around twenty Monk Chat participants. These numbers come from the leaders of the Monk Chat programs at these three temples during October 2016.

7 During Monk Chat sessions, depending on the temple, there are usually about ten monks having small-group conversations with between thirty and forty

tourists seated at tables. Tourists learn about this program through guidebooks and websites about tourism in Chiang Mai or while touring the temples. The monks I spoke to have been attending Monk Chat for two or more years, and more senior ones, who have participated for four or more years, estimated that they have spoken with well over five hundred people.

8   Phra Kyo, adviser to Monk Chat at Wat Suan Dok, confirmed through his calculations of the countries listed in the temple's guest books from 2015 and 2016 that most visitors hail from the United States, Canada, and Australia, followed by European countries, especially England, Germany, and France.

9   This relationship between Thailand and the West has been noted by Rachel V. Harrison in *The Ambiguous Allure of the West: Traces of the Colonial in Thailand* (2010). In the foreword to that volume, Dipesh Chakrabarty (2010, ix) writes that the *farang*, or white foreigner, was the most significant other against whom modern Thai people evaluated themselves.

10   Phra Trilok's preference shows some traces of the biases of modern Buddhism, where some monks involved with Monk Chat will try to explain a kind of "original" Buddhism to their audience, placing this above the particulars of Thai Buddhism. "Modern Buddhism" is a term used most significantly by Donald S. Lopez in his introduction to *A Modern Buddhist Bible* (2002a), and the related term "Buddhist modernism" is used by David McMahan in *The Making of Buddhist Modernism* (2008). These terms can be defined by a kind of Buddhism that privileges a number of modern ideas and processes such as equality, democracy, demythologizing, and deritualizing, among others.

11   The Three Defilements are considered, in Theravada Buddhism, to be three afflictions that keep one from understanding reality. Buddhists regard the Three Marks of Existence as characteristics that all conditioned phenomena share and that describe the nature of experience.

12   The Five Precepts are the rules of moral conduct for lay followers of Buddhism. After taking these precepts, followers commit to training to abstain from killing, stealing, sexual misconduct, lying, and intoxication.

13   Anthropologist of Thailand Marc Askew (2008) discusses Singaporean and Malaysian tourists who visit southern Thailand to seek out sacred monuments for the purpose of making merit.

14   Rebecca Iszatt, "From East to East: The Chinese Tourist Boom in Chiang Mai," *Chiang Mai Citylife*, July 31, 2013, www.ChiangMaicitylife.com/citylife-articles/from-east-to-east-the-chinese-tourist-boom-in-Chiang-mai.

15   Shuan Sim, "Chinese Tourists Behaving Badly in Thailand: Police Hunting Bell-Kicking Culprit," *International Business Times*, February 23, 2015, www.ibtimes.com/chinese-tourists-behaving-badly-thailand-police-hunting-bell-kicking-culprit-video-1824904.

16   Marion Thibaut, "Chinese Tourists Boost Thai Economy but Stir Outrage," *Business Insider*, July 5, 2015, www.businessinsider.com/afp-chinese-tourists-boost-thai-economy-but-stir-outrage-2015-7.

17 James Austin Farrell, "Thailand Doesn't Have a Chinese Tourist Problem: The Problem Is Resentment, and Racism," *Asian Correspondent*, March 25, 2015, https://asiancorrespondent.com/2015/03/thailand-doesnt-have-a-chinese -tourist-problem-the-problem-is-resentment-and-racism.

18 Chinese have migrated to Thailand for over two centuries. Researchers have found that Thai Chinese have both assimilated and integrated into Thai society while also maintaining distinct cultural and language practices. For research into this Sino-Thai group, see Morita (2007) and Tong and Chan (2001). I am focusing not on this group but on Chinese tourists coming to Thailand from mainland China.

19 Iszatt, "From East to East."

20 Anthropologist Jovan Maud (2013) has found that monks are thought to possess supernatural powers and that religious specialists, especially those who are artists of *sak yan*, a type of protective tattoo, are sought after and popular among Chinese Malaysians and Singaporeans visiting southern Thailand.

21 Within Theravada Buddhism the idea of the eventual decline of the Buddha's teachings is pervasive. For more discussion on this topic, see chapter 4 and the conclusion.

22 Historian of religion Alicia Turner (2014) discusses this threat in the context of colonial Burma.

23 Michael K. Jerryson, "The Rise of Militant Monks," *Lion's Roar*, August 23, 2015, www.lionsroar.com/the-rise-of-militant-monks.

24 Theologian Kenneth Fleming (2014, 69) writes of the Buddhism Protection Center of Thailand's plans to restore Buddhism, including founding a Buddhist bank, making Thailand once again the center of the Buddhist world, supporting the two Buddhist universities, increasing quality across monastic education, reforming the Sangha Act and sangha administration, promoting Buddhist festivals, supporting Buddhist nuns, and setting up an association of Buddhist lawyers.

25 A number of monks told me that they observed the groups of young Christian missionaries accompanied by an older person. They believed that the group had come to Monk Chat to try out the conversion techniques they had been practicing with their teacher.

26 This is the opinion of Phra Ruang. I was not able to verify this information about this student population. However, as Monica Lindberg Falk (2013, 40) has found, after the tsunami in 2004, in one of the affected provinces, Phang Nga, some Christian missionaries offered money and other useful things to Buddhists if they converted. The Thai Buddhists who took this offer and converted were looked upon by their community members as untrustworthy and corrupt.

27 French missionaries were also known to be close to the royal court, such as the French Catholic missionary Bishop Pallegoix, who maintained an intellectual friendship with King Mongkut for several decades (Thanet 2009, 408).

28 Sunthorn Plamintr, "Buddhism and Thai Society," BuddhaSasana, www
.budsas.org/ebud/ebdha108.htm, accessed November 29, 2018.

CHAPTER 4: BUDDHIST SPACES OF MISSIONIZATION

1 Glenys Eddy (2015, 90) also finds that Buddhist mission is an overlooked aspect
of Buddhist activity.

2 The Vinaya is one of the three baskets (Tipitaka) of the authoritative texts of
Theravada Buddhism, the Pali Canon. The Vinaya contains the rules for the
monastic community and is made up of a number of parts. One of these parts
is the Mahavagga, which contains rules as well as accounts of the Buddha's
enlightenment, first preaching, and how some key disciples of the Buddha
joined the community. For more translations and information about this text,
see Access to Insight, "Vinaya Pitaka," www.accesstoinsight.org/tipitaka/vin/,
accessed September 30, 2020.

3 The *Saṃyutta Nikāya* is known in English as the *Connected Discourses*. This
collection is part of the *Sutta Pitaka*, one of the three baskets of the Pali
Canon.

4 The *Aṅguttara Nikāya* is often translated as the *Gradual Collection*. This text
is also one part of the larger *Sutta Pitaka*, which are discourses attributed to
the Buddha.

5 This decline narrative represents a reverse order of the building of the Buddhist religious tradition (*sasana*) represented by the gradual dismantling of the
three refuges. The Buddha first established himself as a Buddha-figure, then
the Dhamma, and, finally, the Sangha, or community of practitioners. In the
decline scheme, first the community of monks loses their distinctive identity,
then the Buddhist teachings vanish, and, finally, the Buddha's presence,
through his relics, disappears (Strong 2004, 225).

6 This translation was taken from the English-language chanting book of
Suttajit Bhikkhuni Aram in Doi Saket, Chiang Mai. The *Ayacana Sutta* can be
translated in English as *The Request*. This text is part of the *Saṃyutta Nikāya*,
or *Connected Discourses*, which is located within the *Sutta Pitaka* of the Pali
Canon.

7 I thank Iselin Frydenlund for her insight into the distinctions between centrifugal and centripetal missionizing.

8 Dhammakaya meditation was developed and taught by Luang Por Sot. His
meditation movement claimed that this was the original type of meditation
practiced by the Buddha upon his enlightenment, which Luang Por Sot redis-
covered. The practice's main distinguishing points are a focus on the center
of the body and visualization.

9 Although the *thammacarik* program is propagating and promoting Buddhism,
Prawit Tantalanukul (2002) translates the term *thammacarik* as "pilgrims"
rather than "missionaries."

10 The *thammathut* program is supported by both sects of Thai Buddhism, Mahanikai and Thammayutnikai. The Thammayutnikai has temples in Australia,

NOTES TO CHAPTER 4   189

Canada, Hong Kong, India, Indonesia, Japan, Malaysia, New Zealand, South
Korea, Taiwan, the United States, and nine countries in Europe. Each year since
1995, successive groups of *thammathut* monks have been sent to these countries
through the Thammayutnikai training program, with forty-six *thammathut* monks undertaking training in 2018 (Office of Training *Thammathut*
Monks Traveling Abroad, home page, http://tidga.net/index.php, accessed
September 30, 2020). The Mahanikai sect established a training program
for *thammathut* monks in 1995. In 2014, the Mahanikai's university system,
Mahachulalongkorn University (MCU), established a separate college for
this training, called the Dhammatuta College. Its *thammathut* monks are
sent to thirty-nine temples abroad. The class of 2018 trained 124 monks for
their *thammathut* tasks (Dhammatuta College, home page, www.odc.mcu
.ac.th, accessed September 30, 2020).

11 Buddhist studies scholar Andrew Skilton (2010) has labeled this mission of
Bhikkhu Kapilavaddho a failure.

12 Today, there are fifteen monasteries affiliated with the Ajahn Chah forest
lineage in eleven countries covering four continents. Forest Sangha, "Community," https://forestsangha.org/community/monasteries, accessed September 30, 2020.

13 The English Sangha Trust was established in 1956. For a history of this organization, see the website of Amaravati monastery, a forest temple in the tradition
of Ajahn Chah, "The English Sangha Trust: History," www.amaravati.org
/support/est, accessed September 30, 2020.

14 Luang Por Sumedho, "Gratitude for Luang Por Chah," excerpt from talk given
at the Amaravati Buddhist Monastery, June 17, 2003, *Forest Sangha Newsletter*,
July 2006, www.fsnewsletter.org/html/76/sumedho.htm.

15 This history is recorded in the Thai section of the website of Wat Buddhapadipa,
"Background," www.padipa.org/ความเป็นมา/, accessed February 25, 2019.

16 I thank Anthony Lovenheim Irwin for informing me of this reference.

17 Other scholars, including Donald S. Lopez (2002a), use the term "modern
Buddhism." Here I use "modern Buddhism" and "Buddhist modernism"
synonymously.

18 This approach can be seen in the anthology by Lopez (2002b), *A Modern Buddhist
Bible*, where many famous Buddhists are placed under the label "modern,"
eclipsing their missionizing status.

19 "Religion to Create Peace: Following the Thai Missionary Program to Restore
Faith In Java," [in Thai], *Thai Rath*, March 14, 2017, www.thairath.co.th/content
/883120.

20 These quotations come from my participation in a group discussion with Phra
Kyo at Wat Suan Dok, November 4, 2016.

21 Email correspondence with Phra Ruang, March 14, 2018.

22 I have also found that meditation teachers in Thailand's international meditation
centers perceived foreigners as coming to Buddhism through the door of meditation. They believed that faith and devotion on the part of these foreigners
would come later (Schedneck 2015, 139).

1   Although most of the market of volunteer tourism comes from the global North, Anthropologist Nattaka Chaisinthop (2017) has written about a domestic volunteering organization in Thailand, called the Volunteer Spirit Network. The idea of a volunteer spirit (*phalang chit asa*) has become popular among members of the Thai urban middle class, who, among other activities, take trips into rural Thailand and spend weekends playing games with and teaching children, and stay in the homes of the local people. Nattaka Chaisinthop has found that these domestic volunteers come away with the same "poor-but-happy," romantic, individual-focused, and depoliticized ideas that international volunteers do. Erica Bornstein (2012) has found similarly that domestic volunteer tourism projects in India are more focused on developing the perspective and morals of urban Indian youth than on making a social impact on rural, underdeveloped communities.

2   Anthropologist and geographer Mary Mostafanezhad (2012, 319) finds that volunteer tourism is an important part of the alternative tourism market, with about 1.6 million participants each year who pay to take part in these short-term (six months or less) humanitarian projects. Despite a growing trend of domestic volunteering in some developing countries, international volunteers continue to predominate, with most coming from the United States, Europe, Australia, and New Zealand.

3   Popular websites have also contributed to the critique of volunteer tourism. See, for example, Kim Tran, "Four Reasons Why Volunteer Tourism Won't Save the World," Everyday Feminism, November 10, 2016, http://everydayfeminism.com/2016/11/voluntourism-wont-fix-the-world. The four reasons are that (1) volunteer tourism is more focused on individual gain than helping others; (2) volunteer tourists are untrained and without special skills to solve big problems; (3) volunteer tourism is a neoliberal practice in that it assumes the neediness of the global South without trying to fix underlying structural inequalities; and (4) the temporary fixes of volunteer tourism can stand in the way of more radical change.

4   Nick Kontogeorgopoulos (2014) reports similar findings in his interviews with volunteer tourists in northern Thailand in general.

5   Kontogeorgopoulos (2014, 252) estimates, using data from Far Eastern University in Chiang Mai, that in 2011, northern Thailand received one hundred thousand international volunteer tourists.

6   I have retained the accurate names of volunteer tourism organizations in this discussion.

7   The Wat Doi Saket Project was explicitly marketed as a cultural exchange program offering participants the opportunity to live with and teach English to Buddhist novices and monks in the Doi Saket District, outside of Chiang Mai City.

8   The Wat Doi Saket Project maintained an affiliation with Phra Maha Insorn, principal of the school at Wat Nong Bua. Volunteers taught in this temple and

tutored in nearby temples where novices live. Other projects that volunteers have been involved with are building temple structures, such as the ordination hall at Wat Nong Bua, which an American high school group helped to complete in 2014.

9   Program leaders from the FutureSense Foundation said the move was made because, during an assessment, a greater need was found among the Lawa and Karen people of Mae Sariang (personal communication with Thailand country leader, March 18, 2018). However, when I asked the monastic teachers at Wat Nong Bua why the FutureSense Foundation left, they stated that "the volunteers wanted to be on the mountain" (*yak yu bon doi*), presumably to be located in a more scenic area. They also felt that the volunteers did not like the Doi Saket region because it was too far from Chiang Mai City and there was not much to do.

10 Because of this change, for my research with this project in 2013–14 I refer to this program as the Wat Doi Saket Project and in 2015–17 as the FutureSense Foundation Teaching English to Monks program.

11 I have retained the real name of the director of Friends for Asia, Todd Cikraji, with his agreement.

12 Email correspondence with Jen, June 14, 2016.

13 During my field research and investigation of these programs, I did not encounter any volunteers from Asia.

14 Wat Doi Saket Project, https://atmaseva.wordpress.org/watdoisaketproject, accessed May 3, 2014.

15 Scholars of volunteer tourism have found that authentic encounters are a main motivating factor. See Kontogeorgopoulos 2016; Mostafanezhad 2014; Raweewan 2014.

16 Friends for Asia, "Teaching English to Monks—Volunteer Thailand," www .friendsforasia.org/teaching-english-to-monks-volunteer-thailand, accessed March 5, 2019.

17 Hunaid, "Two Blissful Months in Thailand," Wat Doi Saket Project blog, May 28, 2013, https://atmaseva.wordpress.com/2013/05/28/two-blissful-months-in -thailand.

18 Brady, "The Gist of It," *Campus Y* (blog), September 25, 2013, http://campusyblog .web.unc.edu/2013/09/25/9202913-the-gist-of-it.

19 Email communication with Jonathan, June 6, 2013.

20 Brady, "The Gist of It."

21 Victoria, "Eat, Pray, Love, Give," Wat Doi Saket Project blog, July 31, 2013, https:// atmaseva.wordpress.com/2013/07/31/eat-pray-love-give.

22 Email communication with Mike, July 3, 2013.

23 Email communication with Jonathan, June 6, 2013.

24 Email communication with Jonathan, June 6, 2013.

25 Scott A. Cohen (2010, 118) has been one of the few tourism studies scholars to question the analysis of the self in tourism research, which typically uses a romantic lens to discuss the essential self as something that can be actualized, realized, developed, or discovered.

26 Email communication with Felix, July 24, 2018.

27 Amanda, "In Which I Could Be Offended," *Chitarita* (blog), June 23, 2010, http://chitarita.blogspot.com/2010/06/in-which-i-could-be-offended.html.

28 Brady, "The Size of My Shoes and the Eiffel Tower: A Thank You to ATMA SEVA and My Monks," Wat Doi Saket Project blog, September 14, 2014, https://atmaseva.wordpress.com/2013/09/14/the-size-of-my-shoes-and-the-eiffel-tower-a-thank-you-to-atma-seva-and-my-monks.

29 Email communication with Mike, March 3, 2014.

30 Email communication with Sam, March 15, 2014.

31 Email communication with Jonathan, June 6, 2013.

CONCLUSION

1 PDO has six thousand students plus one thousand novices mixed together in its classrooms. The education along with room and board is free for students because PDO receives donations from Japan, Australia, and Germany. Many of the boys come from the Shan or Kachin States and enter the school already as novices. Those boys who are not novices are encouraged to ordain so the community can feed them and PDO does not have to use as much of its budget on food. The novice life is intentionally not strict for this reason. Interview with Venerable U Nayaka, PDO School, Mandalay, October 12, 2014.

2 Monk-scholar Venerable Khammai Dhammasami (2018, 186) has criticized this approach to education in a Buddhist monastic school. He asserts that PDO gives too much attention to English without any Buddhist material in the curriculum. Instead, he would like to see more of an integration of Buddhism as a pedagogical tool alongside secular subjects.

3 Interview with a local coordinator for World Service Group, Phnom Penh, July 13, 2014. The name World Service Group is a pseudonym.

4 I bring to this discussion my fieldwork at a three-night stay in the Korean Templestay program. I took part in the Templestay program in Beopjusa Temple, October 19–22, 2016.

5 Templestay Korea has a Facebook account (facebook.com/templestay), a Twitter account (twitter.com/templestay/korea), and an extensive website (www.templestay.com). The Templestay Information Center in Seoul provides information about all the programs and participating temples. The Templestay organization publishes a newsletter each season highlighting some of the temples and interviews with participants.

6 Although Korean culture, and the concept of culture more broadly defined, includes more dynamism and nuance, Korean culture as packaged for tourists in the Templestay program centers on activities that neatly fit into a short two- to three-hour program.

7 Didi Kirsten Tatlow, "A Robot Monk Captivates China, Mixing Spirituality with Artificial Intelligence," *New York Times*, June 28, 2016.

8 Harriet Sherwood, "Robot Monk to Spread Buddhist Wisdom to the Digital Generation," *Guardian*, April 26, 2016.

9   Shen Lu and Justin Robertson, "Robot Monk Dispenses Buddhist Wisdom at Beijing Temple," CNN, May 30, 2016, www.cnn.com/travel/article/china-bud dhism-robot-monk/index.html.

10 May Masangkay, "Monk-Run Tokyo Bar Proffers Drinks Even as It Teaches Buddhism," *Japan Times*, April 22, 2017, www.japantimes.co.jp/life/2017/04/22 /food/monk-run-tokyo-bar-proffers-drinks-even-teaches-buddhism.

11 Anthropologist of Japan John K. Nelson (2013, 205) cites statistics that indicate a declining interest in Buddhism among youth and middle-aged people due to increased secularization, access to higher education, and mobility. Other reasons include the perception that Japanese Buddhism is out of touch with contemporary times and further shifts in the Japanese population's perspectives. Instead of Buddhism being the dominant explanatory narrative for Japanese society, there are today many other possibilities to make sense of current events.

12 Delphine Thouvenot and Thanaporn Promyamyai, "Chequebook Buddhism: Threat to Buddhism in Thailand?," *Bangkok Post*, April 9, 2015, www.bang kokpost.com/learning/learning-news/523603/chequebook-buddhism-threat -to-buddhism-in-thailand.

13 For examples in English-language publications, see "Misbehaving Monks in Thailand Test Patience of Faithful," *Gulf Times*, February 28, 2015, www .gulf-times.com/story/428990; "Thailand Cracks Down on Monks Living It Up with Luxuries," *Guardian*, June 17, 2013; "Hardliner Tries to Reform Thailand's Buddhist Monks Behaving Badly," *Guardian*, May 15, 2015; "The Mess Some Monks in Thailand Create," *Strait Times*, April 26, 2018, www .straitstimes.com/asia/se-asia/the-mess-some-monks-in-thailand-create -the-nation.

14 I first expressed my views on this topic in an online article: Brooke Schedneck, "Buddhism in Decline: Media Narratives in Thailand," Association for Asian Studies, *#AsiaNow* (blog), June 15, 2017, www.asianstudies.org/buddhism-in -decline-media-narratives-in-thailand.

15 For examples of this kind of rhetoric in English-language publications, see Cod Satrusayang, "The Crisis in Thai Buddhism," *Asia Sentinel*, February 4, 2013, www.buddhistchannel.tv/index.php?id=52,11302,0,0,1,0; Thomas Fuller, "Monks Lose Relevance as Thailand Grows Richer," *New York Times*, December 18, 2012; Lily Kuo, "Buddhist Monks Are Buying into Thailand's New Religion: Consumerism," July 23, 2013, *Quartz*, https://qz.com/107169/buddhist -monks-are-buying-into-thailands-new-religion-consumerism.

16 Phra Paisal Visalo is one of the most visible and respected monks in Thailand. He is the abbot of Wat Pa Sukato in Chaiyaphum Province. Formerly an activist, he spends much of his time advocating for and writing about end-of-life care from a Buddhist perspective. His second main issue is identifying the causes of what he describes as a crisis of Thai Buddhism and searching for the solutions. Phra Phayom Kalyano is most well known as the abbot of Wat Suan Kaew, a temple outside of Bangkok. Additionally, most Thai Buddhists would know him for his outspokenness concerning materialism and

Buddhism. To relieve some of the suffering due to the 1997 economic crisis, Phra Phayom launched the Thai Help Thai program, where he began a super-market for the poor at his temple.

17 Phra Paisal Visalo, "Spiritual Materialism and the Sacraments of Consumer-ism," Visalo, www.visalo.org/englishArticles/consumer.htm, accessed August 24, 2017.

REFERENCES

SOURCES

Allon, Fiona, and Maria Koleth. 2014. "Doing Good: Transforming the Self by Transforming the World." In *Travel and Transformation*, edited by Garth Lean, Russell Staiff, and Emma Waterton, 11–28. Farnham, Surrey, UK: Ashgate.

Amporn Jirattikorn. 2016. "Buddhist Holy Man Khruba Bunchum: The Shift in a Millenarian Movement at the Thailand-Myanmar Border." *Sojourn: Journal of Social Issues in Southeast Asia* 31 (2): 377–412.

Amporn Marddent. 2007. "Buddhist Perceptions of Muslims in the Thai South." *Silpasat Samnuek* [Liberal arts] 7 (18): 47–63.

Ashley, Sean. 2013. "Narrating Identity and Belonging: Buddhist Authenticity and Contested Ethnic Marginalization in the Mountains of Northern Thailand." *Sojourn: Journal of Social Issues in Southeast Asia* 28 (1): 1–35.

Askew, Marc. 2008. "Materializing Merit: The Symbolic Economy of Religious Monuments and Tourist-Pilgrimage in Contemporary Thailand." In *Religious Commodifications in Asia: Marketing Gods*, edited by Pattana Kitiarsa, 89–119. London: Routledge.

Bao, Jiemin. 2015. *Creating a Buddhist Community: A Thai Temple in Silicon Valley.* Philadelphia: Temple University Press.

Bell, Sandra. 2000. "Being Creative with Tradition: Rooting Theravada Buddhism in Britain." *Journal of Global Buddhism* 1: 1–23.

Benavides, Gustavo. 2005. "Economy." In *Critical Terms for the Study of Religion*, edited by Donald S. Lopez, 77–102. Chicago: University of Chicago Press.

Berger, Peter L. 2018. "Urbanity as a Vortex of Pluralism: A Personal Reflection about City and Religion." In *Religious Pluralism and the City: Inquiries into Postsecular Urbanism*, edited by Helmuth Berking, Silke Steets, and Jochen Schwenk, 27–38. London: Bloomsbury Academic.

Berkwitz, Stephen. 2013. "Hybridity, Parody, and Contempt: Buddhist Responses to Christian Missions in Sri Lanka." In *Cultural Conversions: Unexpected Consequences of Christian Missionary Encounters in the Middle East, Africa, and*

South Asia, edited by Heather J. Sharkey, 99–102. Syracuse, NY: Syracuse University Press.

Bernstein, Elizabeth, and Elena Shih. 2014. "The Erotics of Authenticity: Sex Trafficking and 'Reality Tourism' in Thailand." *Social Politics: International Studies in Gender, State and Society* 21 (3): 430–60.

Blackburn, Anne. 2010. *Locations of Buddhism: Colonialism and Modernity in Sri Lanka*. Chicago: University of Chicago Press.

Bornstein, Erica. 2012. "Volunteer Experience." In *What Matters? Ethnographies of Value in a Not So Secular Age*, edited by Courtney Bender and Ann Taves, 119–43. New York: Columbia University Press.

Braun, Erik. 2013. *The Birth of Insight: Meditation, Modern Buddhism, and the Burmese Monk Ledi Sayadaw*. Chicago: University of Chicago Press.

Brox, Trine, and Elizabeth Williams-Oerberg. 2016. "Buddhism, Business and Economics." In *The Oxford Handbook of Contemporary Buddhism*, edited by Michael K. Jerryson, 504–17. New York: Oxford University Press.

Bruner, Edward. 1991. "Transformation of Self in Tourism." *Annals of Tourism Research* 18 (2): 238–50.

Bruntz, Courtney. 2020. "Taking Tourism into Their Own Hands: Monastic Communities and Temple Transformations in China." In *Buddhist Tourism in Asia*, edited by Courtney Bruntz and Brooke Schedneck, 144–60. Honolulu: University of Hawai'i Press.

Bruntz, Courtney, and Brooke Schedneck, eds. 2020. *Buddhist Tourism in Asia*. Honolulu: University of Hawai'i Press.

Buddhadasa Bhikkhu. 2006. *Christianity and Buddhism*. Silver Spring, MD: Council of Thai Bhikkhus.

Burawatnukoon, Phra Thiraphat. 2009. "The Monkhood in Thailand." In *Thai Buddhism; Monk Chat*, 5–11. Chiang Mai: Mahachulalongkorn Rajavidayalaya Buddhist University.

Burton, David. 2010. "A Buddhist Perspective" In *The Oxford Handbook of Religious Diversity*, edited by Chad V. Meister, 321–36. New York: Oxford University Press.

Butcher, Jim. 2003. *The Moralisation of Tourism: Sun, Sand . . . and Saving the World?* London: Routledge.

Butcher, Jim, and Peter Smith. 2010. "'Making a Difference': Volunteer Tourism and Development." *Tourism Recreation Research* 35 (1): 27–36.

Cabezón, José. 2012. "Buddhist Views of Jesus." In *Buddhism and Religious Diversity: Critical Concepts in Religious Studies*, vol. 2, *Christianity*, edited by Perry Schmidt-Leukel, 205–13. London: Routledge.

Cadge, Wendy, and Sidhorn Sangdhanoo. 2005. "Thai Buddhism in America: An Historical and Contemporary Overview." *Contemporary Buddhism* 6 (1): 7–35.

Cate, Sandra. 2003. *Making Merit, Making Art: A Thai Temple in Wimbledon*. Honolulu: University of Hawai'i Press.

Chakrabarty, Dipesh. 2010. "Foreword: The Names and Repetitions of Postcolonial History." In *The Ambiguous Allure of the West: Traces of the Colonial in Thailand*, edited by Rachel V. Harrison and Peter A. Jackson, vii–xvii. Hong Kong: Hong Kong University Press.

Chansamone Saiyasak. 2003. "The History of Christian Interactions with Buddhist Thais during Pioneer Protestant Missionary Era in Thailand, 1828–1860." Paper presented at the Evangelical Theological Faculty, Doctoral Colloquium, Leuven, Belgium.

Chappell, David W. 1990. "Six Buddhist Attitudes Toward Other Religions." In *Radical Conservatism: Buddhism in the Contemporary World: Articles in Honour of Bhikkhu Buddhadasa's 84th Birthday Anniversary*, 443–58. Bangkok: Thai Inter-Religious Commission.

Cheah, Joseph. 2011. *Race and Religion in American Buddhism: White Supremacy and Immigrant Adaptation*. New York: Oxford University Press.

Chireau, Yvonne, and Nathaniel Deutsch, eds. 2000. *Black Zion: African American Religious Encounters with Judaism*. New York: Oxford University Press.

Chiu, Angela. 2017. *The Buddha in Lanna: Art, Lineage, Power, and Place in Northern Thailand*. Honolulu: University of Hawai'i Press.

Chodok, Phra Raja Sittimuni. 1966. *Dhamma of Interest for Foreigners [Thama Thī Farang Sonjai]: Funerary Volume of Amaateak Prayagitsipumpitak*. Bangkok: printed by Khun Ying Gitsapungpitak.

Choe, Jaeyeon, and Michael O'Regan. 2015. "Case Study 2: Religious Tourism Experiences in East Asia." In *Religious Tourism and Pilgrimage Management: An International Perspective*, edited by Razaq Raj and Kevin Griffin, 191–204. 2nd ed. Wallingford, Oxfordshire, UK: CAB International.

Citrinot, Luc. 2011. "Religious Tourism in South-East Asia." In *Religious Tourism in Asia and the Pacific*, 25–46. Madrid: United Nations World Tourism Organization (UNWTO).

Cohen, Anjalee. 2009. "*Dek Inter* and the 'Other': Thai Youth Subcultures in Urban Chiang Mai." *Sojourn: Journal of Social Issues in Southeast Asia* 24 (2): 161–85.

Cohen, Paul T. 2000. "A Buddha Kingdom in the Golden Triangle: Buddhist Revivalism and the Charismatic Monk Khruba Bunchum." *Australian Journal of Anthropology* 11 (2): 141–54.

———. 2001. "Buddhism Unshackled: The Yuan 'Holy Man' Tradition and the Nation-State in the Tai World." *Journal of Southeast Asian Studies* 32 (2): 227–47.

———. 2017. "Introduction: Charismatic Monks of Lanna Buddhism." In *Charismatic Monks of Lanna Buddhism*, edited by Paul T. Cohen, 1–25. Copenhagen: NIAS Press.

Cohen, Scott A. 2010. "Chasing a Myth? Searching for 'Self' through Lifestyle Travel." *Tourist Studies* 10 (2): 117–33.

Conran, Mary. 2006. "Commentary: Beyond Authenticity: Exploring Intimacy in the Touristic Encounter in Thailand." *Tourism Geographies: An International Journal of Tourism Space, Place and Environment* 8 (3): 274–85.

Cook, Joanna. 2010. *Meditation in Modern Buddhism: Renunciation and Change in Thai Buddhist Monastic Life*. Cambridge: Cambridge University Press.

Cornelio, Jayeel Serrano. 2015. "Global and Religious: Urban Aspirations and the Governance of Religions in Metro Manila." In *Handbook of Religion and the Asian City: Aspiration and Urbanization in the Twenty-First Century*, edited by Peter van der Veer, 69–88. Oakland: University of California Press.

Crossley, Émilie. 2012. "Poor but Happy: Volunteer Tourists' Encounters with Poverty." *Tourism Geographies: An International Journal of Tourism Space, Place and Environment* 14 (2): 235–53.

Cywinski, Pawel. 2015. "Tourist Neo-colonialism as an Indication of the Future of Islands: The Example of Borobodur (Central Java)." *Miscellanea Geographica—Regional Studies on Development* 19 (2): 21–24.

Dhammasami, Khammai. 2018. *Buddhism, Education and Politics in Burma and Thailand: From the Seventeenth Century to the Present.* London: Bloomsbury.

Dhammavaro, Phra Saneh. 2009. *Thai Buddhism; Monk Chat.* Chiang Mai: Mahachulalongkorn Rajavidayalaya Buddhist University.

Durkheim, Émile. (1912) 1995. *The Elementary Forms of Religious Life.* Translated by Karen E. Fields. New York: Free Press.

Easum, Taylor. 2013. "A Thorn in Bangkok's Side: Khruba Sriwichai, Sacred Space and the Last Stand of the Pre-modern Chiang Mai State." *South East Asia Research* 21 (2): 211–36.

———. 2018. "Networks beyond the Nation: Urban Histories of Northern Thailand and Beyond." In *Routledge Handbook of Urbanization in Southeast Asia*, edited by Rita Padawangi, 191–201. London: Routledge.

Eberhardt, Nancy. 2009. "Rite of Passage or Ethnic Festival? Shan Buddhist Novice Ordinations in Northern Thailand." *Contemporary Buddhism* 10 (1): 51–63.

Eddy, Glenys. 2015. "Buddhism." In *World Religions and Their Missions*, edited by Aaron J. Ghiloni, 89–121. New York: Peter Lang.

Eliade, Mircea. 1957. *The Sacred and the Profane: The Nature of Religion.* Translated by William R. Trask. Orlando, FL: Harcourt.

Elverskog, Johan. 2011. *Buddhism and Islam on the Silk Road.* Philadelphia: University of Pennsylvania Press.

Falk, Monica Lindberg. 2007. *Making Fields of Merit: Buddhist Female Ascetics and Gendered Orders in Thailand.* Seattle: University of Washington Press.

———. 2013. "Thai Buddhists' Encounters with International Relief Work in Post-tsunami Thailand." In *Buddhism, International Relief Work, and Civil Society*, edited by Hiroko Kawanami and Geoffrey Samuel, 27–49. New York: Palgrave Macmillan.

Fleming, Kenneth. 2014. *Buddhist-Christian Encounter in Contemporary Thailand.* Frankfurt am Main: Peter Lang.

Fukuura, Kazuo. 2011. "A Ritual Community: The Religious Practices of Spirit Mediums Who Worship the Spirit of the Chiang Mai City Pillar." *Sojourn: Journal of Social Issues in Southeast Asia* 26 (1): 105–27.

Geary, David. 2020. "Peace and the Buddhist Imaginary in Bodh Gaya, India." In *Buddhist Tourism in Asia*, edited by Courtney Bruntz and Brooke Schedneck, 27–43. Honolulu: University of Hawai'i Press.

Gethin, Rupert. 1998. *The Foundations of Buddhism.* Oxford: Oxford University Press.

Gombrich, Richard, and Gananath Obeyesekere. 1988. *Buddhism Transformed: Religious Change in Sri Lanka.* Princeton, NJ: Princeton University Press.

Hansen, Anne Ruth. 2007. *How to Behave: Buddhism and Modernity in Colonial Cambodia, 1860–1930*. Honolulu: University of Hawai'i Press.

Harding, John. 2016. "Trailblazers of Global Buddhist Networks." *Contemporary Buddhism* 17 (2): 390–92.

Harris, Elizabeth J. 2006. *Theravada Buddhism and the British Encounter: Religious, Missionary and Colonial Experience in Nineteenth Century Sri Lanka*. London: Routledge.

———. 2013. "Buddhism and the Religious Other." In *Understanding Interreligious Relations*, edited by David Cheetham, Douglas Pratt, and David Thomas, 88–117. Oxford: Oxford University Press.

Harrison, Rachel V. 2010. "Introduction: The Allure of Ambiguity: The 'West' and the Making of Thai Identities." In *The Ambiguous Allure of the West: Traces of the Colonial in Thailand*, edited by Rachel V. Harrison and Peter A. Jackson, 1–36. Hong Kong: Hong Kong University Press.

Hayami, Yoko. 1999. "Buddhist Missionary Project in the Hills of Northern Thailand: A Case Study from a Cluster of Karen Villages." *Tai Culture* 4 (1): 53–76.

Heine-Geldern, Robert. (1942) 2013. "State and Kingship in Southeast Asia." In *Southeast Asian History: Essential Readings*, edited by D. R. SarDesai, 46–63. New York: Routledge.

Henn, Alexander. 2014. *Hindu-Catholic Encounters in Goa: Religion, Colonialism, and Modernity*. Bloomington: Indiana University Press.

Hitchcock, Michael, Victor T. King, and Michael Parnwell, eds. 2010. *Heritage Tourism in Southeast Asia*. Honolulu: University of Hawai'i Press.

Holland, Patrick, and Graham Huggan. 1998. *Tourists with Typewriters: Critical Reflections on Contemporary Travel Writing*. Ann Arbor: University of Michigan Press.

Holt, John. 2009. *Spirits of the Place: Buddhism and Lao Religious Culture*. Honolulu: University of Hawai'i Press.

Horner, I. B., trans. 1971. *The Book of the Discipline (Vinaya-Pitaka)*. Volume IV. London: Luzac.

Horstmann, Alexander. 2004. "Ethnohistorical Perspectives on Buddhist-Muslim Relations and Coexistence in Southern Thailand: From Shared Cosmos to the Emergence of Hatred?" *Sojourn: Journal of Social Issues in Southeast Asia* 19 (1): 76–99.

———. 2011. "Living Together: The Transformation of Multi-Religious Coexistence in Southern Thailand." *Journal of Southeast Asian Studies* 42 (3): 487–510.

———. 2017. "Charismatic Capitalism, Branding and Aspirations of Theravadin Saints in the Borderlands of Thailand, Laos, Myanmar and Southwest-China." Paper presented at the workshop "Buddhism and Economics: Conceptual and Theoretical Approaches to a Burgeoning Field," Elsinore, Denmark, May 26.

Huysegoms, Henri, and Pierre Liesse, eds. 2012. *Edmond Pezet: A Priest among Buddhist Monks in Thailand; Letters and Writings*. Brussels: Societé des Auxiliaires des Missions.

Irwin, Anthony Lovenheim. 2017. "Partners in Power and Perfection: *Khrubas*, Construction, and *Khu Barami* in Chiang Rai, Thailand." In *Charismatic Monks of Lanna Buddhism*, edited by Paul T. Cohen, 87–114. Copenhagen: NIAS Press.

Iwamura, Jane. 2011. *Virtual Orientalism: Asian Religions and American Popular Culture*. New York: Oxford University Press.

Jackson, Peter A. 2014. "Ascendant Doctrine and Resurgent Magic in Capitalist Southeast Asia: Paradox and Polarisation as 21st Century Cultural Logic." DORISEA Working Paper Series, no. 6. University of Göttingen, Göttingen.

Jakubiak, Cori. 2016. "Moral Ambivalence in English Language Voluntourism." In *Moral Encounters in Tourism*, edited by Mary Mostafanezhad and Kevin Hannam, 93–106. London: Routledge.

Jayatilleke, K. N. 1975. *The Buddhist Attitude to Other Religions*. Kandy, Sri Lanka: Buddhist Publication Society.

Jerryson, Michael K. 2011. *Buddhist Fury: Religion and Violence in Southern Thailand*. New York: Oxford University Press.

———. 2013. "Buddhist Traditions and Violence." In *The Oxford Handbook of Religion and Violence*, edited by Mark Juergensmeyer, Margo Kitts, and Michael K. Jerryson, 41–66. New York: Oxford University Press.

Jobs, Sebastian, and Gesa Mackenthun, eds. 2011. *Embodiments of Cultural Encounters*. Münster: Waxmann.

Johnson, Andrew Alan. 2007. "Authenticity, Tourism, and Self-Discovery in Thailand: Self-Creation and the Discerning Gaze of Trekkers and Old Hands." *Sojourn: Journal of Social Issues in Southeast Asia* 22 (2): 153–78.

———. 2014. *Ghosts of the New City: Spirits, Urbanity, and the Ruins of Progress in Chiang Mai*. Honolulu: University of Hawai'i Press.

———. 2016. "Dreaming about the Neighbours: Magic, Orientalism, and Entrepreneurship in the Consumption of Thai Religious Goods in Singapore." *South East Asia Research* 24 (4) 445–61.

Kamala Tiyavanich. 1997. *Forest Recollections: Wandering Monks in Twentieth-Century Thailand*. Honolulu: University of Hawai'i Press.

Kaplan, Uri, 2010. "Images of Monasticism: The Temple Stay Program and the Re-branding of Korean Buddhist Temples." *Korean Studies* 34: 127–46.

———. 2016. "Updating the Vinaya: Formulating Buddhist Monastic Laws and Pure Rules in Contemporary Korea." *Contemporary Buddhism* 17 (2): 252–74.

———. 2017. "From the Tea to the Coffee Ceremony: Modernizing Buddhist Material Culture in Contemporary Korea." *Material Religion* 14 (1): 1–22.

Katewadee Kulabkaew. 2013. "In Defense of Buddhism: Thai Sangha's Social Movement in the Twenty-First Century." PhD diss., Waseda University.

Keane, Webb. 2007. *Christian Moderns: Freedom and Fetish in the Mission Encounter*. Berkeley: University of California Press.

Keese, James R. 2011. "The Geography of Volunteer Tourism: Place Matters." *Tourism Geographies* 13 (2): 257–79.

Kemper, Steven. 2005. "Dharmapala's *Dharmaduta* and the Buddhist Ethnoscape." In *Buddhist Missionaries in the Era of Globalization*, edited by Linda Learman, 22–50. Honolulu: University of Hawai'i Press.

Keyes, Charles. 1971. "Buddhism and National Integration in Thailand." *Journal of Asian Studies* 30 (3): 551–67.

———. 1975a. "Buddhism in a Secular City: A View from Chiang Mai." In *Visakha Puja B.E. 2518*, 62–72. Bangkok: Buddhist Association of Thailand.

———. 1975b. "Buddhist Pilgrimage Centers and the Twelve-Year Cycle: Northern Thai Moral Orders in Space and Time." *History of Religion* 15 (1): 71–88.

———. 1993a. "Buddhist Economics and Buddhist Fundamentalism in Burma and Thailand." In *Fundamentalisms and the State: Remaking Polities, Economies, and Militance*, edited by Martin E. Marty and R. Scott Appleby, 367–409. Chicago: University of Chicago Press.

———. 1993b. "Why the Thai Are Not Christians: Buddhist and Christian Conversion in Thailand." In *Conversion to Christianity: Historical and Anthropological Perspectives on a Great Transformation*, edited by Robert W. Hefner, 259–84. Berkeley: University of California Press.

———. 2007. "Sexy Monks: Sexual Scandals Involving Monks in Thailand." Paper presented at EUROSEAS Conference, Naples, September 12.

Kiblinger, Kristin Beise. 2005. *Buddhist Inclusivism: Attitudes towards Religious Others*. Aldershot, Hants, UK: Ashgate.

Kim, Hwansoo Ilmee. 2012. *Empire of the Dharma: Korean and Japanese Buddhism, 1877–1912*. Cambridge, MA: Harvard University Asia Center.

Kim, Seung Soo. 2017. "Authenticity, Brand Culture, and Templestay in the Digital Era: The Ambivalence and In-Betweenness of Korean Buddhism." *Journal of Korean Religions* 8 (2): 117–46.

King, Victor T. 2015. "Encounters and Mobilities: Conceptual Issues in Tourism Studies in Southeast Asia" *Sojourn: Journal of Social Issues in Southeast Asia* 30 (2): 497–527.

Knee, Adam. 2015. "Chiang Mai and the Cinema Spaces of Thai Identity." In *Asian Cinema and the Use of Space: Interdisciplinary Perspectives*, edited by Lilian Chee and Edna Lim, 77–92. London: Routledge.

Kom Campiranon. 2011. "Religious Tourism in Thailand." In *Religious Tourism in Asia and the Pacific*, 275–93. Madrid: United Nations World Tourism Organization (UNWTO).

Kontogeorgopoulos, Nick. 2014. "The Relationship between Volunteer Tourism and Development in Thailand." *Tourism: An Interdisciplinary Journal* 62 (3): 239–55.

———. 2016. "Forays into the Backstage: Volunteer Tourism and the Pursuit of Object Authenticity." *Journal of Tourism and Cultural Change* 15 (5): 455–75.

———. 2017. "Finding Oneself While Discovering Others: An Existential Perspective on Volunteer Tourism in Thailand." *Annals of Tourism Research* 65: 1–12.

Korawan Sangkakorn. 2013. "Modern Chinese Tourists' Behavior in Chiang Mai after the Movie 'Lost in Thailand.'" Paper presented at the Second Sino-Thai Strategic Research Seminar, Xiamen, China, October 17.

Learman, Linda, ed. 2005a. *Buddhist Missionaries in the Era of Globalization*. Honolulu: University of Hawai'i Press.

———. 2005b. Introduction to *Buddhist Missionaries in the Era of Globalization*, edited by Linda Learman, 1–21. Honolulu: University of Hawai'i Press.

Lenaerts, Sigrid. 2015. "Visitor Experience and Interpretation at Luang Prabang World Heritage Site." In *UNESCO in Southeast Asia: World Heritage Sites in Comparative Perspective*, edited by Victor T. King, 54–74. Honolulu: University of Hawai'i Press.

Lepp, Andrew. 2008. "Discovering Self and Discovering Others through the Taita Discovery Centre Volunteer Tourism Programme, Kenya." In *Journeys of Discovery in Volunteer Tourism: International Case Study Perspectives*, edited by Kevin D. Lyons and Stephen Wearing, 86–100. Wallingford, Oxfordshire, UK: CAB International.

LeVine, Sarah, and David N. Gellner. 2005. *Rebuilding Buddhism: The Theravada Movement in Twentieth-Century Nepal*. Cambridge, MA: Harvard University Press.

Lewis, Todd, ed. 2014. *Buddhists: Understanding Buddhism through the Lives of Practitioners*. Malden, MA: Wiley-Blackwell.

Liechty, Mark. 2017. *Far Out: Countercultural Seekers and the Tourist Encounter in Nepal*. Chicago: University of Chicago Press.

Lopez, Donald S. 2002a. Introduction to *A Modern Buddhist Bible*, edited by Donald S. Lopez, viii–xli. Boston: Beacon Press.

———, ed. 2002b. *A Modern Buddhist Bible*. Boston: Beacon Press.

MacCarthy, Michelle. 2016. *Making the Primitive Modern: Cultural Tourism in the Trobriand Islands*. Honolulu: University of Hawai'i Press.

Mahadev, Neena. 2015. "The Maverick Dialogics of Religious Rivalry in Sri Lanka: Inspiration and Contestation in a New Messianic Buddhist Movement." *Journal of the Royal Anthropological Institute* 22: 127–47.

Makransky, John. 2003. "Buddhist Perspectives on Truth in Other Religions: Past and Present." *Theological Studies* 64 (1): 334–61.

Maud, Jovan. 2013. "Fire and Water: Ritual Innovation, Tourism, and Spontaneous Religiosity in Hat Yai, Southern Thailand." In *Faith in the Future: Understanding the Revitalizations of Religious and Cultural Traditions of Asia*, edited by Thomas Reuter and Alexander Horstmann, 269–96. Leiden: Brill.

McCargo, Duncan. 2009. "Thai Buddhism, Thai Buddhists and the Southern Conflict." *Journal of Southeast Asian Studies* 40 (1): 1–10.

McGilvary, Daniel. (1912) 2012. *A Half Century among the Siamese and the Lao: An Autobiography*. Reprint, New York: Fleming H. Revell Company.

McMahan, David. 2008. *The Making of Buddhist Modernism*. New York: Oxford University Press.

Mellor, Philip A. 1991. "'Protestant Buddhism? The Cultural Translation of Buddhism in England." *Religion* 21 (1): 73–92.

Meyer, Birgit. 2009. "Introduction: From Imagined Communities to Aesthetic Formations: Religious Mediations, Sensational Forms, and Styles of Binding." In *Aesthetic Formations: Media, Religion, and the Senses*, edited by Birgit Meyer, 1–30. New York: Palgrave Macmillan.

Moran, Peter. 2004. *Buddhism Observed: Travelers, Exiles and Tibetan Dharma in Kathmandu*. London: Routledge.

Morita, Liang. 2007. "Discussing Assimilation and Language Shift among the Chinese in Thailand." *International Journal of the Sociology of Language* 186: 43–58.

Mostafanezhad, Mary. 2012. "The Geography of Compassion in Volunteer Tourism." *Tourism Geographies: An International Journal of Tourism Space, Place and Environment* 14 (2): 318–37.

———. 2014. *Volunteer Tourism: Popular Humanitarianism in Neoliberal Times.* London: Routledge.

Mostafanezhad, Mary, and Nick Kontogeorgopoulos. 2014. "Contemporary Policy Debate: Volunteer Tourism Policy in Thailand." *Journal of Policy Research in Tourism, Leisure and Events* 6 (3): 264–67.

Mostafanezhad, Mary, and Tanya Promburom. 2016. "'Lost in Thailand': The Popular Geopolitics of Film-Induced Tourism in Northern Thailand." *Social and Cultural Geography* 19 (1): 81–101.

Nattaka Chaisinthop. 2017. "Domestic Volunteer Tourism in Thailand: The Volunteer Spirit and the Politics of 'Good People.'" *South East Asia Research* 25 (3): 234–50.

Nelson, John K. 2013. *Experimental Buddhism: Innovation and Activism in Contemporary Japan.* Honolulu: University of Hawai'i Press.

Neumann, Mark. 1992. "The Trail through Experience: Finding Self in the Recollection of Travel." In *Investigating Subjectivity: Research on Lived Experience,* edited by Carolyn Ellis and Michael G. Flaherty, 176–204. London: Sage.

Nidhi Eoseewong. (1991) 2003. "The Thai Cultural Constitution" [Ratthathammanun chabap watthanatham thai]. Translated by Chris Baker. *Kyoto Review of Southeast Asia,* no. 3 (March). https://kyotoreview.org/issue-3-nations-and-stories/the-thai-cultural-constitution.

Nikam, N. A., and Richard McKeon, eds. and trans. 1959. *The Edicts of Asoka.* Chicago: University of Chicago Press.

Norman, Alex. 2011. *Spiritual Tourism: Travel and Religious Practice in Western Society.* London: Continuum.

Novelli, Marina, and Anne Tisch-Rottensteiner. 2012. "Authenticity versus Development: Tourism to the Hill Tribes of Thailand." In *Controversies in Tourism,* edited by Omar Moufakkir and Peter M. Burns, 54–72. Wallingford, Oxfordshire, UK: CAB International.

Oakes, Tim, and Donald S. Sutton, eds. 2010. *Faiths on Display: Religion, Tourism, and the Chinese State.* Lanham, MD: Rowman and Littlefield.

Obadia, Lionel. 2011. "Is Buddhism like a Hamburger? Buddhism and the Market Economy in a Globalized World." In *The Economics of Religion: Anthropological Approaches,* edited by Lionel Obadia and Donald C. Wood, 99–122. Bingley, West Yorkshire, UK: Emerald Group Publishing.

Olsen, Daniel H. 2006. "Management Issues for Religious Heritage Attractions." In *Tourism, Religion and Spiritual Journeys,* edited by Dallen J. Timothy and Daniel H. Olsen, 104–18. London: Routledge.

Parreñas, Rheana "Juno" Salazar. 2012. "Producing Affect: Transnational Volunteerism in a Malaysian Orangutan Rehabilitation Center." *American Ethnologist* 39 (4): 673–87.

Pascal, Eva. 2016. "Buddhist Monks and Christian Friars: Religious and Cultural Exchange in the Making of Buddhism." *Studies in World Christianity* 22 (1): 5–21.

Pattana Kitiarsa. 2010a. "An Ambiguous Intimacy: Farang as Siamese Occidentalism." In *The Ambiguous Allure of the West: Traces of the Colonial in Thailand*, edited by Rachel V. Harrison and Peter A. Jackson, 57–74. Hong Kong: Hong Kong University Press.

———. 2010b. "Missionary Intent and Monastic Networks: Thai Buddhism as a Transnational Religion." *Sojourn: Journal of Social Issues in Southeast Asia* 25 (1): 109–32.

———. 2012. *Mediums, Monks, and Amulets: Thai Popular Buddhism Today*. Chiang Mai: Silkworm Books.

Payutto, P. A. [Phra Prayudh Payutto]. 1984. *Thai Buddhism in the Buddhist World: A Survey of the Buddhist Situation against a Historical Background*. Bangkok: Buddhadhamma Foundation.

———. 1998. *Buddhist Economics: A Middle Way for the Market Place*. Translated by Dhammavijaya and Bruce Evans. Bangkok: Buddhadhamma Foundation.

Phibul Choompolpaisal. 2015. "Political Buddhism and the Modernisation of Thai Monastic Education: From Wachirayan to Phimonlatham (1880s–1960s)." *Contemporary Buddhism* 16 (2): 428–50.

Philachan Kornkrai, Benedetto. 1999. "Missionary Work among Buddhists in Thailand in the Light of Canon 785." PhD diss., Pontificia Università Urbaniana.

Prasit Leepreecha. 2005. "The Politics of Ethnic Tourism in Thailand." Paper presented at the workshop "Mekong Tourism: Learning across Borders," Chiang Mai University, February 25.

Prawit Tantalanukul. 2002. *The History of Wat Srisoda: Where the Regional Dhamma Jarika Project Is Situated in Chiang Mai, Thailand*. Chiang Mai: Saeng Silpa Printing.

Randall, Richard. 1990. *Life as a Siamese Monk*. Bradford-on-Avon, UK: Aukana Publishing.

Ratanaporn Sethakul. 2018. "Lanna Buddhism and Bangkok Centralization in Late Nineteenth to Early Twentieth Century." In *Theravada Buddhism in Colonial Contexts*, edited by Thomas Borchert, 81–100. London: Routledge.

Raweewan Proyrungroj. 2014. "Orphan Volunteer Tourism in Thailand: Volunteer Tourists' Motivations and On-Site Experiences." *Journal of Hospitality and Tourism Research* 41 (5): 560–84.

Reader, Ian. 2011. "Buddhism in Crisis? Institutional Decline in Modern Japan." *Buddhist Studies Review* 28 (2): 233–63.

Reynolds, Craig J. 1972. "The Buddhist Monkhood in Nineteenth Century Thailand." PhD diss., Cornell University.

———. 2006. *Seditious Histories: Contesting Thai and Southeast Asian Pasts*. Seattle: University of Washington Press.

Rickly, Jillian M., and Elizabeth S. Vidon, eds. 2018. *Authenticity and Tourism: Materialities, Perceptions, Experiences*. Bingley, UK: Emerald Publishing.

Rimmer, Peter J., and Howard Dick. 2009. *The City in Southeast Asia: Patterns, Processes, and Policy*. Honolulu: University of Hawai'i Press.

Rocha, Cristina. 2006. *Zen in Brazil: The Quest for Cosmopolitan Modernity*. Honolulu: University of Hawai'i Press.

Saad Chaiwan. 1999. "A Study of Christian Mission in Thailand." *East Asian Journal of Theology* 2 (1): 62–74.

Saeng Chandra-ngarm. 1999. *Buddhism and Thai People*. Chiang Mai: Ming Muang Printing.

———. n.d. *A Buddhist Looks at Christianity*. Chiang Mai: Mahamakut Buddhist University.

Sahlins, Marshall. 1985. *Islands of History*. Chicago: University of Chicago Press.

Salazar, Noel B. 2018. *Momentous Mobilities: Anthropological Musings on the Meanings of Travel*. New York: Berghahn Books.

Salazar, Noel B., and Nelson Graburn, 2014. "Introduction: Toward an Anthropology of Tourism Imaginaries." In *Tourism Imaginaries: Anthropological Approaches*, edited by Noel B. Salazar and Nelson Graburn, 1–30. New York: Berghahn Books.

Samuels, Jeffrey, Mark Rowe, and Justin McDaniel, eds. 2016. *Figures of Buddhist Modernity in Asia*. Honolulu: University of Hawai'i Press.

Sanit Wongsprasert. 1988. "Impact of the Dhammacarik Bhikkhus' Programme on the Hill Tribes of Thailand." In *Ethnic Conflict in Buddhist Societies: Sri Lanka, Thailand, and Burma*, edited by K. M. de Silva, Pensri Duke, Ellen S. Goldberg, and Nathan Katz, 126–37. Boulder, CO: Westview Press.

Sarassawadee Ongsakul. 2005. *History of Lan Na*. Translated by Chitraporn Tanratanakul. Chiang Mai: Silkworm Books.

Schedneck, Brooke. 2014. "Meditation for Tourists in Thailand: Commodifying a Universal and National Symbol." *Journal of Contemporary Religion* 29 (3): 439–56.

———. 2015. *Thailand's International Meditation Centers: Tourism and the Global Commodification of Religious Practices*. New York: Routledge.

———. 2016. "Buddhist International Organizations." In *The Oxford Handbook of Contemporary Buddhism*, edited by Michael K. Jerryson, 398–420. New York: Oxford University Press.

———. 2017a. "Beyond the Glittering Golden Buddha Statues: Difference and Self-Transformation through Buddhist Volunteer Tourism in Thailand." *Journeys: The International Journal of Travel and Travel Writing* 18 (1): 57–78.

———. 2017b. "Presenting 'Lanna' Buddhism to Domestic and International Tourists in Chiang Mai." *Asian Journal of Tourism Research* 2 (3): 102–22.

———. 2018. "Religious Others, Tourism, and Missionization: Buddhist 'Monk Chats' in Northern Thailand." *Modern Asian Studies* 52 (6): 1888–1916.

———. 2019. "An Entangled Relationship: A Lived Religion Approach to Theravāda Buddhism and Economics." *Journal of Global Buddhism* 20: 31–48.

———. 2020. "Loss and Promise: The Buddhist Temple as Tourist Space in Thailand." In *Buddhist Tourism in Asia*, edited by Courtney Bruntz and Brooke Schedneck, 66–83. Honolulu: University of Hawai'i Press.

Schedneck, Brooke, Samran Khansamrong, and Steven Epstein. 2019. "Thai Buddhist Monastic Schools and Universities." *Education about Asia* 24 (1): 37–42.

Schmidt-Leukel, Perry, ed. 2007. *Buddhist Attitudes to Other Religions*. St. Ottilien, Germany: EOS.

Schober, Juliane, and Steven Collins, eds. 2017. *Theravāda Buddhist Encounters with Modernity*. London: Routledge.

Schopen, Gregory. 2000. "The Good Monk and His Money in a Buddhist Monasticism of 'the Mahayana Period.'" *Eastern Buddhist* 32 (1): 85–105.

Schumacher, E. F. 1999. *Small Is Beautiful: Economics as If People Mattered: 25 Years Later. . . with Commentaries*. Point Roberts, WA: Hartley and Marks.

Scott, Rachelle M. 2009. *Nirvana for Sale? Buddhism, Wealth, and the Dhammakaya Temple in Contemporary Thailand*. Albany: State University of New York Press.

———. 2014. "Promoting World Peace through Inner Peace: The Discourses and Technologies of Dhammakāya Proselytization." In *Proselytization Revisited: Rights Talk, Free Markets and Culture Wars*, edited by Rosalind I. J. Hackett, 231–52. London: Routledge.

———. 2017. "Religion, Prosperity, and Lottery Lore: The Linkage of New Religious Networks to Gambling Practices in Thailand." In *New Religiosities, Modern Capitalism, and Moral Complexities in Southeast Asia*, edited by Juliette Koning and Gwenaël Njoto-Feillard, 223–46. Singapore: Springer.

Shulman, David, and Guy G. Stroumsa. 2002. "Introduction: Persons, Passages, and Shifting Cultural Space." In *Self and Self-Transformation in the History of Religions*, edited by David Shulman and Guy G. Stroumsa, 3–16. New York: Oxford University Press.

Skilton, Andrew. 2013. "Elective Affinities: The Reconstruction of a Forgotten Episode in the Shared History of Thai and British Buddhism—Kapilavaḍḍho and Wat Paknam." *Contemporary Buddhism* 14 (1): 149–68.

Skinner, Jonathan, and Dimitrios Theodossopoulos. 2011. *Great Expectations: Imagination and Anticipation in Tourism*. New York: Berghahn Books.

Soares, Benjamin F., ed. 2006. *Muslim-Christian Encounters in Africa*. Leiden: Brill.

Sobhon-Ganabhorn, Phra. 1984. *A Plot to Undermine Buddhism*. Bangkok: Siva Phorn.

Sophorntavy Vorng. 2011. "Bangkok's Two Centers: Status, Space, and Consumption in a Millennial Southeast Asian City." *City and Society* 23 (1): 66–85.

Strate, Shane. 2016. "The Sukhothai Incident: Buddhist Heritage, Mormon Missionaries, and Religious Desecration in Thailand." *Journal of Religion and Violence* 4 (2): 183–203.

Strong, John. 1983. *The Legend of King Asoka: A Study and Translation of the Asokavadana*. Princeton, NJ: Princeton University Press.

———. 2004. *Relics of the Buddha*. Princeton, NJ: Princeton University Press.

———. 2008. *The Experience of Buddhism: Sources and Interpretations*. Ann Arbor: University of Michigan Press.

Suwanna Satha-Anand. 2003. "Buddhist Pluralism and Religious Tolerance in Democratizing Thailand." In *Philosophy, Democracy and Education*, edited by Philip Cam, 206–13. Seoul: Korean National Commission for UNESCO.

Swearer, Donald. 1987. "The Northern Thai City as a Sacred Center." In *The City as a Sacred Center: Essays on Six Asian Contexts*, edited by Bardwell Smith and Holly Baker Reynolds, 103–13. Leiden: Brill.

Swearer, Donald, and Sommai Premchit. 1998. *The Legend of Queen Cama: Bodhi-ramsi's Camadevivamsa, a Translation and Commentary*. Albany: State University of New York Press.

Swearer, Donald, Sommai Premchit, and Phaithoon Dokbuakaew. 2004. *Sacred Mountains of Northern Thailand and Their Legends*. Chiang Mai: Silkworm Books.

Taylor, James L. 1993. *Forest Monks and the Nation-State: An Anthropological and Historical Study in Northeast Thailand*. Singapore: Institute of Southeast Asian Studies.

———. 2008. *Buddhism and Postmodern Imaginings in Thailand: The Religiosity of Urban Space*. Farnham, Surrey, UK: Ashgate.

———. 2015. "Urban Buddhism in the Thai Metropolis." In *Handbook of Religion and the Asian City: Aspiration and Urbanization in the Twenty-First Century*, edited by Peter van der Veer, 219–36. Oakland: University of California Press.

Terwiel, Barend Jan. 1975. *Monks and Magic: An Analysis of Religious Ceremonies in Thailand*. Bangkok: Craftsman Press.

———. 2016. "Bigotry and Tolerance: Two Seventeenth Century Reactions to Thai Buddhist Rituals." In *The Role of Religions in the European Perception of Insular and Mainland Southeast Asia: Travel Accounts of the 16th to the 21st Century*, edited by Monika Arnez and Jürgen Sarnowsky, 67–90. Newcastle upon Tyne, UK: Cambridge Scholars Publishing.

Thanet Aphornsuvan. 2009. "The West and Siam's Quest for Modernity: Siamese Responses to Nineteenth Century American Missionaries." *Southeast Asia Research* 17 (3): 401–31.

Thanissaro, Bhikkhu. 2005. "The Traditions of the Noble Ones: An Essay on the Thai Forest Tradition and Its Relationship with the Dhammayut Hierarchy." Paper presented at the Ninth International Thai Studies Conference, Northern Illinois University, DeKalb, IL, April.

Thelle, Notto R. 2004. "Missionary Religions: A Buddhist Perspective." *Swedish Missiological Themes* 92 (4): 539–42.

Thongchai Winichakul. 2015. "Buddhist Apologetics and a Genealogy of Comparative Religion in Siam." *Numen* 62 (1): 76–99.

Toh, Mun Heng. 2012. "Competitive Cities and Urban Economic Development in Southeast Asia." In *Urbanization in Southeast Asia: Issues and Impacts*, edited by Yap Kioe Sheng and Moe Thuzar, 115–38. Singapore: Institute of Southeast Asian Studies.

Tomazos, Kostas, and Richard Butler. 2009. "Volunteer Tourism: The New Eco-tourism?" *Anatolia* 20 (1): 196–211.

Tong, Chee Kiong, and Kwok Bun Chan, eds. 2001. *Alternate Identities: The Chinese of Contemporary Thailand*. Singapore: Brill.

Tran, Anh Q. 2018. *Gods, Heroes, and Ancestors: An Interreligious Encounter in Eighteenth-Century Vietnam*. New York: Oxford University Press.

Truschke, Audrey. 2016. *Culture of Encounters: Sanskrit at the Mughal Court*. New York: Columbia University Press.

Tsing, Anna Lowenhaupt. 2005. *Friction: An Ethnography of Global Connection*. Princeton, NJ: Princeton University Press.

Turner, Alicia. 2014. *Saving Buddhism: The Impermanence of Religion in Colonial Burma*. Honolulu: University of Hawai'i Press.

Tweed, Thomas. 2006. *Crossing and Dwelling: A Theory of Religion*. Cambridge, MA: Harvard University Press.

UNWTO (United Nations World Tourism Organization). 2011. *Religious Tourism in Asia and the Pacific*. Madrid: UNWTO.

Urry, John, and Jonas Larsen. 2011. *The Tourist Gaze 3.0*. London: Sage.

van der Veer, Peter. 2015. "Introduction: Urban Theory, Asia, and Religion." In *Handbook of Religion and the Asian City: Aspiration and Urbanization in the Twenty-First Century*, edited by Peter van der Veer, 1–20. Oakland: University of California Press.

Van Esterik, Penny. 1992. *Taking Refuge: Lao Buddhists in North America*. Tempe: Arizona State University, Program for Southeast Asian Studies.

Veidlinger, Daniel. 2016. "On the Road: The Appeal of Buddhism to Travellers." *Contemporary Buddhism* 17 (2): 439–52.

Vélez de Cea, J. Abraham. 2013. *The Buddha and Religious Diversity*. London: Routledge.

Viehbeck, Marcus, ed. 2017. *Transcultural Encounters in the Himalayan Border-lands: Kalimpong as a "Contact Zone."* Heidelberg: Heidelberg University Press.

Vrasti, Wanda. 2013. *Volunteer Tourism in the Global South: Giving Back in Neo-liberal Times*. London: Routledge.

Walter, Pierre G. 2015. "Travelers' Experiences of Authenticity in 'Hill Tribe' Tour-ism in Northern Thailand." *Tourist Studies* 16 (2): 213–30.

Walters, Jonathan S. 1992. "Rethinking Buddhist Missions." PhD diss., University of Chicago.

———. 2005. "Missions: Buddhist Missions." In *Encyclopedia of Religion*, edited by Lindsay Jones, 9: 6077–82. 2nd ed. Detroit: Macmillan Reference USA.

Warayuth Sriwarakuel. 2009. "Christianity and Thai Culture." In *Relations between Religions and Cultures in Southeast Asia*, edited by Gadis Arivia and Donny Gahral Adian, 91–102. Washington, DC: Council for Research in Values and Philosophy.

Wearing, Stephen. 2001. *Volunteer Tourism: Experiences That Make a Difference*. Wallingford, Oxfordshire, UK: CAB International.

Wearing, Stephen, Adrian Deville, and Kevin D. Lyons. 2008. "The Volunteer's Journey through Leisure into the Self." In *Journeys of Discovery in Volunteer Tourism: International Case Study Perspectives*, edited by Kevin D. Lyons and Stephen Wearing, 63–71. Wallingford, Oxfordshire, UK: CAB International.

Weber, Max. 1958. *The Religion of India: The Sociology of Hinduism and Buddhism*. Translated and edited by Hans H. Gerth and Don Martindale. Glencoe, IL: Free Press.

Wickens, Eugenia. 2011. "Journeys of the Self: Volunteer Tourists in Nepal." In *Volunteer Tourism: Theoretical Frameworks and Practical Applications*, edited by Angela M. Benson, 42–52. London: Routledge.

Wyatt, David. 1969. *The Politics of Reform in Thailand: Education in the Reign of King Chulalongkorn*. New Haven, CT: Yale University Press.

Zahra, Anne. 2011. "Volunteer Tourism as a Life-Changing Experience." In *Volunteer Tourism: Theoretical Frameworks and Practical Applications*, edited by Angela M. Benson, 90–101. London: Routledge.

INTERVIEWS

Names marked with an asterisk are real names. Those without asterisks are pseudonyms.

Plik Wiwek Dhamma Center

Novice monks, monks, and Phra Ajahn Dr. Thani Jitawiriyo, July 14–17, 2016.
Phra Bong, July 16, 2016.
Phra Jing, July 16, 2016.
Phra Sukkasem, July 17, 2016.
*Phra Ajahn Dr. Thani Jitawiriyo, July 17, 2016.

Wat Sri Boen Ruang Temple Stay and Retreat Program

Program coordinators and participants, November 10, 2009; March 2, 2010; October 13, 2013; September 24–28, 2014; July 15–17, 2015.
*Phra Ajahn Dr. Abhisit Pingchaiyawat, October 13, 2013.
Program coordinator, July 10, 2014.
Naen Pairat, September 24, 2014.
Naen Somchai, September 24, 2014.

Wat Nong Bua

Monastic and lay teachers, June 24, 2016.
Phra Maha Aat, June 30, 2018.
*Phra Maha Insorn Khunawuttho, June 10, 2016; July 13, 2016; June 30, 2018.

Student Monks

Phra Aakash, Wat Suan Dok, March 16, 2017.
Phra Akara, Wat Chedi Luang, June 20, 2018.
Phra Atid, Wat Chedi Luang, June 20, 2018.
Phra Bunma, Wat Phan Sao, July 12, 2018.
Phra Bunmi, Wat Suan Dok, May 30, 2017; June 20, 2018.
Phra Canda, Wat Chedi Luang, March 24, 2017.
Phra Chaiya, Wat Chedi Luang, March 31, 2017.
Phra Chandra, Wat Suan Dok, October 22, 2016.
Phra Chet, Wat Chedi Luang, March 31, 2017.
Phra Daeng, Wat Chedi Luang, June 26, 2018.
Phra Day, Wat Chedi Luang, February 17, 2016; October 22, 2016.
Phra Decha, Wat Chedi Luang, June 12, 2018.
Phra Dipankara, Wat Suan Dok, February 23, 2016.
Phra Gamon, Wat Phra Singh, June 30, 2018.
Phra Jaya, Wat Srisuphan, February 27, 2016; October 29, 2016.

Phra Jiu, Wat Chedi Luang, February 17, 2016; October 22, 2016.
Phra Jor, Wat Chedi Luang, February 17, 2016; October 22, 2016.
Phra Kai, Wat Suan Dok, June 19, 2018.
Phra Maha Mitra, Wat Suan Dok, March 1, 2016; Wat Doi Saket, March 25, 2017; May 28, 2018.
Phra Myo, Wat Suan Dok, March 16, 2017.
Phra Neyya, Wat Suan Dok, March 21, 2017.
Phra On, Wat Suan Dok, February 2, 2017.
Naen Pong, Wat Chedi Luang, June 12, 2018.
Phra Ravi, Wat Suan Dok, May 23, 2018.
Phra Ruang, Wat Chedi Luang, February 20, 2016; January 18, 2017.
Naen Samrin, Wat Suan Dok, June 4, 2018; Wat Chedi Luang, June 20, 2018.
Phra Sarit, Wat Chedi Luang, June 20, 2018.
Phra Sek, Wat Suan Dok, March 6, 2017; Wat Phra Singh, June 30, 2018.
Phra Sonalin, Wat Suan Dok, March 20, 2017; June 19, 2018.
Naen Supakorn, Thammaraj School, Wat Phra Singh, June 8, 2018.
Phra Thet, Wat Suan Dok, March 1, 2016; March 16, 2017; March 29, 2018.
Phra Thach, Wat Srisuphan, March 5, 2016.
Naen Maha Tri, Wat Chedi Luang, March 24, 2017; June 12, 2018; June 26, 2018.
Phra Trilok, Wat Chedi Luang, February 23, 2016.
Phra Tummarat, Wat Chedi Luang, March 24, 2017.
Phra Udom, Wat Suan Dok, February 22, 2016.
Phra Vin, Wat Suan Dok, January 11, 2016.
Naen Win, Thammaraj School, Wat Phra Singh, June 8, 2018.

Senior Monks

*Phra Maha HaOrn, Wat Phan Sao, July 12, 2018.
Phra Ajahn Jong, Wat Suan Dok, June 13, 2018.
Phra Ajahn Kaew, Wat Chedi Luang, March 6, 2017; Wat Phra Singh, May 17, 2018; June 30, 2018.
Phra Kyo, Wat Suan Dok, March 29, 2017.
*Phrakru Tirasuttapot, Wat Palad, June 30, 2018.
Phrakru Winay, Wat Chedi Luang, November 4, 2016.

Volunteer Tourism

Ann, Wat Suan Dok, July 15, 2018.
Bridget, Chiang Mai, May 27, 2013.
Chanel, Thammaraj School, Wat Phra Singh, June 1, 2018.
Felix, Friends for Asia Office, June 1, 2018; Thammaraj School, Wat Phra Singh, June 4, 2018.
Jim, Chiang Mai, July 10, 2013.
Joanie, Chiang Mai, July 10, 2013.
Lauren, Chiang Mai, July 10, 2013.
Mary, Friends for Asia Office, June 1, 2018.
Nina, Chiang Mai, July 9, 2013.

Sally, Chiang Mai, June 4, 2018.
*Todd Cikraji, Friends for Asia Office, Chiang Mai, June 11, 2018.

Outside of Thailand

*Venerable U Nayaka, Phaung Daw Oo (PDO) School, Mandalay, October 12, 2014.
Venerable Sopheara, Phnom Penh, July 15, 2014.

INDEX

A

alms collection, 106, 113, 148, 153; as tourist attraction, 139, 140, 144
Amaravati Monastery, 189n13
Amporn Marddent, 89, 90
amulets, 112; Chatukham, 168; as magical, 78, 86–87; sales of, 51, 64, 65
"ascendant doctrinalism" versus "resurgent magic," 77–78, 83, 86–87, 98–99, 185n3
Asian Correspondent (website), 85
Asian economic crisis (1997), 54
Askew, Marc, 186n13
Aśoka, King, 107–8
ATMA SEVA, 152, 178n25
authenticity: and modernist Buddhism, 114; monks' lack of concern with, 161, 170; sought by tourists, 20, 131, 134, 137, 145, 150, 160; urbanization and, 158. *See also* Buddhist authenticity
Ayutthaya, 25, 26, 29; Wangnoi campus of MCU, 81

B

Bachelorette, The (TV show), 30
Bangkok: Buddhist temples, 54, 56, 76, 109, 110, 113, 193n16; language and values of, 174n6; religious encounters in, 11; urbanization of, 6, 9, 19, 23. *See also* Wat Dhammakaya
Bangkok Post, 29, 30, 51, 53, 55; article "Chequebook Buddhism," 166–67
Bangladesh, monks from, 36; Phra Dipankara, 86; Phra Kyo, 80, 89, 93–94, 101, 117–18, 186n8
Bao, Jiemin, 47
barami (charisma), 49, 50, 182n12

Benavides, Gustavo, 47
Beopjusa Temple, 192n4
Best Together Foundation, 179n31
bhikkhunis, 175n20
Bhuridatta, Ajahn Man, 48
Blackburn, Anne, 12
blog posts, 15, 41, 142, 152, 156, 165, 168
Boon Raksa coffee shop, 68
Bornstein, Erica, 149, 190n1
Bradley, Dan Beach, 27
Bua, Luangda Maha (Luangda Maha Bua Nanasampanno) forest lineage, 49
Bua Kam, Princess, 26, 27
Buddha: attitudes toward religious others, 78; "great commission," 105; legends of presence in Chiang Mai and northern Thailand, 5, 17–19, 22, 182n7; relics of, 5, 17, 18, 52, 106, 108, 188n5; in Theravada texts, 105–7, 188nn2,4–5
Buddha images, 5, 17, 55, 86, 102; image halls, 55, 60; wish-granting, 64
Buddha lands (*buddhadesa*), 5, 19, 182n7
Buddha statues, 26, 68, 82, 114, 138, 142, 156; tourist misbehavior involving, 28, 29
Buddhadasa Bhikkhu, 95, 97
Buddhaghosa, *Commentary on the Gradual Collection* (Aṅguttara Nikāya), 106, 188n4
Buddhism: central Thai, 79, 108–9; and colonialism, 12; commercialization of, 51–54, 167–68; compared with Christianity, 97–98, 117–19; decline of, 87–88, 96, 106, 166–70, 171–72, 188n5, 193n11; in the diaspora, 176n25; and economics, 46–51; explanations of, to tourists, 83–84, 186n10, 161; insulting of, as

Lightning Source UK Ltd.
Milton Keynes UK
UKHW011033170822
407424UK00005B/312